Tea

Lear

Teaching in the Lifelong Learning Sector

Peter Scales

 Open University Press

Open University Press
McGraw-Hill Education
McGraw-Hill House
Shoppenhangers Road
Maidenhead
Berkshire
England
SL6 2QL

email: enquiries@openup.co.uk
world wide web: www.openup.co.uk

and Two Penn Plaza, New York, NY 10121-2289, USA

First published 2008

Reprinted 2009

A catalogue record of this book is available from the British Library

ISBN-13:   9780335222407 (pb)   9780335222391 (hb)
ISBN-10:   0335222404 (pb)   0335222390 (hb)

Library of Congress Cataloguing-in-Publication Data
CIP data applied for

Typeset by BookEns Ltd, Royston, Herts.
Printed in the UK by CPI Antony Rowe, Chippenham, Wiltshire

The **McGraw·Hill** Companies

Contents

To my wife, Vanessa, for her love and support while this book has had me 'in a trance' and to my father, Cyril Walter Scales, who lived in a different age.

Acknowledgements

The author and publishers would like to thank the following: Craig Raine for permission to reproduce his poem, *A Martian sends a postcard home*; MICA Management Resources (UK) Inc for permission to reproduce the figure from Edward de Bono's *The Greatest Thinkers*; The Plain English Campaign for permission to reproduce material from their website; the Qualifications and Curriculum Authority, and the Department for Education and Skills.

I would like to thank my students for the past 27 years, from whom I have learned so much. In particular I want to thank Martyn Watson, Russell Godber, Lisa Adamiec, Jasvir Girn, Becca Wildey, Zaheera Sidat and Terry Doherty for permission to reproduce extracts from their journals.

Special thanks to my colleagues at the University of Derby for their advice, support and reading draft chapters; Jo Pickering; Lynn Senior; Kath Headley; Beth Claridge; Des Hewitt; Dave Foord; Marie Parker-Jenkins and Gill Julian (Derby College) and to my sister, Carole Bagnall for reading and suggestions.

Abbreviations

ADHD	attention deficit hyperactivity disorder
AfL	assessment for learning
ALI	Adult Learning Inspectorate (now disbanded, inspection duties incorporated within Ofsted)
AOC	Association of Colleges
APEL	Accreditation of Prior Learning and Experiential Learning
APL	Accreditation of Prior Learning
AQA	Assessment and Qualifications Alliance
AVCE	Advanced Vocational Certificate of Education
BECTA	British Educational and Communications and Technology Agency
BTEC	Business and Technology Education Council
CASE	Cognitive Acceleration through Science Education
CPD	continuing professional development
CTTLS	Certificate in Teaching in the Lifelong Learning Sector
DDA	Disability Discrimination Act
DED	disability equality duty
DfES	Department for Education and Skills (replaced by DCSF, Department for Children, Schools and Families and DIUS, Department for Innovation, Universities and Skills)
DRC	Disability Rights Commission
DTTLS	Diploma in Teaching in the Lifelong Learning Sector
EBD	emotional and behavioural difficulties
ECM	Every Child Matters
ERIC	Educational Resource Information Centre
ESOL	English for speakers of other languages
FE	further education
FENTO	Further Education National Training Organisation (now replaced by LLUK)
FERL	Further Education Resources for Learning
GNVQ	General National Vocational Qualification
GCSE	General Certificate of Secondary Education
ICT	information and communications technology
ILP	individual learning plan
ILT	information and learning technologies

IQ	intelligence quotient
IT	information technology
JISC	Joint Information Systems Committee
LLUK	Lifelong Learning UK
LLN	language, literacy and numeracy
LSC	Learning and Skills Council
NIACE	National Institute of Adult and Continuing Education
NQF	National Qualifications Framework
NRDC	National Research Development Centre for Adult Literacy and Numeracy
NVC	nonverbal communication
NVQ	national vocational qualification
OCN	Open College Network
OCR	Oxford, Cambridge and RSA examinations
OHP	overhead projector
OHT	overhead transparency (used on OHP)
PBL	problem-based learning
PCET	post-compulsory education and training
PDJ	personal development journal
PLTS	personal, learning and thinking skills
PTTLS	Preparing to Teach in the Lifelong Learning Sector
QCA	Qualifications and Curriculum Authority
QIA	Quality Improvement Agency
QTLS	Qualified Teacher Learning and Skills
RSA	Royal Society for the encouragement of Arts, Manufactures & Commerce
SATs	standardised assessment tasks
SfL	Skills for Life
SpLD	specific learning difficulties
VAK	visual, auditory, kinaesthetic
ZPD	zone of proximal development

Introduction

By instructing students to learn, unlearn and re-learn, a powerful new
force is added to education ... Tomorrow's illiterate will not be the man
who can't read; he will be the man who has not learned how to learn ...
(Alvin Toffler *Future Shock* 1970: 367)

Although written nearly forty years ago, Toffler's predictions seem uncannily
accurate and chime very well with current thinking on lifelong learning. The
term *lifelong learning* is so common in educational circles that there seems a
danger we might lose sight of what it actually means and it will become just
another 'buzz phrase'. Lifelong learning is not just an educational fashion;
it's what people have always done and they were doing it long before formal
education and schools were invented. Learning is natural; formal education
isn't. However, we are living in the real world of schools, colleges,
universities and workplaces and we have to work within those structures.
Eventually, by changing the learning and teaching we might begin to change
the structures.

Traditional forms of learning have been heavily reliant on learners being
able to correctly recall a fairly arbitrary body of knowledge (chosen by
educators and politicians) in a formal assessment, generally an examination.
One of the underlying assumptions of this system was that people were
genetically endowed with fixed levels of intelligence – some were 'bright',
some 'less 'bright'; some 'academic', some 'vocational' – and that the job of
education was to identify and select these different performers and assign
them to the appropriate institutions where they would meet others very
much like themselves to be taught by teachers who were habituated to
teaching only those kinds of pupils. Education was designed on an industrial
model to suit the needs of an industrial society – with a standardised body of
learning (the curriculum), a limited range of teaching and learning methods
(pedagogy) and a standardised product (assessment and qualifications) used
to grade learners and to slot them into a job at the appropriate level of the
economy. All of this was delivered in formal, hierarchical settings governed
by the clock – just like a factory.

This rather gloomy scenario does great discredit to many people working in
all levels of education who are passionate about learning and strive to make
education more meaningful and valuable. Things are, undoubtedly, getting

better. But, to a greater or lesser extent, the industrial model of education still prevails. So what can we do? We can develop lifelong learning.

Why 'lifelong learning'?

The 'industrial model' of education may have been appropriate for an industrial age; unfortunately we don't live in an industrial age any longer. This may be a matter of regret for many, but that's just the way it is. Others might regard it as liberation.

In a post-industrial age, there is no longer a job for life. People will have different jobs, even a 'portfolio' of several jobs at the same time. There will be a need for learning and re-learning throughout our lives. Non-standard jobs will increasingly require non-standard and non-uniform learning. People will probably need skills more than knowledge. All this within a globalised economy in which people will work in many different places – real or virtual. These developments are echoed by moves within education to develop more personalised and individualised forms of learning. There will always be a need for shared bodies of knowledge and skills but, increasingly, these will be decided by the needs of the learners rather than the traditions and expertise of the providers.

We are said to be living in a 'knowledge economy' in an 'age of information'. It could be argued that knowledge and information in themselves are not particularly useful. Real education has never been about just passing on parcels of knowledge from one generation to the next: knowledge has to be used, interpreted, changed, developed, discarded, become the building blocks for something new. At school, I learned the currency of pounds, shillings and pence – no longer required. As an adult, I learned to programme my VHS recorder – now irrelevant. In the 'information age' knowledge will rapidly become outdated and new learning will be required. We will need to learn how to learn.

In the 'information age' there is a great danger that we will become mindless consumers of information from a bewildering variety of sources but not be able to discriminate or make judgements about its reliability or validity. We will need to develop our skills of selection, judgement, interpretation, criticism and argument. If we are to become active citizens we must become active learners.

We are frequently reminded of the importance of skills and the need for a 'skills-based' economy. There can no argument against this, but it depends on how wide is our definition of skills. Poor literacy and numeracy skills have blighted the lives of many people and affected their health, their life spans, their relationships and their job prospects. The drive to improve literacy and numeracy, as well as developing information and communication technology (ICT), is part of the job of every teacher in the lifelong learning sector. I would argue, however, that the wider skills – communication, team-working, self-management, creativity and innovation – are more important. Skills don't just pop up out of nowhere; they are created in particular contexts at particular times. The Industrial Revolution was a product of creativity, imagination and innovation; of people questioning how things were done and how they would need to change in a changing world. The pioneers of the Industrial Revolution didn't come up with a set of skills and sit around until they'd thought of a use for them.

Lifelong learning is central to social and economic inclusion. We know that education has failed many people and left them disadvantaged in many ways – emotionally, psychologically, economically and socially. Inclusive learning and widening participation go hand in hand. It is the job of lifelong learning to reach out to people and bring them in and provide learning that meets their needs. Older people need to be brought back into the habit of lifelong learning; younger people not to lose it in the first place.

Another set of arguments for lifelong learning can be found in brain research. There is much neurological evidence to support the benefits of learning throughout life and the ways in which our brains develop at different stages of our lives (see, particularly, Blakemore and Frith 2005). Old dogs should learn new tricks; it makes our lives more varied and interesting and, as research suggests, can help to ward off the onset of conditions such as Alzheimer's.

The development of lifelong learning also reflects changes in the system of education and the blurring of age boundaries between different education sectors. The 14–19 agenda is blurring the boundaries between school and college in an effort to improve our poor staying-on rates post-16; many 14–16-year-olds attend vocational courses in further education (FE) colleges. There are considerable numbers of higher education students studying in FE colleges, many of them mature students. At the time of writing, several FE colleges are planning to sponsor city academies; in one county there is even discussion of creating a combined school, college and university. Many schools see themselves as community learning facilities.

These are just a few arguments in favour of lifelong learning. I'm sure you can think of many more.

What does all this mean for teaching and learning?

In a nutshell, it means that learning will be different from what it was in the past. The emphasis is moving away from *teaching* towards *learning*; away from students being filled up with knowledge and tested. We are moving away from a teacher-centred system to a learner-centred system.

This book is about *active learning*. Precisely what this means will become more apparent as you read but, essentially, it describes the kind of learning where individuals are actively involved in creating meaning, knowledge and skills; the kind of learning which encourages questioning, discovery and exploration; the kind of learning which uses assessment as a means of continual improvement rather than as a way of ascertaining at what point people will fail; the kind of learning which believes everyone can continually develop and achieve.

Teachers are lifelong learners

Teachers are not exempt from the need to 'learn, unlearn and relearn'. The Lifelong Learning UK (LLUK) standards for teachers, tutors and trainers in the lifelong learning sector put reflection and continual improvement at the heart of professional practice. Lifelong learning makes considerable demands on teachers because they have to update both their subject-specific skills and their teaching and learning methods. As Norman Longworth says:

> For teachers, lifelong learning enforces a double whammy. It changes not only the content, but also the methodology of their profession. They become transformed into organisers of all the considerable educational and human resources at their disposal in the interests of actively stimulating learning.
>
> (Longworth 2003: 29)

There's an old adage which goes something like this, 'If you really want to learn about something, write a book about it'. Having worked in post-compulsory education for more than 25 years, I thought I knew pretty well everything about teaching and learning in the sector. However, I've learned a great deal more by writing this book; in fact it's been an excellent piece of continuing professional development. The point I wish to make is that all good teachers are good learners – indeed, lifelong learners. If you're not learning, you're not teaching very well. Not only will you lack up to date skills and knowledge, you will have little to enthuse or excite you and, consequently, your learners.

Who is this book for?

The lifelong learning workforce includes those in further education, adult and community learning, work-based learning and offender learning. In addition, the public services, the armed services and the health service all have considerable numbers of people involved in training and continuing professional development.

This book is designed for all these, and more, including:

- any pre-service or in-service trainee teachers taking courses leading to: Preparing to Teach in the Lifelong Learning Sector (PTTLS); Certificate in Teaching in the Lifelong Learning Sector (CTTLS); Diploma in Teaching in the Lifelong Learning Sector (DTTLS).
- those who have qualified to teach since 2001 who wish to gain Qualified Teacher Learning and Skills (QTLS) status or 'brush up' their knowledge and skills;
- teachers in colleges working with 14–16-year-olds;
- teachers in sixth forms and sixth-form colleges;
- trainers in private training providers.

This book might also be useful to lecturers in higher education who want to develop new ideas and methods. During its writing I have been influenced by John Biggs's excellent book on teaching in universities (Biggs 2003).

How to use this book

The simplest way to use this book is just to read it. However, I would urge you to read Chapter 1, 'The reflective teacher' and Chapter 2, 'Communication and the teacher' first because these provide the foundations of good practice upon which everything else is built. The rest you can read in any order you like or as you need.

The LLUK standards

LLUK has produced the standards which underpin all teaching in the lifelong learning sector. You should download a copy of the 'New overarching standards for teachers, tutors and trainers in the lifelong learning sector' from their website *www.lifelonglearning.org.uk*. To provide an overview, the standards are divided into six main domains. These are:

Domain A	Professional values and practice
Domain B	Learning and teaching
Domain C	Specialist learning and teaching
Domain D	Planning for learning
Domain E	Assessment for learning
Domain F	Access and progression

Each domain has a series of competence statements detailing scope, knowledge and practice:

- *S = Scope.* These statements provide an overview of the domain and the underpinning values. For example, BS1 'Maintaining an inclusive, equitable and motivating learning environment'.
- *K = Knowledge.* These statements are derived from the scope statement and describe what a teacher in the lifelong learning sector should know and understand. For example, BK1.1 'Ways to maintain a learning environment in which learners feel safe and supported'.
- *P = Practice.* These statements are also derived from the scope statement and describe the professional practice of teachers in the lifelong learning sector. For example, BP1.1 'Establish a purposeful learning environment where learners feel safe, secure, confident and valued'.

Each chapter in the book indicates the standards covered. However, you should remember that not all the standards will be met by reading a book; the standards are as much about what you do as what you collect. The standards are based on a competence system which breaks the teacher's job down into a series of competences which should be common to all. You will be asked to provide evidence of how you meet the standards as part of your teacher training. However, all jobs, especially that of the teacher, are more than the sum of the individual parts. Teaching is a holistic activity which brings together a range of elements – planning, methods, assessment – to work together in concert. The final chapter of this book encourages you to make connections and see the big picture beyond the separate elements.

Terminology

Throughout this book I have used the term *learner* to include, at least, the following: student, trainee and apprentice. *Teacher* is used to indicate teacher, lecturer, trainer and tutor. I have generally used the term *lifelong learning sector* to include, at least: further education, post-compulsory education and training (PCET), colleges, work-based learning, adult and community learning and offender learning.

I hope you will excuse the slight bias towards English, communication studies and media studies in the examples. These, and teacher training, are the main things I delivered during my 22 years in further education.

1 The reflective teacher

The most distinctive of these very good teachers is that their practice is the result of careful reflection ... They themselves learn lessons each time they teach, evaluating what they do and using these self-critical evaluations to adjust what they do next time.

(Why Colleges Succeed, Ofsted 2004, para. 19)

What this chapter is about

- Reflective practice – what is it? Why and how should we do it?
- Reflection 'in' and 'on' action
- Some models of reflective practice
- Using reflection as a basis for improving learning and teaching
- Writing your personal development journal (PDJ)
- Your individual learning plan (ILP)
- What makes a good teacher in lifelong learning?

LLUK standards

This chapter covers, at least, the following standards:

AS 4; AK 4.2; AP 4.2; AK 4.3; AP 4.3
CK 1.1; CP 1.1; CK 4.1; CP 4.1
DS 3; DK 3.1

What is reflective practice?

The LLUK Professional Standards for teachers, tutors and trainers in the lifelong learning sector state that those working in the sector should value 'Reflection and evaluation of their own practice and their continuing professional development as teachers' (AS 4). In addition, their professional knowledge and understanding includes: 'Ways to reflect, evaluate and use research to develop own practice and to share good practice with others'. As part of their professional practice, they should: 'Share good practice with others and engage in continuing professional development through reflection, evaluation and the appropriate use of research'.

Qualified Teacher Learning and Skills status requires trainees to begin the practice of continuing professional development (CPD) right from the start of their training by keeping a development journal. This practice continues after completion of training; all teachers in lifelong learning are required to provide evidence of a minimum of 30 hours CPD each year in order to maintain their licence to practice.

There is one quality above all that makes a good teacher – the ability to reflect on what, why and how we do things and to adapt and develop our practice within lifelong learning. Reflection is the key to successful learning for teachers, and for learners. As the LLUK standards make clear reflection is an underpinning value and is the key to becoming a professional teacher.

A commonsense view of reflection is that it involves just thinking about things. Perhaps, thinking about the structure of the universe or why you disagreed with your partner last night could be regarded as reflection – others might consider it nothing more than idle and self-indulgent speculation. Most of us spend time thinking about what we do and the effects we have on others, but we don't always take it a step further and reflect on our actions and make plans to do things differently.

In a professional setting, reflection is:

- deliberate;
- purposeful;
- structured;
- about linking theory and practice;
- to do with learning;
- about change and development – becoming a reflective teacher.

Jenny Moon suggests:

> Reflection is a form of mental processing that we use to fulfil a purpose or to achieve some anticipated outcome. It is applied to gain a better understanding of relatively complicated or unstructured ideas and is largely based on the reprocessing of knowledge, understanding and, possibly, emotions that we already possess.
>
> (Moon 2005: 1)

From 'help!' to 'second nature'

The process of reflection helps us to monitor our own development from raw beginner to experienced professional. Reynolds's (1965) model of developing competence in social work suggests the stages seen in Figure 1.1. Those of you who recall learning to drive will recognise these stages. Mastering, for example, clutch control is a deliberate practice of trying, sometimes failing, trying again, becoming confident, until it eventually becomes an unconscious process. Our teaching careers follow a similar process: early fears about the timing of activities or the use of information technology (IT) are initially difficult, even frightening, but eventually become second nature.

Another, uncredited model, suggests a movement through the stages of:

- *unconscious incompetence* – in which we are unaware of what we can't do or don't know;
- *conscious incompetence* – in which we become aware of our development needs and start to do something about them;
- *conscious competence* – where we are using our new skills and knowledge, but watching and monitoring ourselves;
- *unconscious competence* – the skills become naturalised. This is like Reynolds's notion of 'second nature'.

Many of our skills, our knowledge and competences will become, like driving a car, second nature. However, we must ensure that 'second nature' doesn't become complacency. Success in teaching requires us always to challenge and develop our practice by regular reflection and review.

David Berliner (2001) outlines the stages of teacher development as going from the Novice – raw recruit who is learning the basics and is relatively inflexible – to the Expert, who is very much like the racing driver or the

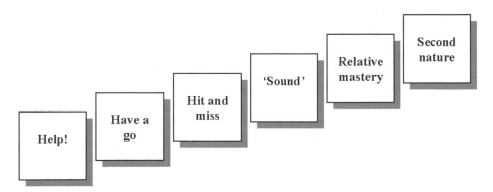

Figure 1.1 From Reynolds's (1965) model of developing competence.

professional footballer who is completely at one with their art, performing effortlessly and naturally. Experience and length of service do not, however, necessarily make an expert; experience needs reflection if we are to become expert teachers.

Rollett (2001) describes what it means to be an expert teacher. This is a very useful model and is worth quoting at length:

> Experts rely on a large repertoire of strategies and skills that they can call on automatically, leaving them free to deal with unique or unexpected events ... The wealth of knowledge and routines that they employ, in fact, is so automatic that they often do not realise why they preferred a certain plan of action over another. However, when questioned, they are able to reconstruct the reasons for their decisions and behaviour.
>
> (Rollett 2001: 27)

Reflection – some theory

John Dewey was a leading educational philosopher of the late nineteenth and early twentieth centuries whose ideas are still influential. He believed that traditional education, as then practised in his native America, was rigid, static and inadequate for the rapidly developing society and economy of the time. (The same criticism is frequently made of education today!) Dewey advocated child-centred learning and stressed the importance of each individual's lived experience as a starting point for learning.

Key to Dewey's philosophy was the development of thinking, particularly, reflective thinking. In *How We Think*, he states that:

> Thought affords the sole method of escape from purely impulsive or purely routine action. A being without capacity for thought is moved only by instincts and appetites, as these are called forth by outward conditions and the inner state of the organism. A being thus moved is, as it were, pushed from behind.
>
> (Dewey 1933: 15)

Such a person is, in other words, not in control. They are dragged along by events, unable to understand or change them. To use more up to date terminology, such a person is merely reactive, rather than active or proactive – things happen to them; they don't make things happen. We must, as Dewey says, move from routine action to reflective action which is characterised by ongoing self-appraisal and development.

Dewey believed that reflection begins in a state of doubt or perplexity which, for teachers, is most likely to be encountered when working with learners, particularly new or unfamiliar learners. When we are faced with difficulties and uncertainties in practice, when things don't go according to plan or don't fit with the theory, we may feel powerless and unable to resolve the situation. For, Dewey, however, these are key moments for learning; we can reflect on these problems to solve the perplexity and learn from it.

Donald Schön (1983) developed the notions of *reflection in action* and *reflection on action*. For the purposes of this book I will explain these two concepts very simply as 'reflecting while you're doing it' and 'reflecting after you've done it'. When delivering the learning you have so carefully planned and prepared, you need to be constantly aware and monitoring the session as it develops. This awareness allows you to make changes as the situation demands, to be able to 'think on your feet'. When the session is complete you can reflect on, analyse and evaluate the learning and teaching. This post-action reflection then informs your subsequent planning and preparation leading to a cycle of continuing improvement. We can represent the process as in Figure 1.2.

A further development in Schön's work is the distinction between *technical rationality* and *tacit knowledge*. This distinction could be characterised more simply as the 'theory-practice gap'. Like Dewey, Schön believed that reflection begins in working practice, particularly those areas of practice where professionals are confronted with unique and confusing situations – 'the swampy lowlands of practice' as Schön calls them. Teachers may have acquired the theoretical knowledge (technical rationality) of their subject or of the practice of teaching and learning, but whilst this might explain their classroom practice as it should be, it might not explain it as it actually is. From these real-life experiences teachers can develop tacit knowledge – a synthesis of theory and practice which they have developed for themselves. It is vital that these learning experiences are recorded in journals and discussed with mentors and fellow trainees.

Trainee teachers might express the opinion that 'this theory stuff is all very well, but it doesn't work in the real world'. Teacher trainers may be offended by such rejections of theory, but their trainees may have a point – theory is only of any use when it is applied and developed in practice. The real teaching environment is where theory is applied, tested and evaluated. Theory is never used rigidly, nor does it provide all the answers to the problems teachers encounter. It is, however, the starting point for developing teaching and learning in practice. Reflection, in and on action, allows teachers to continually improve their practice and even to the development of *practice-based theory*.

During your training, and as a result of reading this book, you will acquire a body of theoretical knowledge related to teaching and learning which you will want to apply in your learning sessions. For, example, humanist theories of teaching and learning stress the development of the whole person and the

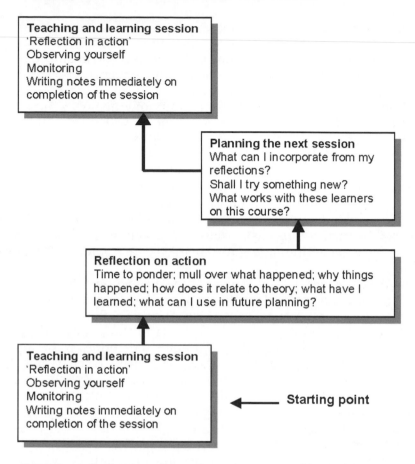

Figure 1.2 Using reflection *in* and *on* action to improve teaching and learning.

creation of a non-threatening, positive learning environment. In practice, this might not be as easy as the theory suggests. However, this does not invalidate the theory, but it does mean you will need to adapt and experiment with it in practice. Schön calls this application and development of theory in the real world *theory-in-use*.

The notion of reflection linking theory and practice underlies the work of Kolb and of Gibbs. The models of learning and reflection they developed are sometimes called 'iterative' because they are based on a repeating, but continually evolving and improving, cycle of learning.

Kolb (1984) is explained in detail in the chapter on learning theory. Essentially, his Experiential Learning Theory shows a four-stage cycle of activity. These four elements are:

- concrete experience;
- reflection;
- abstract conceptualisation;
- active experimentation.

The learner, in this case the teacher, can begin the cycle at any point but must follow each step in order.

Consider, for example, that a trainee teacher uses role play in a session (concrete experience). The role play is partially successful. The teacher reflects on the use of this learning method and considers how it could be improved and made more effective (reflection). She reads up on the use of role play and talks to more experienced colleagues and, as a result, formulates an improved version of the activity (abstract conceptualisation). The next time she plans to use role play she incorporates her new ideas into the planning (active experimentation). This leads to a new concrete experience and the repetition of the cycle.

Activity

Consider a recent example from your own teaching when you have tried a new method or resource. Using Kolb's four stages, consider the development of the technique in practice.

Several writers on reflective practice have emphasised the importance of the teacher's feelings as part of the reflective process. This fits in with the development of emotional intelligence, which is discussed later in the book. We may experience a wide range of feelings during and after our teaching – elation, confusion, anger, helplessness, blaming the learners – and it is important to recognise and reflect on them.

Gibbs (1988) adds feelings to his model of 'learning by doing'. See Figure 1.3 for the stages of learning in his model.

Gibbs's model provides key points in development, especially description, evaluation, analysis and action, which we will consider further in the section on methods of reflection. Before then we need to examine the reasons for reflective practice.

Reflective practice – why should we do it?

An obvious answer is because we've got to! However, this is not a good reason for doing it.

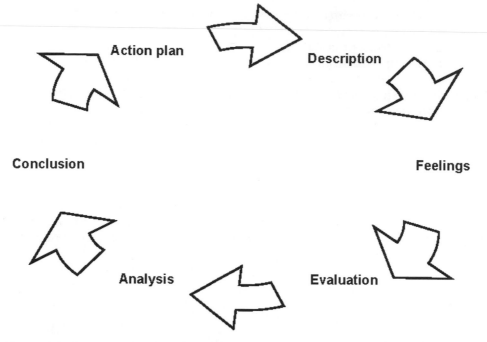

Figure 1.3   Gibbs's model of 'learning by doing'.

As we have already agreed, reflective practice is a professional requirement that we have to provide evidence of, usually in a journal or log. This requirement brings teachers in the lifelong learning sector up to date with other professionals, such as nurses, social workers and human resource professionals. Just as we wouldn't want to be cared for by a nurse who wasn't familiar with the latest techniques, we probably won't want to be taught by someone who doesn't know their subject or the best ways of teaching and learning.

Another reason for reflective practice is because it encourages us to understand our learners and their needs and abilities. Every learner is different and there are likely to be varying interpretations of what we say and do within any group of learners. There are 'different worlds' within our classrooms and skilled teachers will try to see themselves as their students see them. Stephen Brookfield believes that: 'Of all the pedagogic tasks teachers face, getting inside students' heads is one of the trickiest. It is also the most crucial' (Brookfield 1995: 92).

This book is based on the principle that active learning is preferable to passive learning and that active learning requires reflection. Reflective teachers are more likely to develop reflective learners. If we practise reflection we can more effectively encourage learners to reflect on, analyse, evaluate and improve their own learning. These are key skills in active learning and the development of independent learners.

Reflection can also help us to develop our emotional intelligence, particularly if we include a consideration of feelings as part of our reflections. The concept of emotional intelligence, developed by Daniel Goleman (1995, 1998), encourages the development of self-awareness of feelings and the recognition and management of emotions.

Finally, and most importantly, reflective practice is the key to improvement. If we don't think about, analyse and evaluate our professional practice we cannot improve.

Activity

Empathy (see Chapter 4, 'Communication and the teacher') is important in developing your reflective practice, particularly the ability to imagine what it would be like as a learner in your own class.

I can well recall a staff development session in which a colleague talked to us for more than an hour. At the end of it I was extremely annoyed at just being a passive object. It was a salutary experience and made me realise what it would be like to be a student in a passive, non-stimulating environment.

When you're teaching you have considerable freedom of movement and activity – you can stand up; sit down; walk around and, generally, direct operations. This is not usually the case for learners.

Next time you're in 'learner mode', at a conference or staff development session, think about how you feel. Do you feel stimulated, interested, engaged, or restless and fidgety? Would you like to move around a bit, stand up for a while, say something, do something?

Reflective practice – how to do it

Reflection is a process and an activity which teachers undertake primarily for themselves. It is not about the production of mountains of paper evidence at the behest of teacher trainers or managers – such 'other-directed' activity becomes a chore for trainees and teachers from which they will derive little value. Reflection will, however, lead to a product – diary, log, PDJ – which will contribute to assessment and, subsequently, be used as evidence of CPD.

The right mental attitude

We should remember that reflection is not an end in itself; it is the starting point of becoming a reflective practitioner. For Jenny Moon reflection is used, 'with the sense of saying something not so much about what a person does as what they are' (Moon 1999).

The basis of all reflection is a willingness to undertake the process and to value it as means of improvement and development. Reflection can be difficult, even threatening, because it forces us to be honest with ourselves and recognise not only our successes but areas where we need to improve. It makes us take responsibility for our teaching and learning. Being a reflective practitioner is like being your own observer and your own critical friend. We can refer to this willingness to reflect and develop as the 'right mental attitude', without which the whole process of reflection is pointless.

The professional development journal (PDJ)

There are many forms of reflection and occasions on which you will reflect, but as a trainee teacher the main form of reflection will be through your reflective journal, commonly referred to as the professional development journal.

Your PDJ is a written record of your experiences of, and feelings about planning, preparing and delivering teaching and learning. It will contain general accounts of learning sessions but, more importantly, will identify critical incidents which can be the basis for learning and continuing professional development (CPD).

The PDJ is subjective; it is written by you and for you and gives an opportunity to conduct a dialogue with yourself. You must remember, however, that as a trainee your tutors and mentors will see the journal, so it pays not to be indiscreet or make personal comments. The journal is also a place where you can relate theory to practice. We have already established that theory is only useful if it is used, tested and evaluated in your teaching and learning.

Success, or otherwise, in teaching is not just a matter of luck. It results from thorough planning and preparation, knowing your students, and reflection on, and evaluation of, your practice. You will experience the wonderful feeling you get after a class has gone well; the learners, and you, have enjoyed themselves and, above all, learned. You will also experience the depths of despair following a session which just hasn't worked, where the learners don't seem to want to learn and you just long for the end of it all. The reflective teacher uses both extremes to learn and develop. If it went well, are there general conclusions you can draw to try with other learners? Are there specific points you can use with this group again – remember each group of learners is unique and reflection helps you to get to know them and work effectively with them. After the dreadful session, you might be chastising yourself (or worse, your learners) for the failure. Neither course is appropriate. You must reflect, analyse, evaluate, learn and change.

One of the most valuable functions of your PDJ is to help you identify development points for action planning. You should review your journal regularly to see if there any recurring themes which you need to pick up on for your training and development. It will be useful to summarise your journal at the end of your course. This summary can have two functions; first, you can see how far you have come since you started your training and, second, you can use it as the basis for your CPD. Remember, evidence of CPD is a requirement in getting and maintaining QTLS.

Writing your PDJ

Many trainee teachers in PCET worry about writing their journals – what form should it take; typed or handwritten; how much; how often; is it right? The main message is – don't worry. When it comes to journals, you can't do them wrong! There are, however, guidelines and advice to help you make them more useful and more effective.

Writing and written style

Writing is a very effective way to make sense of experience – to organise, evaluate and learn from it. Creative writing is often used as a form of therapy by which people can work things out and find solutions for problems. Cognitive behavioural therapy requires clients to recognise and write down examples of mistaken thinking and to imagine more positive scenarios – in other words to reflect, analyse, evaluate and, most importantly, change.

It is important to get into the habit of writing and to do it as soon as possible after the event. It's a good idea to include a reflection box at the end of your session plans in which to record some immediate thoughts which will form the basis of your journal entry. When you start writing, don't spend too much time thinking about it. Let the writing flow and try to capture the experience and some critical incidents (see below). Once you've recalled the events, then you can start to learn from them.

Little and often is a good rule, particularly in the early days of journal writing. You should always be regular in your journal writing habits. You might find it useful to track a particular group of learners or, perhaps, to compare groups. Your course tutors will advise you regarding how much you should write and what period of time your journal should cover.

As for writing style, you should be free, spontaneous and informal. There's no need for the impersonal, academic style; some of the best journals I've seen are quirky and idiosyncratic. You must, however, avoid inappropriate language or too much slang or colloquialism and never make personal comments about teachers or colleagues – unless, of course, you are referring to their good practice. There will be times when you are frustrated and annoyed in your training or in your work. You can use your journal to get some of this out of your system, it can even be therapeutic, but you must use it as a basis for learning and development – extended moaning is not acceptable.

In keeping with the spontaneous and informal approach you will probably write your journal by hand, but it's best to check if your tutors have any preferences regarding written or word-processed documents. Some of you will prefer to type your reflections straight on to your computer, possibly using a template you have designed to suit your needs. When you are reviewing your journal it's useful to highlight key points for your summary, for action plans, or as discussion points for tutorials.

I have known trainees who recorded their journals on to dictation machines (digital rather than tape). This can increase the spontaneity but, obviously, necessitates transcription into written form – if you've got voice-activated software this is less of a problem. Increasingly, trainees are experimenting with using blogs for their reflective journals. This provides some interesting opportunities for sharing ideas with a whole range of people and even the development of 'communities of practice'. Again, you must check with your tutors regarding the acceptability of this format.

Communities of practice don't have to be online. You can share your reflections with fellow trainees in taught sessions or group tutorials. It can be very helpful to find that colleagues are experiencing the same uncertainties or difficulties as you and, hopefully, enjoying successes. Sharing ideas and developing strategies together is an extremely valuable collaborative activity. You may even wish to build in presentations to colleagues on particular issues.

Many teachers, like many learners, have a visual learning preference and, as such will want to include diagrams, drawings or any other visual modes. I always encourage this, particularly as visuals can help you get the big picture and explore relationships between ideas. One of my former students who taught art produced a wonderful journal full of written entries, pictures, sketches, quotes and jokes – quite a work of art in itself. Personalise your journal by all means, but remember you will need to share it with your tutors, and possibly submit it for assessment, so be prepared to summarise and translate as necessary.

More than just description

The most inadequate reflections are those which merely describe what happened in a teaching and learning session. On its own, this is of no value.

But it is a start. To the *description* (what happened?) you need to add *analysis* (how, why?); *evaluation* (how effective was it?) and *conclusions* (suggestions for future practice).

Driscoll and Teh (2001), working in nursing and clinical practice, provide a simple but very useful framework for reflection based on three questions:

- What?   Description of the event
- So what?   Analysis of the event
- Now what?   Proposed actions following the event

They also provide a range of 'trigger questions' for each stage. For example:

WHAT?

- What happened?
- What did I see/do?

SO WHAT?

- How did I feel at the time?
- What were the effects of what I did (or did not do)?

NOW WHAT?

- What are the implications of what I have described and analysed?
- How can I modify my practice?

Perhaps the most complete model of reflection is provided by Gibbs (1988). This makes explicit the need for conclusions and action plans. The trigger questions he suggests are shown below:

Description: What happened? Don't make judgements yet or try to draw conclusions; simply describe.

Feelings: What were your reactions and feelings? Again, don't move on to analysing these yet.

Evaluation: What was good or bad about the experience? Make value judgements.

Analysis: What sense can you make of the situation? Bring in ideas from outside the experience to help you. What was really going on? Were different people's experiences similar or different in important ways?

Conclusions: What can be concluded, in a general sense, from
(general) these experiences and the analyses you have undertaken?

Conclusions: *(specific)*	What can be concluded about your own specific, unique, personal situation or way of working?
Personal *action* *plans:*	What are you going to do differently in this type of situation next time? What steps are you going to take on the basis of what you have learned?

Critical incidents

When writing your journal you will almost inevitably identify critical incidents. These are specific occurrences within teaching and learning sessions which you consider significant or important. Critical incidents may be positive or negative. They can be moments in which you suddenly become aware of a problem, or a solution to a problem; when you realise that you have a particular development need or a particular strength. They could be described as 'light bulb' moments when there is a particular incident or a sudden realisation. For example, as young and naïve teacher, I made what I considered to be a humorous comment about a student's name. His strong, negative reaction was a critical, and memorable, incident for me when I realised that people's names are precious to them and should be respected.

You will have many critical incidents in your training and during your working life as a teacher; they are all occasions for learning. You might, for example, be faced with behavioural difficulties with learners or a refusal by one, or all, of a group to engage. You might suddenly realise that you have talked for too long and the answer is to provide a change of activity. Critical incidents will often lead to generalisable ideas and solutions which are transferable to other groups and learning situations.

Layout and form of your PDJ

PDJs can take many forms – notebook; a ring-binder with loose-leaf pages; a file on your computer – whatever is easiest for you. Again, you should check with your course tutors to see if they have any preferences, although generally teacher trainers avoid giving too many guidelines for PDJs, for fear of producing uniformity and stifling the student's own approach. If you use a notebook, an A4 size with perforated and hole-punched pages will be the easiest to use. You can design your own template for use with word-processing, perhaps using categories such as:

- description;
- analysis and evaluation;
- conclusions for future practice.

I favour just a straightforward written narrative without too much preconceived structure which might detract from the spontaneity.

A useful device has been developed by Heath (1998) which involves a split-page or two page approach, using the left-hand side to record the description of the events and the right-hand side is used for reflection.

Left-hand page	*Right-hand page*
Time/date/contextual details	Reflection
Description of the session	Analysis and evaluation
Describe critical incidents	Reference to theory (if appropriate)
Initial feelings	Thoughts added during review or tutorials

Individual learning plans (ILPs)

In your work or on your teaching placements you will very likely have negotiated and used ILPs with your learners; you will be expected to do the same as a trainee on a course leading to QTLS.

Your ILP can be considered as the starting point of reflection and of your CPD. It can take the form of an audit of your existing knowledge, skills, attitudes and personal qualities; to identify your strengths, and to highlight any uncertainties you have about becoming a teacher in the lifelong learning sector. It is most likely that your course tutors will provide an ILP format which you will be expected to use as an initial audit, but also as a document to refer to during tutorials and as a measure of the distance you have travelled at the end of your course. The important point is to use the ILP to kick-start your personal and professional development, not merely something you produce because you've been asked to.

If you haven't been provided with an ILP pro-forma, here are a few areas you might wish to consider for your development. You can develop a rating scale for these so that you can see your starting point and the distance travelled.

What do you know about or how confident are you about:

- the roles and responsibilities of a teacher?
- learning styles?
- planning a course?
- planning a session?
- how people learn?
- Skills for Life and Key Skills?
- communication skills?
- presentation skills?
- demonstration skills?

- questioning and explaining?
- using a range of teaching and learning methods?
- designing and using resources?
- using ICT?
- health and safety?
- assessing learning?
- reflection?
- equality, inclusion and diversity?
- subject knowledge and skills?
  - how up to date are you?
  - latest ideas in teaching and learning
  - sources of information
  - subject specialist professional development.

An 'autobiographical' approach to your ILP

Stephen Brookfield (1995) suggests we have four 'critically reflective lenses' through which we can reflect on our teaching. These are:

- our autobiographies as learners and teachers;
- our students' eyes;
- our colleagues' experiences;
- theoretical literature.

We will concentrate here on the first of these lenses – our autobiographies as teachers and learners.

Our preferred learning style will significantly affect our teaching style. Without reflection, there is a danger that we will teach in the ways we ourselves like to be taught. For example, if your school experience was of didactic, teacher-centred lessons or of formal lectures at university, these could become your dominant mode of teaching. If you have happy memories of making discoveries in science or researching a project for history, you will probably want to incorporate such methods into your teaching. Many people have bad memories of school and how these affected their learning. Maths, for me, was just an alternative spelling of the word 'fear'; answers were either right or wrong and wrong meant trouble. No one told me that maths could be interesting and useful, even fun.

So, a useful starting point on your critically reflective journey might to be recall and discuss some of your experiences of being a student and of being taught.

What makes a good teacher?

When you start teaching it's useful to have some sort of guidelines or role models of good teachers to provide something to aim at, especially when you're starting your ILP.

'Good teachers are born not made'

You might have heard this old maxim and thought yourself not suited to be a teacher. The main problem with this saying is that it's wrong. True, there are those who exhibit confidence and an ability to inspire and motivate groups of people. Such people, however, are not necessarily good teachers. They may struggle to plan classes, to explain properly, to assess, and are deficient in a whole range of other necessary skills. They might occasionally provide a stimulating session – but they fly by the seat of their pants. This is no way to teach. Teaching in lifelong learning is a profession and requires you to behave like a professional by learning and developing the necessary skills and practice.

Activity

Best and worst teachers.

1 Think back to your days at school, college or university. Think of someone who was a particularly good teacher.

2 List the top five personal qualities, skills or attitudes which made them so good.

3 Think of your worst teacher.

4 List the top five personal qualities, skills or attitudes which made them so bad.

5 As a group, identify any recurring themes.

6 Produce a top five for the group.

The introductory statement to the LLUK standards states that:

> Teachers in the lifelong learning sector value all learners individually and equally. They are committed to lifelong learning and professional development and strive for continuous improvement through reflective practice. The key purpose of the teacher, tutor or trainer is to create

effective and stimulating opportunities for learning through high quality teaching that enables the development and progression of all learners.

(LLUK 2006: 1)

Lifelong learning is a diverse sector with millions of learners in a wide range of settings. You will need a variety of teaching and learning methods in your toolbox if you wish to be successful. In addition, you will need to know about your learners and what elements of good practice will develop effective learning. Fortunately, there is plenty of research to help you.

Rosenshine (1971) developed the following list of effective teaching behaviours. Although this research is over 30 years old now and is based on teaching in schools, it is still relevant today, to both the compulsory and post-compulsory sectors. According to Rosenshine, good teachers show these characteristics:

1   introducing (structuring) topics or activities clearly
2   explaining clearly with examples and illustrative materials
3   systematic and business-like organisation of lessons
4   variety of teaching materials and methods
5   use of questions, especially higher-order questions
6   use of praise and other reinforcement (verbal and nonverbal)
7   encouraging learner participation
8   making use of learners' ideas, clarifying and developing them further
9   warmth, rapport and enthusiasm, mainly shown nonverbally

A simpler and more reliable guide to teacher skills and qualities is provided by the Association of Colleges (AOC) and FENTO publication *Mentoring Towards Excellence* (2001). As part of this project 700 learners were asked what they thought makes for good teachers and teaching.

Top five professional characteristics:

Understanding and supportive
Committed, dedicated and hardworking
Fair with an inclusive and respectful approach
Warm
Humorous

Top five teaching skills:

Clear instruction and presentation
Strong communication and active listening

Patience
Motivation and encouragement
Organisation and classroom management

Top five favourite teacher qualities:

Sound subject knowledge
Understanding and gives good advice
Creative, interesting and imaginative
Warm and cheery
Clear instruction and presentation.

Adult expectations of teachers

Across the whole lifelong learning sector most learners are adults, some returning to learning after a considerable time away from it. Research, especially by Malcolm Knowles (1978), suggests that adults have particular characteristics. In addition to the guidelines above, adults expect teachers to:

- treat them as adults – this sounds obvious but adult learners often report that they have felt patronised or treated like children;
- recognise their life experiences – adults will have many experiences relevant to your sessions. They will expect to have them acknowledged and, wherever possible, integrated into the teaching and learning;
- provide them with support and guidance – despite their life experiences many adult learners will feel anxious and ambivalent about returning to learning, especially if they have bad memories of school;
- respect their self-concept – adults will want to take increasing responsibility for their own decisions and are capable of self-direction;
- help them develop autonomy and independence as learners.

Above all, teachers need to understand their learners, their characteristics, needs and motivations. They need to be able to adapt and adjust content and style to suit the needs of groups and individuals. Most importantly, they must be good communicators – this takes us neatly to the next chapter.

For your PDJ

If you are just starting your career in lifelong learning, the important thing is just to get yourself a notebook or set up a document on your computer and just begin writing.

You can begin by reflecting on your feelings of meeting learners for the first time. It's easy to be negative and just concentrate on what you feel went wrong, but try to consider the positives as well. If the learners became more attentive or responsive, try to work out what you did that made the difference.

Start reading and researching your subject and general texts on teaching and learning. Talk to colleagues and students; get some feedback.

Journal extract: Martyn, training to teach popular music

My journal ... records not just the disconsolate musings that follow an unsuccessful session but also episodes of naïve joy and moments of sudden enlightenment that the Japanese call 'satori'. Each evening at 8:00 pm my mobile phone alerts me to the need to complete my PDJ and it is in this *regularity* that I find most reward as it determines that *all* of the emotional ebb and flow of 'learning to teach and teaching to learn' is recorded. The mixed media format of my journal reflects not just an abiding passion for collage but also the cut and paste/record and overdub nature of 'pop'. My PDJ is a 'visual representation of (my) values, opinions and philosophy' and a working document to which I constantly refer. It is not simply a diary of critical incidents but something to read, question, amend and augment.

Further reading

Brookfield, S. (1995) *Becoming a Critically Reflective Teacher*. San Francisco: Jossey-Bass.

Gibbs, G. (1988) *Learning by Doing*. London: Further Education Unit.

Moon, J. (1999) *Reflection in Learning and Professional Development*. London: Kogan Page.

Moon, J. (2005) *Guide for Busy Academics No. 4: Learning Through Reflection*. Higher Education Academy.

2 Communication and the teacher

It is important that the training of teachers incorporates knowledge of the processes of interpersonal communication that lie at the heart of effective learning and teaching. ... Is it not surprising that professional communicators should not be trained to communicate?

(Harkin, Turner and Dawn 2001: 72)

What this chapter is about

- What is communication?
- Communication theory for teachers
- Barriers to communication
- How learners construct meaning
- Communication skills, including: nonverbal communication (NVC); listening; speaking; empathy; giving and receiving feedback
- Communication 'climate' and emotional intelligence

LLUK standards

This chapter covers, at least, the following standards:

AK 5.1; AP 5.1: AK 5.2; AP 5.2
BS 3; BK 1.1; BP 1.1; BK 1.3; BP 1.3; BK 3.1; BP 3.1; BK 3.2; BP 3.2; BK 3.3
BP 3.3; BK 3.4; BP 3.4;

What is communication?

This book is based on the belief that effective communication is the foundation of all successful teaching and learning, not just a peripheral concern. There seems to be an assumption that communication and communication skills cannot be taught; that communication is something you are either good at or not. But, there are many successful courses and therapeutic procedures which can and do improve people's communication skills. We could argue that communication is the most important element of teacher training and that becoming a successful teacher entails identifying, evaluating and developing your communication skills. It has frequently been said that, 'One cannot not communicate'. Therefore, as reflective teachers, we need to be aware that everything we do is communicative and will have an impact on the success and effectiveness of our teaching.

There are many definitions of communication, but it's a difficult beast to tie down and define precisely and accurately. Communication is the glue that holds societies together; it makes connections and interactions between people possible. Communication is the start and end point of all human interaction and it makes possible everything we want to do. We communicate to achieve particular needs and purposes – to make friends, to persuade, to form relationships, to teach and to learn. Many introductory teacher training texts add a piece about communication as an afterthought, but it is important to remember that communication is what makes it all possible. As teachers our primary function is to communicate; our purpose is to teach and to facilitate learning.

The study of communication basically comprises two schools of thought. The first sees communication as a process involving the transmission of messages from senders to receivers. The second sees communication as a social activity which people create and exchange meaning. We do not need to concern ourselves here with the debates between these two schools; we can learn something from both of them.

Contrary to popular opinion, communication does not involve the transmission of thoughts. This simple principle underlies all communication theory. You can prove this by a simple experiment. Think of something and focus all your attention on that thought. Now turn to the person next to you and, without speaking or moving or any form of physical action, transfer this thought to that person. I can fairly safely predict that the thought remained in your head and stubbornly refused to cross to the mind of your colleague.

So, if we can't exchange thoughts, how is communication possible? Whenever we need to communicate we have to find a way of encoding this need into a form that can be transmitted – spoken or written words, a gesture, a facial expression. This message is then sent to, and received by, someone who decodes it and, hopefully, understands it. This, put simply, is the process school.

However, we can immediately see some problems with this explanation of communication as a process when someone says 'I don't understand what you mean' (a frequent complaint of learners, it seems). The sender of the message, in this case the teacher, could easily blame the receiver for not paying sufficient attention or not being sufficiently intelligent; it's all too easy to blame learners for not understanding. Alternatively, the teacher might assume there is a problem in the process of transmission which can be solved, perhaps, by speaking more slowly or clearly, using a different explanation, or making the handouts more readable. A third explanation is possible – the receiver (the learner) just doesn't understand because they have no previous experience or concepts that they can connect the new information and ideas to. People can't just be given meanings; they have to create them for themselves and fit them into the things they already know. This is the essence of the school of communication which sees communication as the creation of meaning.

The teacher's job is to help learners create meanings by connecting with their existing knowledge and understanding. As we shall see in subsequent chapters, this relates to the ideas of constructivism and meaningful learning. Equally, however, the teacher's role is to create the best conditions for learning and the most effective ways of communicating.

Some communication theory

As we have seen in Chapter 1, theory is really only useful for teachers if they test it out in practice and make use of it. In the same way, the models of communication shown here are to be used to analyse, evaluate and develop your communication skills.

Sender–Receiver model

The simple model shown in Figure 2.1, developed from the work of Shannon and Weaver, shows communication as a process and is sometimes known as a Sender–Receiver model.

Take an example of a teacher using a PowerPoint presentation to explain behaviourism. The process goes something like this:

1   The teacher needs to explain behaviourism in a psychology class simply because the specifications demand it and, therefore, the learners have to know it.
2   The information is encoded in written language and visual images on the PowerPoint slides.
3   The information is transmitted, using the medium of the PowerPoint presentation via the visual channel.
4   The message is received by the learners.
5   The message is decoded by the learners.
6   The message is understood – or not.

We can use this model as an analytical tool to identify barriers and diminish

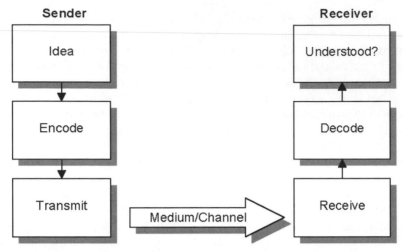

Figure 2.1 Sender–Receiver model of communication.
Source: Based on Shannon and Weaver (1949).

difficulties in the process of communication. A communication barrier is anything which prevents a message from a communicator reaching the receiver – from teachers to learners. When Shannon and Weaver developed their model, they identified three categories of barriers which could interfere with effective communication – physical or mechanical barriers; semantic barriers; psychological barriers. Using the model and the three types of barriers we can consider stages at which communication might be problematic and some of the possible causes.

Physical or mechanical barriers

These barriers are about the physical transmission and reception of the message. Examples could be the readability and focus of the overhead projector (OHP) or data projector; the volume of the teacher's voice; and noise inside or outside. Students who are uncomfortable because of excessive heat, cold or thirst will find it difficult to concentrate. You might have learners who have hearing or sight difficulties for whom you need to adapt materials and presentations.

Semantic barriers

Semantic barriers are essentially to do with meaning and the extent to which meanings are successfully shared or generated. At one level this could be to do with spoken or written language – possibly the use of jargon or technical language which is not yet understood by the learners. For example, students doing a simple research project for a level 2 will be mystified by discussions of epistemology or ontology. Equally, a generation gap between learners and students might result in the use of unfamiliar concepts or reference points – if you're over 50, your younger learners will know little of The Beatles, let alone The Small Faces or The Troggs! Problems with meaning can also occur at a nonverbal level, for example if teachers or learners use unfamiliar or culturally-specific gestures, such as the thumb and first finger forming a ring. In America and many western countries this means 'A-OK'. In some cultures it says, 'You're worth nothing'. In yet other cultures, the meaning of this gesture is far too offensive even to discuss here.

Psychological barriers

The ways in which we perceive other people affect how we approach them and how we communicate with them. But our perceptions are influenced by our beliefs, values and attitudes. The attitudes we have towards individuals and groups can be positive or negative – even the most well-intentioned and sensitive of us will have some element of prejudice which will affect our perceptions of our learners. These kinds of prejudice can lead us to make assumptions about learners, which, if we don't subsequently adjust them as we get to know people, will affect our communication with them. At their worst these types of barriers can lead to sexism and racism and assumptions that those of a particular race or gender will be less or more able than others. Psychological barriers can lead to teachers taking contributions from some learners more favourably than others or treating some learners with less respect than others. Similarly, insensitivity or uncertainty can lead us to make assumptions about the disabilities and abilities of learners.

Using the Sender-Receiver model and its associated barriers we can consider how, and at what points in the process, the teacher's communication could go wrong.

- *Motivation for teaching and learning* – this is the first step in our example of the psychology teacher explaining behaviourism. If, even unconsciously, you give the impression you are only doing this because the specifications demand it then students will regard it as little more than drudgery. You must always explain why a particular topic is important, relevant and, above all, something learners can connect to their own experience and make meaningful. For example, students who are not interested in statistics can suddenly become enthused if they are encouraged to apply them to their favourite sport.
- *The idea* – the content or the idea might not be fully realised or organised in the teacher's mind. Teachers need to be clear about the ideas they are communicating.

- *Encoding* – there may be problems with using jargon or inappropriate technical language, particularly if learners are new to this area of work. Encoding and decoding will only be successful if teachers and learners share, as far as possible, the same concepts and reference points.
- *Encoding and transmission* of the message can give learners an excellent concise, visual overview of the new concept. Conversely, if it is the third PowerPoint presentation they've seen that day they could be less receptive to the message.
- *Transmission* of the message can be ineffective in many ways, for example, the pace and volume of the teacher's voice; the visibility of visual aids; the size and layout of the room; the ability of all learners to see in a demonstration. It should be an easy job for teachers to check these things but, unfortunately, they are often overlooked.
- *Transmission of messages* – thought given to the transmission will aid the reception of the message. However, we need to ensure that we create an environment in which students are willing to receive messages. Even the most attentive adults can only listen and concentrate for relatively short periods of time – excessive teacher talk will, eventually, lead to inattentive learners. Consider the tone, pace and variability of your voice and keep teacher input lively. Learners are less likely to concentrate and attend to you if it's too hot or cold; if the session is too long; if they are thirsty or uncomfortable. Most importantly, learners will not be receptive to learning if they feel that the learning environment is not emotionally safe – if they are likely to be humiliated, ignored or not valued.
- *Decoding and encoding* are two sides of the same coin. Teachers have a responsibility to check learning and understanding. This is not done effectively by saying 'Is that alright?' or 'Does everybody understand?' Many learners, particularly younger ones, will find it too easy not to put their heads above the parapet and admit that they don't understand. Checking understanding can be done much more effectively by, for example, using open questions to get students to discuss and explore their learning.

Activity

Think of a recent learning session you have organised and delivered.

Use the Sender–Receiver model and associated barriers to analyse the *process* of communication in the session.

What specific conclusions can you draw to improve your future practice?

Who? What? To whom? How? Why?

Harold Lasswell, an American political scientist concerned with propaganda techniques, developed his general model of communication in 1948 (see Figure 2.2). It is a deceptively simple yet powerful tool which can be used to analyse virtually any communication event. Lasswell's original five questions were: Who? Says what? In which channel? To whom? With what effect? (Lasswell 1948). I have adapted the questions as follows:

- Who?
- Says what?
- To whom?
- How?
- Why?

To help you understand this model, I'll begin with a personal anecdote. When I rediscovered education as a mature student, I studied O Level sociology. Our first teacher was extremely erudite and knowledgeable sociologist with a real passion for his subject. Unfortunately, he didn't know how to adjust his teaching to suit a group of students keen to learn but with little or no sociological grounding. He wasn't able to consider how he would select what we needed to know from what he knew, and how to present it in a way that would gradually bring us into the subject and give us confidence. His approach just frightened off some of my fellow students. We are all experts in something but it can be all too easy to forget that our audience, our students, do not yet share our knowledge and skills.

Who?

The starting point of any effective communication is to consider you, the communicator, in this case the teacher. You may be highly qualified and knowledgeable in your subject but you must consider how you will select from your knowledge the necessary content for your learners at this stage in their learning. For example, a teacher with a Masters in English will not need to discuss Bernstein's theories of restricted and elaborated code with GCSE English language students.

You should also consider your personal style, your motivation for teaching, and your experience – how similar to or different from your learners are you? Equally importantly, you need to consider your experience as a learner: did you have a preferred learning style? If you did, you need to take care that this doesn't become your preferred teaching style. Just because you liked lectures, for example, this doesn't mean your learners will. This requires reflection.

Says what?

This develops from the point above. What are the elements of content, skills, knowledge and understanding which your learners need at this time? This may be related to the level (entry, foundation, intermediate or advanced) or the requirements of the specification. What must you include? What can you omit at present and return to when learners have the big picture? There will be many instances, particularly in adult and community education, where you will be able to negotiate content with your learners. Rogers (2001) outlines the concepts of *action learning* and *self-managed learning* by which learners can take some responsibility for what they learn and how they learn it.

To whom?

A key question for all lifelong learning teachers is 'who are your learners?' The LLUK standards stress the importance of teachers knowing their learners and their needs. You need to consider, for example: the age and gender composition of the group; the cultural mix of the group; their previous experience; and what existing knowledge and skills they have. One of your first tasks when you meet a new group of learners is to find out about them and what they already know and can do. As this book emphasises on many occasions, effective teaching and learning starts with what people already know.

How?

This includes, for example, what teaching and learning methods you will choose for this group and for this purpose. We will consider teaching strategies later but you will need to develop a wide range of different methods to suit different learners. There will be times when you need concentrated teacher input but others where you will want to develop more active or discovery learning strategies. When planning your teaching, you will have to consider how you can differentiate the learning for different members of the group.

Why?

A very basic question we may frequently overlook is, 'Why am I doing this?' Why am I teaching this class or why am I using this particular strategy? The answers will be many and varied. It might be because you've got to – because the specifications say you should; it could be that you wish to change people's attitudes or behaviour; it might be to develop particular skills in your learners. If you want to be an effective teacher you will definitely want to enthuse and motivate your learners.

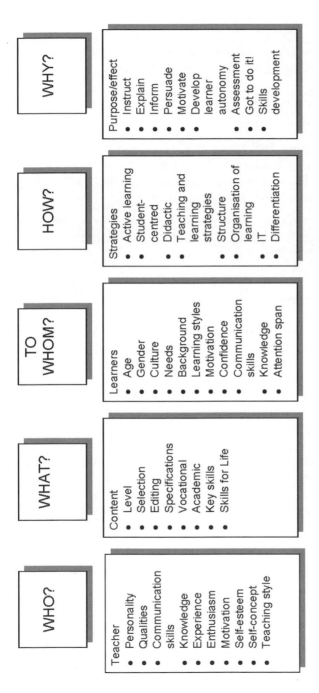

WHO?

Teacher
- Personality
- Qualities
- Communication skills
- Knowledge
- Experience
- Enthusiasm
- Motivation
- Self-esteem
- Self-concept
- Teaching style

WHAT?

Content
- Level
- Selection
- Editing
- Specifications
- Vocational
- Academic
- Key skills
- Skills for Life

TO WHOM?

Learners
- Age
- Gender
- Culture
- Needs
- Background
- Learning styles
- Motivation
- Confidence
- Communication skills
- Knowledge
- Attention span

HOW?

Strategies
- Active learning
- Student-centred
- Didactic
- Teaching and learning strategies
- Structure
- Organisation of learning
- IT
- Differentiation

WHY?

Purpose/effect
- Instruct
- Explain
- Inform
- Persuade
- Motivate
- Develop learner autonomy
- Assessment
- Got to do it!
- Skills development

Figure 2.2 Lasswell's model of communication (modified).

Note: Each box contains a range of factors which a teacher should consider in their planning, preparation and delivery of teaching and learning. In each case, the list is not exhaustive – add others you think appropriate.

Activity

All the key questions of Lasswell's model will be explored in subsequent chapters, however it might be useful to start to apply it now.

1 If you're already teaching, see if you can answer each question (Who? What? To whom? How? Why?) and use them as reflective questions to improve your teaching.

2 Effective learning is about making connections and developing thinking skills. Work out ways in which each question impacts on the others. For example, in what ways does Whom affect What? What's the relationship between How and Why?

3 Use this model to analyse the planning, delivery and effectiveness of a session you have recently delivered. Start with Who and How.

The problem of meaning

When I was doing a philosophy module at university, I was asked to write an essay on 'The meaning of meaning'. This was no easy task, in fact I didn't really know what it meant. As we saw earlier, it is all too easy to interpret the statement 'I don't know what you mean', as a learner's failure.

Let's start with a controversial statement – words have no meanings. You might initially be shocked by this statement, but a moment's reflection suggests that it must be true. If words contained meanings we wouldn't have to learn languages – foreign, technical, occupational, or others – we would simply listen and unpack the meaning. Teachers wouldn't have to teach – they would simply tell people things and they would then know the meaning.

David Berlo (1960) makes a series of statements about meaning:

- Meanings are in people.
- Communication does not consist of the transmission of meanings, but of the transmission of messages.
- Words do not mean, only people mean.
- People can have similar meanings only to the extent that they have had, or can anticipate having, similar experiences.
- Meanings are never fixed: as experience changes, so meanings change.
- No two people can have exactly the same meaning for anything.

This last statement could seem particularly hopeless for teachers. If we can't share meanings, what's the point? Things are not this bad; we can and do share meanings and teachers do help learners to understand and create meaning. However, we must remember that merely transmitting messages doesn't necessarily mean that we have transmitted meaning. Many of our communication problems result from the assumption that my message means the same to you as it does to me.

How does this, seemingly obscure, discussion relate to teaching and learning? First, it relates to constructivist theories of learning which suggest that learners have to actively create meaning – they can't just be given it (see Chapter 3, 'Learning theories'). Second, it reminds us that successful teaching and learning rely on identifying those areas of shared experience which teachers and learners can use as a common pool from which to develop further learning. To illustrate this Wilbur Schramm (1973) devised a simple model to show this in graphic terms (see Figure 2.3).

To encourage successful communication and successful learning we need to find areas where the circles overlap – shared areas of experience and understanding. For example, someone teaching *Romeo and Juliet* to 16-year-olds may find the language of Shakespeare a barrier to understanding the story and the plight of the 'star-crossed lovers'. However, a shared reference point might be a comparison with a similarly doomed love affair in a film or soap opera. Purists might regard this as 'dumbing down', but it's a starting point for increasing learners' understanding of the play. Similarly, English for speakers of other languages (ESOL) teachers can overcome cultural differences by finding common ground, perhaps through examples from music, food or sport.

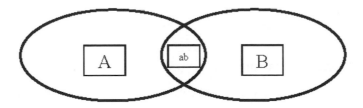

Figure 2.3 Wilbur Schramm's model (1973).
Note: A = the teacher; B = the learners. The area ab represents the area of shared knowledge or experience.

Communication skills

We normally take the word 'skill' to mean a physical skill, such as sporting skill, skill in playing musical instruments, or art and craft skills. When we watch an artist dashing off a quick portrait, we are impressed by their talent and their, seemingly, effortless skill. We can be certain, however, that even though they may be naturally gifted, they haven't developed this gift without a great deal of hard work and practice. Similarly we might observe a teacher who can enthuse, motivate and engage learners and assume that they are just naturally gifted communicators; this is rarely true. In the same way that sports players can develop physical skills, teachers can develop their communication and interpersonal skills. As with all other professional development, however, this can only be achieved by reflection and a willingness to change and develop.

The social psychologist, Michael Argyle, has written extensively on interpersonal and social skills. He compares physical, motor skills with social and interpersonal skills by saying that: 'In each case the performer seeks certain goals, makes skilled moves which are intended to further them, observes what effect he is having and takes corrective action as a result of feedback (Argyle 1994: 117). In other words, we watch what we're doing while we're doing it; evaluate the effectiveness, and try new strategies to achieve our goals. There is a very clear connection here with theories of reflective practice, especially Schön's 'reflection in action'. There are several components of interpersonal and communication skills. In addition to reflection (Chapter 1, 'The reflective teacher') and questioning (Chapter 6, 'Questioning and explaining'), the following are the most relevant to teaching and learning:

- nonverbal communication (NVC)
- listening
- speaking
- empathy
- feedback
- written communication

Nonverbal communication

Activity

Think about meeting a group of learners for the first time.

- Even before much has been said, what do you notice most about the group and the individuals in it?

- How do you get information about their feelings, attitudes and behaviour? How is this information shown?

- To what extent do you think they will notice the same things about you?

Nonverbal communication (NVC) refers to all the body signals we send, deliberately or unconsciously, when we are communicating with others. It includes the following:

- eye movement and eye contact
- gestures
- posture
- proximity and orientation
- facial expression

These elements are commonly referred to as body language, but NVC also includes:

- Vocal elements of speech (sometimes called 'paralanguage'). This comprises: stress, intonation, pitch, tone, volume, and speed of speech, as well other sounds such as sighs, grunts and gasps. We will consider this further when we look at speaking.
- Appearance, including fixed elements such as your size and stature, and relatively fixed elements including hairstyle and colour, clothing, and bodily adornments such tattoos and body piercing.

Despite the claims of some pop psychologists and tabloid newspapers, NVC is not an exact science. Folded arms *can* mean that a person is being defensive or feeling vulnerable; it is also possible that the person is happy and relaxed but just like folding their arms. Nonverbal communication signals cannot reliably be read in isolation; we need to consider the total package of what we see and hear.

Unlike verbal communication we cannot cease NVC; it is a constant stream, occasionally accompanied by speech. Communication specialists refer to the 'primacy of NVC', which means the content of messages, especially emotional content, is transmitted primarily by NVC (including vocal elements) rather than by the verbal elements of speech. Mehrabian (1972) researched this and concluded that, on average, the total impact of a message owes 7 per cent to the words, 38 per cent to the paralanguage, and 55 per cent to nonverbal signals. Parents of small children and pet-owners are generally well aware that how you say something has more effect than what you say.

Activity

Recall a teacher from your own educational experience – school, college, trainers, university.

What were their most noticeable and annoying nonverbal habits?

Why were they so annoying?

Did they affect your learning?

Eye contact and eye movement

Eye contact and eye movements are probably the most expressive elements of our nonverbal repertoire. They enable us to react to other people and to influence and change their behaviour in various ways. We are frequently nervous of eye contact, especially when prolonged, because it can be too intimate. We may have the feeling that eyes are 'the window of the soul' and that when we look at people too intensely they will know what we are thinking.

Eye movements have a number of functions in social interaction, particularly in teaching.

Opening and controlling channels of communication. Making eye contact with particular learners is a way of opening a channel of communication to them. If you want someone to answer a question or offer a contribution to the session, looking at them invites them in. Similarly, when that person's contribution is finished you will switch eye contact to another contributor to open the channel of communication. Eye contact makes connections between people – indicating liking, interest, or sometimes, threat.

Eye contact shows attention and interest. You may have experienced a teacher or lecturer who doesn't look the learners in the eyes, perhaps tending to look down or speak over people's heads; you may also know how this made you feel – inferior, not valued, just a member of another group to be taught. We should remember, however, the proviso that NVC is not an exact science. Much of our school experience will suggest that not looking at the teacher, doodling, or gazing out of the window are signs that the learner is not paying attention but there is evidence to suggest that such behaviours can actually increase concentration and help to visualise and internalise what they are hearing.

During interaction, participants will look at each other between 25–75 per cent of the time; listeners will look more than speakers. For teachers, particularly in a classroom setting, it is important to include all the learners by distributing eye contact around everyone in the group. It is especially important to include those at the periphery. Individual eye contact will normally last between 5 and 15 seconds; to each individual in a group it is usually between 4 and 5 seconds. Don't, even unconsciously, pick favourites in the group who always return your eye contact – include everyone.

To give and receive feedback. When we are speaking we like to know that people are listening. When teachers look at their learners, they make connections with them. Learners feel that the teacher is taking an interest in them and are also likely to feel that the speaker is more confident and more believable. Avoiding eye contact looks shifty and is often associated with lying. Learners, generally, look while they are listening to teachers to get extra visual information to supplement the words and to gauge their feelings and emotions.

To affect and control behaviour. Eye contact can be a very powerful signal in behaviour and motivation. If you have a small group of people who talk while you are talking or interrupt others, a slightly longer than usual gaze, combined with a serious facial expression, is almost guaranteed to induce quiet, even if only for a short period of time. Eye contact can indicate authority, as well cooperation and friendliness.

Gestures

Gestures are actions which signal meaning, deliberately, or unconsciously to those who are watching. Unfortunately, we all have to some extent habitual, unwitting, gestures which are distracting or annoying. Such gestures may be more prevalent when we are nervous or meeting a new group for the first time. Excessive hand and arm movements might suggest confidence and exuberance but can easily become more fascinating to the learners than the content of the teacher's input. You may recall the television scientist, Dr Magnus Pyke, who is remembered more for the extravagance of his gestures than for the content of his programmes. It's a good idea to video yourself to identify any idiosyncratic movements or gestures, or even ask your learners.

Conversely, a teacher or trainer, who stands or sits still can be uninspiring, to say the least. Gestures and body movement indicate excitement and enthusiasm, which, hopefully will transfer to your students. Certain gestures, known as 'baton gestures', are particularly important in supporting and reinforcing key points or punctuating speech. Baton gestures include a raised finger, a sweep of the hand, or a hand-chop, but don't use threatening gestures, such as pointing.

Posture

Posture refers to the way in which we arrange our bodies when we stand, sit or walk. Much of our posture is unconscious; we may not be aware that our shoulders are drooped, head down, or we have a generally slumped appearance. But, as teachers we need to be aware of our posture and to adjust it to suit the circumstances and purposes of the session.

Posture is a key indicator of our feelings and emotions and, as such, communicates a great deal to our learners and helps to set the tone for the session. We might wish to be authoritative for a group of young learners who need a structured environment, but more relaxed for a group of adults with whom we are working on a more collaborative basis.

An effective posture for most teachers is one which is poised yet relaxed with the body upright; weight spread evenly on both feet; shoulders not slumped and the chin level. This posture suggests a quiet, business-like authority combined with approachability. A bad posture, hunched shoulders; clasped hands, and feet pointing inwards, sends messages which could be interpreted as vulnerability or lacking confidence.

Not for nothing did parents, guardians and teachers tell us to 'walk tall'. An erect posture, extending yourself to your full height, not only makes you appear more confident, it makes you feel physically better; you will breathe more efficiently, which will bring more oxygen to the brain, and you will speak more clearly and project your voice better. Try leaning forward – a seated person leaning forward towards individuals or groups of learners gives the impression of being more interested in the participants and the topic under discussion than a person leaning backwards or away from their audience.

You should also consider the posture of your learners. Without wishing to return to a rigid school style with students sitting bolt upright, try to discourage over-relaxed postures – students will feel better and work more effectively when they are comfortable. Balancing on the back two legs of chairs is not desirable, even if only for health and safety reasons.

Proximity and orientation

Proximity refers to the distance between people who are communicating and, in teaching, sends very powerful messages concerning relationships, status, attitude and emotions. We frequently refer to our personal space, particularly the invasion of it by others. There are personal and cultural differences in our use of personal space but there are some guidelines we can use in estimating what is appropriate in various settings.

Edward T. Hall divided space into four zones:

- intimate – 0–50 centimetres – generally inappropriate in teaching and learning!
- personal distance – about 50 centimetres to 1.2 metres. Most English people will talk in the street about 1–1.5 metres apart. For teachers this distance might be appropriate when working one-to-one or with a small group;
- social distance – about 1.2 to 3.5 metres. This is the distance at which most transactions, including classroom-based teaching, takes place;
- public distance – 3.5 metres and upwards. University lecturers addressing large groups of students in lecture theatres will tend to inhabit this zone.

Clearly, the perception and use of space will vary according to situation and purpose. Moving closer to individuals and groups, especially when sitting, can create a relaxed and collaborative atmosphere. Standing over a seated learner can suggest authority and control. As with all other aspects of communication, reflection and sensitivity should guide the use of space.

Orientation refers to the spatial positions people adopt in interaction. This is most apparent in classroom layouts – even experienced teachers sometimes pay too little attention to the way in which chairs, tables and equipment are set out in learning spaces. I have frequently observed small numbers of learners spread out all over a classroom set up for 20–30 learners. While you are using a room, you can organise it however you want – provided you remember to put things back as you found them. The physical environment is just one of the many elements a skilled teacher can manipulate to create a positive learning environment. If you've got a small group, try making a small island of desks around which you and the learners can sit. You will notice an immediate difference in the feel and atmosphere. If you feel the need to be more 'traditional' in style and presentation, stand up and move away from the learners.

While we're on the subject of rooms – keep them tidy. Scruffy rooms with desks and chairs all over the place don't send messages of professionalism and a business-like attitude to teaching and learning. The appearance is even more depressing when empty drinks bottles, crisp packets and piles of unclaimed handouts are strewn around.

Activity

Consider the following room layouts and discuss how they might positively or negatively affect the learning environment.

- desks and chairs set out in rows – school style;

- a horseshoe or three-sided arrangement;

- an island of desks;

- several islands of desks round the room;

- a circle of chairs, including the teacher, with no desks;

- all the desks and chairs cleared to the edges to make an open space.

Finally, under this heading, we can include your movement and position around the learning space. A teacher seated behind a desk at the front of the room can appear imposing and authoritative and, in some situations, you might feel the need to do this. At other times, however, try moving your desk out of the way completely and avoid any physical barriers between you and your learners. Moving around the class creates added visual interest and allows you to involve all the learners yet easily move to a position where you can work at close quarters with individuals or small groups.

Journal extract: Terry, trained to teach in the Ambulance Service

We have just opened up a small off-site classroom. The furniture had just been placed in the room in no particular arrangement. Our normal classroom layout is very much the horseshoe with the projector or overhead projector taking centre stage.

For a change I decided I would not use that format but rather keep the tables together in a block formation in the centre of the room. My thoughts were that this particular course was extremely difficult for the students and with everyone sitting around the same set of tables it would help to bond the group of nine students. Obviously on the odd occasion I used the projector some movement was required to ensure everybody could fully see the screen.

This arrangement was to last for the first week. The subsequent week I was accompanied by another teacher who is less open to change. It became obvious he was not comfortable with this arrangement. And by the end of week two he had achieved his aim of returning the room to what he perceived as being the correct layout, namely the horseshoe.

Trying not to show friction between the teachers I went along with this arrangement but mainly because I would be leaving the course in a couple of days to take up other duties. It was interesting to note the indirect the comments passed by students about how they had liked the original classroom layout.

Did it work? Yes, I feel it did, right from the outset there was a terrific feeling of belonging, being part of a team. Students were more willing to be involved by contributing to the lesson nobody seemed to be left out on the wings. I felt there was a sense of ownership. There was a feeling that everyone was of equal value. Obviously this could have been associated with us being off site in a remote location thus creating a much more relaxed atmosphere. From a practical point of view it was considerably easier to influence and direct the group when in the block formation. All the students very quickly got to know each other and started using individual's names.

Facial expression

The face and the eyes are the most noticeable parts of the body but are also the most complex and difficult to interpret channel of NVC. One reason for this is that facial expressions change rapidly, providing a continuous commentary while we are speaking or listening. As teachers we can, and should, consciously control our facial expressions, particularly to send messages of support, encouragement and interest. It is equally true, however, that our faces often flash indications of our 'true' feelings – sometimes contradicting our spoken words- and even the slightest expression of disapproval can discourage learners. Social psychologists call this phenomenon 'leakage'.

Michael Argyle (1994) refers to research which concludes that there are six major facial expressions, which correspond to these emotions:

- happiness
- surprise
- fear
- sadness
- anger
- disgust or contempt

These expressions are innate and found in all cultures and in young children. Argyle also points out that:

> The area round the mouth adds to the running commentary by varying between being turned up (pleasure) and turned down (displeasure). These facial signals lead to reactions from others, for example, looking puzzled may lead to clarification, and a smile acts as a reinforcement, encouraging the kind of act which led to it.
>
> (Argyle 1994: 26)

Listening

We spend more time listening than we do speaking, writing or reading but we rarely have any training in listening. Listening is considered a passive activity; something we just do. It is rarely considered a skill, still less a skill which we can develop and improve. Many surveys of learners at all ages suggest that what they dislike most is not being listened to. In a survey of adult learners' perceptions of teachers' communication skills, listening was ranked highest (Wolvin 1984).

Hearing is not the same as listening. If we go back to our Sender–Receiver model of communication, it's easy to see that hearing is equivalent to the reception of the message; listening is about decoding the message.

There are many barriers to listening, including the following:

- being distracted by another task or by thoughts and personal concerns;
- being put off by the speaker and/or what they are saying;
- making assumptions about speakers and allowing prejudice and stereotypes to affect our perceptions of what they are saying;
- thinking about how we will respond before we've heard everything the speaker says;
- 'pseudo-listening' – the face and body language suggest an attentive listener, but they're not taking any notice;
- 'hogging the limelight' – these people don't listen attentively because they'd prefer to be talking;
- selective listening – just listening for and attending to those things that interest you.

Effective listening requires that we 'forget' ourselves to some extent so that we can make space for the experiences of our learners. Alan Mortiboys, writing about teaching and emotional intelligence, points out that:

> sometimes your readiness to jump in with your own analysis or wealth of anecdotes and experiences can take away from what the learner is

actually saying. You can fail to truly value the learners' experience and sometimes not even hear correctly what they have said because of your rush to contribute.

(Mortiboys 2005: 70)

Listening well is hard work and we need to make conscious efforts to listen closely and to *show* that we are listening. We don't just listen with our ears; we use our eyes, face and body to show others that we are listening to them. This applies whether we are in a one-to-one situation, such as a support or tutorial session, or with a group of learners. Willingness to listen actively is likely to encourage learners to offer their ideas and join in discussion. Active listening is a key element of active learning. Hargie and Dickson state that:

Research has shown that speakers want listeners to *respond appropriately* to what they are saying rather than just listen. In other words, they desire active listening in the form of both verbal and nonverbal behaviours. Although verbal responses are the main indicators of successful listening, if accompanying nonverbal behaviours are not displayed it is usually assumed that the individual is not paying attention, and *ipso facto* not listening.

(Hargie and Dickson 2004: 194)

Tips for effective listening

Avoid distractions. No matter how busy you are, stop what you're doing and listen to the speaker. Carrying out any physical activity will be interpreted as not listening. Attention will fade quite quickly and you need to be aware when this is happening.

Remember body language. Your posture will show that you are actively attending. Sitting more forward or inclining yourself towards the speaker will show interest.

Keep an open mind. You might hear things you don't agree with or contradict you ideas and beliefs but you still need to listen. Try to avoid making assumptions about people based on their appearance or their personal style.

Listen for the main ideas. These are likely to come at the beginning, middle and end of the speaker's message. Try to summarise the main points in your mind, then check them with the speaker.

Let the speaker finish. Be sure that the person has finished speaking before you begin. Even a pause does not necessarily mean they've said all they wanted to say.

Try to avoid thinking of your response while you're still listening. Concentrate on what the person is saying.

Give feedback while the person is speaking. Listener responses show that you are listening. Occasional head nods and smiles assure the speaker that you are attending to them.

Reflecting back. Training in counselling skills encourages listeners to 'reflect back' to the speaker. This generally means summarising or paraphrasing what the person has said in a way that reflects both the feelings and the thoughts of the speaker. This can be useful for checking and for showing empathy but if overused can sound contrived and unsympathetic.

Speaking

Just as we have an obligation to be good listeners, as teachers we also have a duty to ensure that we speak in ways which encourage listening and understanding.

The major components of effective speaking are:

- structure;
- clarity and use of language;
- voice qualities.

Structure

Delivering teaching and learning requires clearly structured presentations, logically organised which help learners to follow the teacher's input and to grasp the main points. Clearly, effective lesson planning will contribute significantly to this end but even unplanned discussions which occur during a session need to be managed in order to ensure that all learners are able to see their structure. This aspect of communication will be discussed in more detail in Chapter 6, 'Questioning and explaining'.

Clarity and use of language

To be a good teacher you need to be able to express yourself clearly and to help people learn, understand and develop. It is a teacher's job to enlighten, not to impress people by how much they know or by using long words and convoluted phrases.

All spheres of human interest – occupational or educational – have their own particular language. Teachers will discuss standardised assessment tasks (SATs), spiral curricula and constructivism; bricklayers talk about 'compo' and Flemish Bonds; solicitors know about *habeas corpus, ultra vires,* ABH and GBH. Used appropriately, this kind of language represents effective communication because it is shared by the users and represents a kind of verbal shorthand to refer to complex ideas. When such language is used with an audience that is unfamiliar with them, this is ineffective and inconsiderate communication. All disciplines require specialised language and no teaching and learning materials can be jargon free. Becoming a doctor, for example, is to a great extent about acquiring medical language and concepts but, like a foreign language, it has to be *learned*; it is part of the training. Education, particularly post-compulsory education and training, has become littered with initialisations and acronyms which are frequently used as if understood by all. Trainee teachers will find glossaries of such terms invaluable (see the list of abbreviations at pages ix–x).

Activity

Identify some words or phrases peculiar to your area of work, an interest or hobby.

Try to explain these to others in your group.

Did you try to find any areas of shared knowledge/experience to explain?

Voice qualities

Every voice is unique and makes a certain impression on those hearing it. Our voices reflect our personality and our self-esteem – assertive and emotionally expressive people tend to have loud voices; shy people tend to have soft voices. We should recognise our unique vocal qualities but also remember that, like all aspects of communication, we can change and develop them.

Activity

- Think of how many different ways you can say, 'I love you'. How do you make it sound convincing?

- Try saying 'Hello' to express surprise, pleasure, annoyance, boredom, seduction.

- Say the words *import* and *export* as verbs. Now say them as nouns. How do you make the difference?

From the above activity you should have been able to deduce that voice qualities include: stress, intonation, pitch, volume and speed of speech. We can also mention the 'ums' and 'ers' of hesitation and a variety of sounds including gasps, grunts and sighs. These features are extremely important because, as we have seen earlier, the way we say something is usually more important than what we say. In teaching, vital messages of support, encouragement, enthusiasm or disapproval are conveyed largely by vocal qualities. Use of voice should be considered carefully for, as Michael Argyle points out: 'the voice is "leakier" than the face; that is, true emotions which are being concealed tend to show through' (Argyle 1994: 33).

> *Intonation.* We don't have to be Laurence Olivier reciting Shakespeare to arouse and interest our learners but we need to ensure that we avoid a monotonous tone when speaking. Intonation, or tone, is the rise and fall of the voice and variations will add to interest and emphasis.
> *Pitch* indicates the use of a high voice or a low voice. When speakers are nervous they speak in a higher voice, which listeners quite easily interpret as nervousness. Anxiety means that your vocal chords are stretched tightly and you are not relaxed and, eventually, this will affect your voice.
> *Volume* is easier to control than pitch. Teachers need to be able to adjust the volume of their speaking according to the size of the venue, the number of people and to signal their intentions clearly. Learning to project your voice is crucial and is clearly linked to posture and confidence. Voice is part of a repertoire of non-verbal elements by which we indicate, for example, confidence, knowledge and authority, as well as support and encouragement.
> *Speed.* When teachers, particularly trainees, are nervous or feel under-prepared, they tend to speak rapidly, basically because they want to get the whole thing done and leave as quickly as possible. The main problem, of course, is that learners won't be able to hear what you are saying or keep up with you. Another problem with speaking too quickly is that there are no gaps in which your learners can seek clarification or ask questions. In your early days of teaching you will need to slow right down to what might seem feel a ridiculously slow pace, but you will adjust and find your natural level. Don't forget that silence can be effective; leave gaps and scan the faces of learners for feedback. The keys to avoiding fast delivery are thorough preparation, confidence that you are an expert in your subject, and relaxation.
> *Stress.* English is a stress-language which means that every word of more than one syllable relies on stress to make the meaning clear.

Empathy

Empathy is not the same as sympathy. To sympathise is to feel for somebody, often to feel sorry for them. Empathy goes a stage further: it is a particular kind of perception by which we can 'tune in' to the others' feelings and communicate more sensitively. Those who lack empathy find relationships and communication difficult, even to the point of being dysfunctional. Unable to understand or recognise their own feelings, people who lack empathy find it hard to recognise, and therefore understand, the feelings of others. Egocentric people have problems because empathy requires a genuine interest in others and their feelings, be they joy, pain, anger or happiness.

As we saw in the previous chapter reflection requires self-awareness. Empathy grows from self-awareness and the more we can recognise and manage our own feelings the better we can understand others, particularly our learners. Empathy requires the ability to recognise and interpret nonverbal signals. Daniel Goleman, the leading figure in emotional intelligence, says, 'just as the mode of rational mind is words, the mode of the emotions is nonverbal' (Goleman 1995: 97). The nonverbal signals discussed above provide vital information for teachers to gauge the feelings and attitudes of their learners. Without the ability to recognise such signals we are unable to adjust and adapt our teaching.

Feedback

Feedback in teaching and learning is generally understood as written or spoken comments provided as part of assessment. We will examine this in the chapter on assessment.

Feedback has a more general meaning in the communication process. Gill and Adams (1998: 74) define it as, 'a response from the receiver which gives the communicator an idea of how the message is being received and whether it needs to be modified'. Good teachers look for and seek feedback from their learners, particularly about whether the messages have been received and understood. It may be that the form of communication does not suit everyone. For example, many learners will struggle to understand a spoken or written explanation, but will see the point, quite literally, when a visual representation is used or an appropriate example or analogy given.

Feedback is clearly linked to empathy, in that it requires you to notice nonverbal feedback from your learners, interpret it and respond accordingly. Good teachers notice and respond to feedback and make efforts to obtain it; bad teachers carry on regardless of, or even fail to notice, feedback.

Activity

In what ways, nonverbal and verbal, do your learners give you feedback?

How do learners indicate they are: interested, attentive, bored, distracted?

Does all feedback have to be responded to by the teacher?

Written communication

Writing is frequently overlooked in advice on effective communication. Like all other forms of communication, writing must be produced with the audience and purpose in mind: writing is usually for other people to read and, hopefully understand. This does not mean 'dumbing down', it means writing clearly, concisely and effectively.

Writing which does not consider the needs, level and experience of the learners or, worse still, is designed to impress rather than inform is bad writing. Some academics seem to be scared to write plainly. Clearly there are the necessary conventions of academic writing – objectivity; being impersonal; referencing sources – but these requirements should not hinder readability and understanding. Michael McCarthy, in an article on academic writing, states, 'Texts are for readers, not for their writers, and we should respect our readers by choosing our grammar appropriately, so that it helps, not hinders, the processing of the specialist vocabulary and concepts.' (McCarthy 2006)

Jargon, as we discussed earlier, is the language of particular groups of people in specific occupations or disciplines. It is a useful shorthand between these people but is often used, consciously or unconsciously, to exclude others.

Some of the most valuable advice on writing clearly and avoiding jargon is available from the Plain English Campaign. The Basic Skills Unit also provides guides on producing readable documents. The Plain English Campaign does 'exactly what it says on the tin', that is to identify and publicise instances of bad use of language and to persuade anyone who issues written documents to consider their readers by writing simply and directly. In addition, they publish examples of jargon and cliché on their website for amusement and as anti-role models. Here's an example from their 'before and after' section:

Before:
'High quality learning environments are a necessary precondition for facilitation and enhancement of the ongoing learning process.'

After:
  'Children need good schools if they are to learn properly.'
  (© Plain English Campaign)

We will consider elements of written language in more depth in Chapter 8.

Communication climate and emotional intelligence

I want to conclude this chapter by discussing two concepts which bring together the various elements of communication. The first comes from Adler, Rosenfeld and Towne (1998) who refer to *communication climate*. The second element is the more recent concept of *emotional intelligence*, developed mainly by Daniel Goleman (1995). Later, having read Chapter 3, 'Learning theories' you will be able to make links with the humanist theory of learning, especially the ideas of Carl Rogers.

In teaching, like so many other areas of human activity, the most obvious things are frequently overlooked, even ignored. Emotions, and the understanding of their effects, have had no real place in mainstream education. Some people have traced this back to the French philosopher René Descartes and his separation of mind and body, emotion and reason, head and heart. The life of the mind became superior; emotions, human weaknesses to be overcome or ignored. Most of us, however, will be able to recall times when emotions got in the way of our learning and, in many instances, negative emotions were induced by the learning environment. Nobody ever learned effectively or meaningfully by being bored, frightened, humiliated or anxious. Recently, I have heard stories of teachers who physically or emotionally separate pupils they consider to be achievers and non-achievers. Clearly, such acts will produce negative emotional states which will impede learning. Learners perceived as failing and labelled as such are more likely to fail – this is often referred to as a 'self-fulfilling prophecy'.

Successful teaching and learning requires, perhaps fundamentally, the creation of a positive emotional environment. Adler et al. (1998: 327) define communication climate as: 'the social/ psychological tone of a relationship. A climate doesn't involve specific activities as much as the way people feel about each other as they carry out those activities.' They go on to suggest that a positive communication climate is one in which people feel valued. Feeling valued comes from communication between learners and teachers. Simple things such as knowing and using learners names, listening, congratulating achievement and using eye contact, are referred to by these authors as *confirming responses*. Responses and teacher behaviour which result in a negative communication climate are *disconfirming responses*.

Activity

Bearing in mind the elements of communication in this chapter, give examples of behaviour, particularly nonverbal, which are likely to be:

- confirming;

- disconfirming.

Remember, this could include unexpected elements such as the tone and the style of a written handout.

The essence of emotional intelligence, particularly as propounded by Goleman, is that emotional intelligence is at least as important as intelligence quotient (IQ). The area of our brains which deals with emotions is, in evolutionary terms, older than the neo-cortex which deals with cognitive aspects such as logic and reasoning. Because the emotions are more fundamental than intellect and reasoning, if emotions and feelings are not recognised and managed by teachers and learners, then effective learning cannot occur. As Goleman says, 'emotions enrich; a model of mind which leaves them out is impoverished' (1995: 41).

Learners bring many things to our sessions – some of which we don't know about – which can positively or negatively affect their learning. They bring their needs; their life experiences; their fears and uncertainties; their hopes and aspirations; their prejudices and assumptions; their happy or unhappy homes. We cannot and should not try to uncover these feelings, neither should we expect them simply to put them aside and concentrate on learning, but we can be certain they are there. Awareness of emotional intelligence helps us to create a positive learning state in which learners feel 'valued, curious, safe, relaxed, connected and motivated' (Mortiboys 2005: 29).

Activities to develop communication skills

The back-to-back exercise

This is designed to develop understanding of communication as a process and the identification of stages at which problems can occur and the consideration of barriers to communication (and learning).

Process

Group members split into pairs and sit back-to-back. One is nominated the sender; the other is the receiver.

The sender is given an A4 sheet which has between five and eight different shapes or objects drawn on it. The sender's job is to describe these to the receiver so that he can reproduce them as accurately as possible. This is done twice – once without any communication from the receiver; the second time the receiver can seek as much clarification as he wishes.

At the end of the exercise, the results are compared and conclusions drawn.

Using video

An amusing way to study NVC is to watch television with the sound off. The removal of the verbal channel makes the nonverbal more obvious. You can try to deduce characters emotions, relationships and personality from this activity.

It can also be instructive to make a recording of yourself teaching. This will allow you to analyse and evaluate your communication skills. If you are brave enough, share and discuss it with colleagues.

For your journal

A communications skills audit

The following questions can be used as the basis for an audit and evaluation of your communication skills in teaching and learning. Some of the conclusions might inform your PDJ. You can adapt and add to these questions in any way you wish, possibly by adding a rating scale. You might want to use them to get feedback from your learners.

1 I use eye contact to include all learners.
2 I am aware of my posture when sitting or standing.
3 My posture communicates, e.g. confidence, authority, approachability.
4 I move around the room and get amongst my learners.
5 I adjust the room layout to suit the number of learners, purpose and communication climate.
6 My students can hear me clearly.
7 I am aware of my voice and adjust speed, pause, pitch, volume and stress to suit learners and purpose.
8 I am a good listener.
9 I let learners finish speaking before I reply.

10 I know learners' names.
11 I avoid unnecessary use of jargon/specific language and ensure that learners understand new words and phrases.
12 I consciously try to reduce mechanical/physical barriers to communication.
13 I am aware of the effects of emotions on teaching and learning.
14 I try to create a safe and positive communication climate conducive to learning.
15 I recognise that I might make assumptions about learners.
16 I notice feedback from learners.
17 I am prepared to adjust how and what I am teaching in response to learners' feedback.
18 I consider carefully the structure and clarity of written material.

Journal extract: Jane, training to teach childcare

This was my first session with the childcare group and I felt very nervous, even though I was very well prepared. When I walked into the room I felt all eyes were on me and scrutinising me. Looking back, I'm aware that I was probably looking a bit apologetic for being there; I think I was hunched and avoiding eye contact.

My first questions to the group were met with silence, even a few sniggers – this made me feel even worse. As the session developed I began to relax and take my time. I started to look at the learners and the responses began, gradually, to improve.

Further reading and useful websites

Adler, R., Rosenfeld, L. and Towne, N. (1998) *Interplay: The Process of Interpersonal Communication*, 7th edn. New York: CBS Publishing.
Argyle, M. (1994) *The Psychology of Interpersonal Behaviour*. London: Penguin.
Burton, G. and Dimbleby, R. (1995) *Between Ourselves: An Introduction to Interpersonal Communication*, 2nd edn. London: Arnold.
Goleman, D. (1995) *Emotional Intelligence*. London: Bloomsbury.
Hartley, P. (1999) *Interpersonal Communication*, 2nd edn. London: Routledge.
www.basic-skills.co.uk The Basic Skills Agency has a downloadable free guide, 'Readability', on how to design and write accessible texts.
www.plainenglish.co.uk The Plain English Campaign provides downloadable free guides on 'How to write in plain English' and 'The A–Z of alternative words'.

3　Learning theories

What this chapter is about

- How people learn
- How people learn most effectively
- Discussion of a range of theories of learning
- Discussion of learning styles
- Summary of key points of theory and implications for practice in lifelong learning

LLUK standards

This chapter covers, at least, the following standards:

AK 4.1; AP 4.1
BK 2.1; BP 2.1; BK 2.2; BP 2.2; BK 2.3; BP 2.3
CK 3.1; CP 3.1

How do people learn?

Different people learn in different ways; some may have a preference for a particular style of learning and teaching. Learners will become more effective if they extend their range of learning styles and experiences. Teachers in lifelong learning need to understand that people do not all learn in the same way and that they must provide a range of teaching and learning experiences if learners are going to achieve. An understanding of learning theory is essential for teaching in post-compulsory education and training. However, theory is most useful and more readily understood when it is put into practice. This chapter will provide clear summaries of the implications of theory for teaching and learning.

The main schools of learning theory are:

- behaviourism;
- cognitivism and constructivism;
- humanism;
- brain-based learning;
- learning styles;
- adult learning;
- situated learning.

None of these theories is definitive or provides the 'correct' answer to how people learn. Some are more favoured by educationalists; others may be less fashionable. However, there is something for trainee teachers to learn from each of them. Successful teaching and learning is likely to be an amalgam of elements from a range of theories and ideas.

It is important that we avoid a 'common-sense' approach to the question of how people learn and don't assume that how we learn best is how everyone will learn best. A simple, but mistaken, theory of learning is the one I refer to as the 'empty bucket' theory. You might see this referred to as transmission learning. The basic elements are:

- teacher knows everything;
- students know nothing ('empty buckets');
- teacher's job is to fill the empty buckets with knowledge;
- students' job is to learn and retain the knowledge;
- teacher tests students to assess if they have retained the knowledge;
- students who have retained and can regurgitate the knowledge are successful;
- students who cannot retain the knowledge are considered 'leaky buckets' who need further teaching or are deemed less intelligent.

You should be able to work out a number of reasons why this approach is flawed (e.g. teachers don't know everything) – more criticisms will become apparent by the end of this chapter.

Behaviourism

Early psychologists were mainly concerned with introspection – that is the interior, mental processes of individuals' thinking. Behaviourists rejected the notion that psychology was basically concerned with individuals' mental processes. They considered such approaches to be unscientific and subjective, arguing that the mind could not be studied objectively. Behaviour, however, was observable and could be studied and measured scientifically. Much of the early work in behaviourism was carried out in the 1920s and 1930s by Pavlov, Skinner and Thorndike.

Behaviourism is concerned with observable changes in behaviour and suggests that we learn in response to external stimuli. A stimulus is an internal or external factor which stimulates an organism and causes action. It could be anything – a sound, a hunger-pang, a pleasant or unpleasant smell, a colour, a particular classroom.

A response is any action or activity generated by a stimulus. A simple example is that stroking and speaking softly to a dog will likely cause it to roll over in expectation of tummy-rubbing. Shouting and rapid movement may cause the animal to run away. The dog example takes us to the often referred to, but frequently misunderstood, Pavlov's dogs.

Ivan Pavlov

Pavlov (1849–1936), a Russian physiologist, during his research into the digestive system of dogs, observed occasions when dogs salivated merely at the sight of the food bucket. In subsequent experiments he trained dogs to salivate at the sound of a bell, having previously accompanied the sound with the arrival of food. This, essentially, is learning by association – the dog associated the sound of the bell with the arrival of food and began to salivate. This is known as *classical conditioning*.

However, if a response is to be repeated there needs to be some kind of reinforcement. In *operant conditioning* responses are strengthened or weakened by the consequences of reactions to the behaviour. Desired behaviour is reinforced; undesired behaviour is ignored or punished.

E.L. Thorndike

Thorndike (1874–1949) developed Pavlov's work in a series of experiments using kittens in boxes. The sequence goes roughly like this:

- hungry kitten placed in box which has a release latch
- fish placed outside box
- kitten tries (unsuccessfully) to get out
- eventually hits release latch
- in repeats of the experiment kitten spends less and less time jumping about aimlessly
- kitten is said to have 'learned' that hitting the latch leads to release and fish.

As a consequence of these experiments Thorndike coined the term *law of effect,* that is, behaviour leading to pleasant consequences is likely to be repeated.

B.F. Skinner

Skinner (1904–1990) is, perhaps, the most well-known behaviourist. His chosen animals for experimentation were rats and pigeons; his equipment, the Skinner Box. Skinner showed that these animals could be trained to carry out increasingly complex tasks. Essentially, an animal would be placed in the Skinner Box and through a process of trial and error would learn to obtain food pellets by pressing a lever.

Skinner's main contributions to behaviourism were the notions of *positive* and *negative reinforcement*. He maintained that positive rewards were far more effective than negative rewards or punishment in developing desired behaviour. Skinner also developed the idea of *behaviour shaping*, that is training humans or animals to carry out new tasks through a series of increasingly complex activities leading to the completion of the desired task. Shaping can be used to help learners who have severe learning difficulties, for example in the acquisition of language.

What can we learn from behaviourism?

At this point it seems appropriate to consider what salivating dogs; hungry kittens and trained pigeons have got to do with human learning. The answer from many psychologists and educationalists would be – not very much. As with all experiments involving animals the main problem, apart from the obvious cruelty, is the extent to which the results can be generalised to human behaviour.

Behaviourism is frequently criticised for being too simplistic and reducing human behaviour and learning to nothing more than a process of stimulus and response. Pavlov, Thorndike and Skinner may well have produced learning in their animals but we can be fairly certain that it was learning without understanding. Human learning, it is argued, is much more complex and involves thinking, reasoning and social factors.

Clearly there are instances in early child education where the role of behavioural learning is obvious. Discipline can be reinforced by rewarding appropriate behaviour and punishing inappropriate, although the child might learn to carry out inappropriate behaviour where it cannot be seen. We may, however, find it hard to understand how behaviourism can provide any useful insights into post-compulsory and adult education. The following points summarise some useful aspects of behaviourism:

- Positive rewards and encouragement are more effective than negative responses. For learners in post-compulsory settings, encouraging comments in response to class contributions, for example, are likely to encourage further learner involvement. Constructive and developmental comments on learners' work are preferable to the old-school style 'could do better'.

- For many adults considering a return to learning, memories of authoritarian and rigid schools can act as negative stimulus and affect their willingness to enrol and participate. It is up to us to provide friendly and supportive learning environments.
- There are instances where teacher demonstration followed by student practice and repetition are appropriate, for example in learning and developing skills such as bricklaying, drawing, or playing a musical instrument. Skills cannot be acquired without frequent practice. Active learning is more effective than passive learning. 'Learning by doing' is important.

Cognitivism and constructivism

Cognitive psychology is the scientific study of mental processes – the acquisition and organisation of knowledge. Cognition refers to thought and thinking. It is concerned with the ways in which people perceive, learn, reason and create their own understanding of the world. *Cognitivism* differs from behaviourism in that it sees humans not as organisms which simply react to stimuli but as meaning-making individuals who actively select, interpret, organise and use information from the world around them.

Constructivism is based on the idea that learning is a result of mental construction whereby new information is connected to what we already know and our mental frameworks adapt and develop. Constructivist theory suggests that we must provide, and help learners to create, frameworks for learning. (Note the frequent use of construction metaphors in this theory – building, scaffolding, framework). The most effective learning is active, student-centred learning – the opposite of the 'empty buckets' view, outlined earlier. This idea of 'meaning-making' suggests that:

> We never really understand something until we can create a model or metaphor derived from our own unique personal world. The reality we perceive, feel, see and hear is influenced by the constructive process of the brain as well as by the cues that impinge upon it. It is not the content stored in memory but the activity of constructing it that gets stored ... Humans don't *get* ideas; they *make* ideas.
>
> (Costa, quoted in McGregor 2007: 68)

This section will consider the following key theories and theorists:

- Gestalt
- Jean Piaget
- Jerome Bruner
- Lev Vygotsky
- David Ausubel

Gestalt

'The whole is greater than the sum of the parts.' This frequently made observation captures the essence of gestalt psychology. Gestaltists believe that psychologists should be concerned with the total, structured forms of people's mental experiences rather than individual elements. Gestalt psychologists refer to the notion of 'insight' when a learner suddenly becomes aware of the significance or relevance of something, rather like when the last piece of a jigsaw goes into place. These moments of illumination might be when a mental framework becomes complete or when a major connection is made. Such insight, however, is not just a matter of luck; it depends on teachers and learners building frameworks for learning.

Applied to learning this means, simply, that learners need the 'big picture'. This idea is at the heart of gestalt and of constructivism. In the same way as it is difficult to do a jigsaw without the picture on the box, it is difficult for learners to start with details and elements without a structure in which to locate them. Film studies students will benefit from a textual analysis of a film's camera work, sound, lighting and script, but a film is more than just the total of its elements – it is a complete work. Gestalt links to the left brain–right brain theory in which the left side of the brain deals with logic, sequence and analysis whilst the right side deals with patterns and wholes (see the section on brain-based learning, pp. 72–6).

Jean Piaget

Piaget's (1896–1980) most notable contribution to constructivism is his 'developmental stage' theory which relates child development (from 0–11+) to age-specific stages of development. However, given that our current concern is post-16 learning, we will concentrate on other areas of Piaget's work.

Piaget was one of the main theorists in the development of *schema* theory. Schemas are mental models or frameworks which every individual creates to organise and understand the world and to store this in the long-term memory. Each schema consists of discrete pieces of information which are connected together in ways which are meaningful to the individual. Every human has a need to categorise and schemas provide a sort of mental store for this to happen. An adult may have thousands of schemas and, although individuals may have similar schemas, everyone is unique.

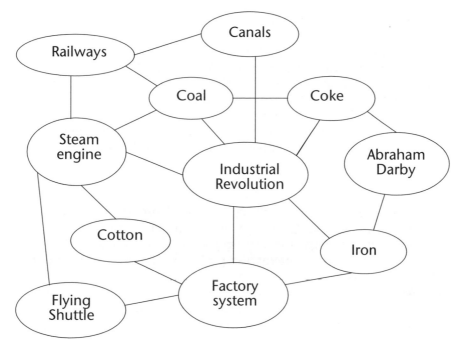

Figure 3.1 Concept map representing schema of Industrial Revolution.

Concept maps and diagrams are useful because they are analogues of schema. They allow learners and teachers to build a framework in which to connect ideas and locate new information. Figure 3.1 shows a concept map representing the Industrial Revolution, a historical period which can be difficult to understand because of the interlinking of so many technological, economic, social and business elements. Producing a map like this can help teachers to plan and students to learn. For teachers and learners these kinds of devices can serve a *heuristic* function – that is, to discover things and to make connections. It should be possible to explain the connection between any two elements joined by a line, even to add others. When I have used this concept map with trainee teachers many have liked the way in which it is presented and the opportunities it provides for exploration and the linking of ideas. However, others have complained that it is too 'busy' and is confusing. Several would prefer to modify it by simplifying, using hierarchy and structure or by introducing colour. This is fine; the key point is that advance organisers, including concept maps, can be adapted and modified to suit individuals. Above all, they provide a starting point for discussion and thinking, either of the content or the methods.

Schemas, like concept maps, are not fixed; they are incomplete and always evolving. Constructivism is concerned with how they grow, develop and adapt. Piaget used the terms *assimilation* and *accommodation*. Assimilation is the process in which new information and ideas are added to existing schema leading to an increase in knowledge. The schemas do not change but they grow to include the new information. We can understand an increasing amount of information, but there will be times when new knowledge conflicts with existing. Piaget uses the term accommodation to describe the process by which schema change to make sense of new knowledge and ideas. Assimilation adds to existing schema; accommodation changes schema. These additions and changes happen throughout our lives.

Jerome Bruner

Bruner (1915–) believed that learning is a social process in which learners construct their understanding of the world through communicative interaction. In addition he regarded learning as a continuous, active process involving intellectual development and problem solving, not the production of a body of knowledge.

From Bruner we get two important, connected educational theories: a theory of learning and a theory of instruction (teaching).

Bruner's *theory of learning* has three elements.

1 *acquisition*: the acquisition of new knowledge which (in Piaget's) terms may be assimilated or accommodated;
2 *transformation*: basically the learner does something with this new knowledge. They manipulate it and apply it work out problems. It might be used in a new situation (transference);
3 *evaluation*: the learner assesses and evaluates the utility of the new knowledge in relation to the problem or task.

His theory of instruction has four elements:

1 *readiness*: learners should have a predisposition to learning. He believed the most effective motivation was for learners to be confronted with problems to be solved. The problem/s should arouse curiosity and uncertainty.
2 *structure*: the content must be structured so that the learner can understand it. He suggested, perhaps controversially, 'that any idea or problem or body of knowledge can be presented in a form simple enough so that any learner can understand it in a recognisable form' (Bruner 1966). The content can, according to Bruner be represented in three main ways:
   • by a set of actions or *enactive representation*: for example, a lecture in plumbing could provide a demonstration;

- using images or *iconic representation*: the plumbing lecturer can provide the information using pictures or a PowerPoint presentation;
- *symbolic representation*: the lecturer may present the information in the form of a diagram using symbols specific to plumbing and heating. The learners interpret this information using their prior experiences.

3 *sequence*: material must be presented in the most effective sequence to allow learners to acquire, transform and transfer learning. Bruner uses the term *spiral curriculum* to denote the method by which students revisit ideas and concepts over a period of time but at increasingly complex levels. In history, the very difficult question of the origins of World War I could be encapsulated in a visual chart showing the main combatants, alliances, etc., and revisited to develop an increasingly sophisticated understanding;

4 *motivation*: the final element is concerned with the nature and pacing and rewards. Initially, learners may be motivated by positive feedback from teachers (extrinsic motivation) but, ideally will move towards intrinsic motivation which comes from the satisfaction of solving problems and developing new ones to be solved. This intrinsic motivation can make the process cyclical, in that the learner will become ready to start a new, related stage of learning.

Bruner advocated the use of *discovery learning* as the most effective method to encourage the kinds of active, problem-solving learning implicit in his theories of learning and instruction. Problem-based learning is a very similar method, frequently used in health education and training in which learners start from a problem to be solved. They then draw on their learning and develop the new learning and research required to solve the problem. An excellent overview can be found in Harkin, Turner and Dawn (2001). Project-based learning, in which learning is based around an integrated theme, can include a discovery element.

Discovery learning is, essentially, an active student-centred approach in which the teacher's role is to provide opportunities for learners to work out problems and evaluate and transfer their learning. As Geoff Petty points out it is 'teaching by asking' rather than 'teaching by telling' (2004). Petty goes on to stress that in many cases teachers will need to provide initial information and examples to kick-start active learning and, to ensure differentiation and motivation, some learners will need more support than others – this he describes as 'guided discovery'.

Activity

Consider an element from a course or module you teach. Briefly outline a task/s which would encourage discovery learning with your students.

For example – Motor Vehicle students could be confronted with a car which fails to start and asked to find out why and what can be done to rectify it.

Lev Vygotsky

Vygotsky (1896–1934) developed his ideas during the Stalinist period in Russia. His works were forbidden to be discussed, disseminated or reprinted until 20 years after his death. He believed education should liberate children (and people) by developing their thinking, learning skills and, particularly, the development of language.

Like other educationalists – those we now refer to as constructivists – Vygotsky maintained that education is an active process. However, people need help to learn and, for Vygotsky, the teacher is a more knowledgeable person who challenges the learner to achieve more by providing *scaffolding* to help them climb to higher levels. He refers to the difference between what the learner can do alone and what they can do with help as the *zone of proximal development* (ZPD). Alan Pritchard (2005: 31) explains the ZPD as 'a theoretical space of understanding which is just above the level of understanding of the given individual. It is the area of understanding into which a learner will move next.' This move will be facilitated and aided by the teacher. Although the most effective learning will aim for the higher levels of the ZPD, the zone will be different for each learner and, consequently, we must know our learners as individuals in order to assess how high we can ask them to aim and to provide the right amount of scaffolding – too high unsupported will feel threatening for some learners; a small rise with too much support will not represent a challenge for others possibly leading to a decrease in motivation. As with scaffolding in construction the framework is temporary. Once the higher levels have been attained and made safe for the learner to access alone the scaffolding is removed.

David Ausubel

Unlike Piaget Ausubel (1918–) does not advocate discovery learning, which he considers can be too time-consuming and is not necessarily experiential learning. He favours the use of *expository teaching*, or direct explanation by the teacher. In this respect, we could argue that this is teacher-led and, hence, has no place in a survey of constructivism. However, as Legge and Harari (2000: 32) suggest:

> What is interesting about this approach is that although it is presented as completely teacher-led, Ausubel actually argues that it is constructivist because the student is not a passive recipient of information, but actively learns from it. The outcome of expository teaching is reception learning. The student receives the information from the teacher, rather than discovering it for themselves.

Ausubel is concerned with the development of meaningful learning – the acquisition of new meanings which are incorporated into the learner's cognitive structure. This is where Ausubel takes on a constructivist perspective in that he asserts that learners must make their own meaning from what they have received, connect it to previous knowledge and develop existing schemas.

In Ausubel's theory the key method by which teachers provide structure for the delivery and reception of learning is by the use of advanced organisers. These are devices for providing organisational frameworks which teachers present to learners to prepare them for what they are about to learn. They link previous knowledge and learning to the coming topic or provide the 'big picture' for new learning. As well as preparing for learning to come, organisers can be used for revising learning, connecting learning and discovering new ideas and concepts, analysing and thinking. Examples of advanced organisers include:

- concept maps;
- flow charts;
- diagrams;
- written overviews;
- charts;
- timelines;
- maps;
- tree diagrams;
- bullet points;
- series of steps.

What these organisers do most effectively is to 'fix' an idea or concept so that new learning can be related to it. The communication models shown in Chapter 2, 'Communication and the teacher', are examples of advanced organisers. In English literature, a teacher can fix the structure and characters in a play or novel by a visual representation. Organisation charts help business studies students to see clearly, and to analyse, the structure of businesses. Advanced organisers which use a visual element are sometimes called 'graphic organisers'. Edward de Bono's book *The Greatest Thinkers* (1976) provides essays outlining the work and ideas of significant thinkers from Moses to Sartre. Each essay is introduced by a diagrammatic overview of the ideas. Figure 3.2, from the essay on Darwin, shows a simple, visual representation of the prevailing notion that God created all creatures and they remained unchanged. This is contrasted with the model after the publication of the *Theory of the Origin of the Species* which represents evolution as a series of adaptations and changes with some branches dying out, others adapting and surviving.

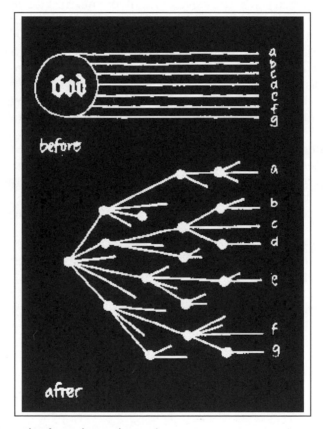

Figure 3.2 Example of an advanced organiser.
Reproduced from Edward de Bono's *The Greatest Thinkers*. Permission from MICA Management Resources (UK) Inc. copyright 1976. All rights reserved. No copying permitted.

Activity

Think of an idea or concept you want your learners to understand, or an overview of a module or unit of learning. Design an advanced organiser, preferably graphic, to give an overview.

Try asking your learners to design their own organisers to help them organise and understand their learning.

Deep and surface learning

Surface learning is characterised by rote learning, memory and low-level cognitive activities rather than understanding. It can only usually be reapplied in the same situation in which it was learned. Whilst memorisation is not in itself undesirable – learners may be required to memorise the periodic table or the lines of a play – real learning only occurs when the information is connected to previous learning. I learned my times tables as a chant but for all I understood it might just as well have been a shopping list in Serbo-Croat. If I was asked what 7 × 8 made, I would mentally go through the chant until I reached that point and tentatively suggested that 56 might be the answer.

Deep learning is about really understanding a subject, making connections and recognising underlying principles. It is learning which is based on student-centred activities, such as problem-based learning, reflection, case studies, application, evaluation and analysis. Deep learning is long lasting. Deep learning is associated with constructivism in that it requires the development of schema and the making of connections. Deep learning is best achieved when learners have their curiosity aroused and are set challenging problems.

It could be argued that our current education system, with its emphasis on testing and the acquisition of paper-based qualifications, encourages both teachers and learners to adopt surface learning techniques. As Gavin Reid (2005: 3) points out:

> Education is about learning; qualifications are by-products of that learning. Yet often the reverse is the case. A school may pride itself by referring to the number of students obtaining high grades in national examinations, but that in itself is not evidence that these students have become effective and autonomous learners.

The challenge for those working in education, not just lifelong learning, is to meet the needs of a qualifications-driven system whilst developing the questioning, autonomous lifelong learning necessary for the twenty-first century.

Active and passive learning

Constructivism is, above all, about *active learning*. Active learning doesn't mean learners are busily involved in physical activity, although they might be. Active, in this sense means being actively involved in making meaning rather than just being given information. *Passive learners* are reactive rather than proactive and, typically, are involved in taking notes, listening, copying – just being 'filled up' with information. In passive learning the content is structured and organised by the teacher. Deep learning is the result of active learning; surface learning the result of passive.

This book is, essentially, about active learning and the development of learning and teaching techniques which make learners connect ideas and develop their own schemas. Active learning requires learners to operate at a higher level and to develop thinking skills and to become increasingly independent in their learning.

Humanism

In essence, humanism in education could be summed up as the removal of barriers to learning. It is particularly concerned with creating an emotionally safe and secure learning environment. It also revolves around the simple notion that we all need to feel good about ourselves.

You might have memories of your own or of friends' school experiences. Most of us can provide examples of teaching which has been threatening, humiliating and, occasionally, frightening. My own memories of maths in school are associated with fear – of failure, punishment or humiliation. Consequently, my number skills did not develop until I got my first job in a shop; a good example of 'situated learning'. These kinds of barriers are not confined to schoolchildren. 14–19-year-olds and adult learners may well have similar psychological baggage which affects their learning and their feelings about learning. For adults returning to learning, the creation of a non-threatening environment is one of the keys to success. This, it could be argued, is an instance where humanism links to behaviourism.

Activity

Consider your own, or another person's, experience of education (in school; college or university).

- Identify an experience which was negative or something which was a barrier to learning

- In what ways did it impede learning?

- How did it make you feel about that subject; about the school or college; about education?
- How did it make you feel about yourself?

The activity above may have illustrated the notion of the *self-fulfilling prophecy*, whereby an individual's self-perception is moulded by what others say about them and how they act towards them. Thus, someone who is frequently told they are a failure will come to believe they are a failure, with negative consequences for their future learning. Often in lifelong learning we are faced with the task of helping to repair those who have been damaged by early educational experiences. Humanist theorists regard every human as unique. Their aim is the education of the whole person and the development of individuals with positive self esteem. Positive self-esteem is both a goal of education and a basis for lifelong learning.

Carl Rogers

Rogers (1902–1987) is generally associated with the fields of counselling and psychotherapy but he provides much useful advice for learning and teaching.

As a therapist he believed that most people had the solutions to their problems within them and that the role of the therapist is to provide a safe environment in which they can express themselves openly and reach their own conclusions for the best way to deal with their problems. In this way the clients will develop confidence and self-esteem. Similarly, in education, Rogers argues that the most effective learning is student-centred learning in which the teacher acts a facilitator who creates a safe and secure learning environment and provides the necessary opportunities and resources for learning.

For Rogers one of the keys to learning, as well as psychological well-being, is the development of a positive *self-concept*. Self-concept is the view you have of yourself as an individual – this may be positive or negative – and it arises from your communication with others since childhood. As Legge and Harari point out:

> We all have a self-concept, but are we conscious of what that self-concept is and how it affects our lives? For example, individuals may feel they are too unlovable to form successful interpersonal relationships, but once they become aware of, and acknowledge this feeling, they can begin to understand why their relationships fail.
>
> (Legge and Harari 2000: 11)

Self-concept and *self-esteem* are closely linked but easily confused. Briefly, the former is how we view ourselves; the latter is how we feel about ourselves. Both are dependent on our communication with others, not least with our teachers. In the same way that teachers can contribute towards negative self-esteem by the self-fulfilling prophecy they can positively affect learners by what some psychologists refer to as the 'Pygmalion effect' in which people can be encouraged by positive, friendly attentions. If they feel that they are valued by others, they may begin to value themselves. The 'Pygmalion effect' links to Rogers's notion of *unconditional positive regard* in which teachers have respect for learners and value them whatever they do. This might seem a very tall order when faced with a particularly difficult or demanding learner but a refusal to be aggravated and the use of continued politeness may, eventually be 'modelled' by the learner.

Abraham Maslow

Maslow (1908–1970) provided a hierarchy of needs which he developed from his experience as a psychologist and psychotherapist (see Figure 3.3). In his hierarchy Maslow suggests there is a range of human needs from basic to higher levels. The lower levels, particularly physiological, safety and belonging needs are deficiency needs which must be satisfied before others can be addressed. Obviously, if we are homeless, cold, hungry, and/or unloved we will not be especially concerned about our intellectual development. The higher levels, relating to our learning and cognitive needs and our need for self-fulfilment cannot be attained until the basic needs have been met.

For teachers in lifelong learning, Maslow's hierarchy makes us think about the total experience of our learners. From physiological factors (is the room too hot or too cold?) to relationships (do we give positive regard and developmental feedback?) to self-esteem needs ('I'm no good at English'), his hierarchy provides a useful device to help us understand learning and motivation.

Brain-based learning

Brain-based learning sounds like a tautology because we assume that all learning has something to do with the brain. This, of course is true, but recent developments in neuroscience research and cognitive psychology have provided new ideas about how the brain functions and how we can promote effective learning. Brain-based theories of learning are contentious for some educationalists who consider they are, as yet, insufficiently supported by research. However, these theories are still worthy of your attention.

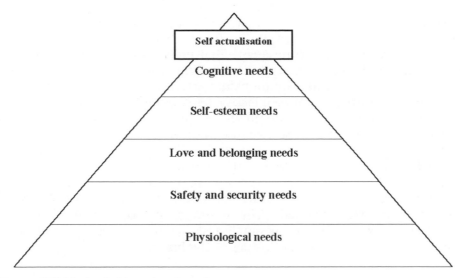

Figure 3.3 Maslow's hierarchy of needs.

The main elements of this section are:

- left brain/right brain dominance;
- the triune brain;
- the brain's search for meaning and patterns;
- the brain's need for fuel.

Left brain/right brain

The brain comprises two hemispheres. The left hemisphere controls the motor movement of the right side of the body; the right hemisphere controls the left side of the body. As for cognitive processes and intellectual development it is suggested that the left hemisphere is concerned with logic and sequencing; the right with wholes, creativity and patterns.

Left brain (sometimes called the *analyser*)	*Right brain* (sometimes called the *integrator*)
Sequences	Imagery
Logical	Similarities
Detail	Patterns
Categorising	The 'big picture'
'Step-by-step'	Integration
Linear	Intuition and creativity

Each individual tends to have either left-brain or right-brain dominance. We can draw two conclusions from this. The first is that we should use activities to engage the right brain for those with that preference; left-brain activities for those with left-brain preference. Conversely, the second conclusion could be that we challenge learners by providing activities which do not fit their hemispherical dominance. To be effective we should do both. For example, we can ask those with left-brain dominance to produce concept maps; we can use or create advance organisers or use metaphors to explain ideas and concepts. 'Right-brainers' can be encouraged to categorise, produce sequences or lists. Much work has been done with 'brain gyms' for young children in schools, a key element of which is the provision of activities to connect the two hemispheres. We should be wary, however, of categorising learners as 'left-brained' or 'right-brained'. The brain is one organ and the two hemispheres work together; even simple tasks such as decoding words and recognising numerals require both sides of the brain.

The triune brain

A more recent view of the brain suggests a triune, or three-part, structure. The three parts are:

1 *The basic, or reptilian brain:* this part controls our primitive responses (fear; 'flight or fight') and autonomic functions such as breathing and heartbeat. If learners feel threatened or under stress, this basic part of the brain will take over and higher functions will not be possible.
2 *The emotional brain, or limbic system:* this part deals with values; emotions and memory (particularly long-term). Our feelings and attitudes about learning and places of education are held in this part of the brain. Adults with memories of authoritarian schools or bullying are likely to associate education with these unpleasant experiences. As teachers we have to positively engage the emotional brain by creating safe and positive learning environments.
3 *The neo-cortex:* the higher part is known as the neo-cortex. It is divided into the left and right hemispheres and is where the higher cognitive functions occur – patterns of meaning; models for understanding; problem-solving and language. This part of the brain, however, cannot function satisfactorily if the other two don't allow it to. Therefore, we must create calm and secure learning environments in which the needs of the basic brain and the emotional brain are met. The formula of low threat – high challenge is the most appropriate. There is a clear connection to Rogers's humanist ideas here.

This view of the brain reminds us that the emotional element of learning is at least as important as the cognitive element. For a fuller discussion of this, see Goleman (1995, Chapter 2).

The brain's search for meaning and patterns

Our senses are bombarded by stimuli throughout our lives and all humans need to make sense of what they experience and to look for meaning. Learners in post-compulsory education and training are faced with new knowledge, ideas and concepts which they have to comprehend, integrate and evaluate. It is part of our task as teachers to present learning in ways which make structuring and patterning easier for learners. We must ensure that learners:

- know why they are doing things;
- know what they have to do;
- can connect it to previous learning;
- can see the big picture;
- can construct their own personal version of the learning.

If learning is about constructing patterns and models, we must remember that they consist of two elements – parts and wholes – that is, the individual elements and the ways in which they are organised and combined. As has already been stated the brain has two hemispheres but operates as one unit. We need to provide learners with both the jigsaw pieces and the picture to guide them in its construction.

The brain's needs for fuel

Brains, like people, need water, nutrition, exercise and rest. The brain is 75 per cent water and we need to ensure that we are properly hydrated in order to keep our brains functioning effectively and efficiently. Dehydration can lead to headaches, drowsiness and a loss of concentration – not very conducive to learning. Estimates vary as to how much water we should drink, but 5 or 6 large glasses per day is about the average recommendation. Whilst coffee, tea and fizzy drinks are not allowed in some learning environments, water should be. One of the key elements in 'brain gyms' being developed in schools is an adequate supply of water. Similarly, brains need nutrition. We all know the feeling of reduced energy when hungry. Research underlines the importance of essential fatty acids – such as those found in oily fish – as an essential component of brain development and functioning. P.G. Wodehouse's Bertie Wooster was probably right when he attributed Jeeves's phenomenal brainpower to a fish-rich diet.

Brains need to be exercised. One way to do this is by learning, particularly challenging, new learning that reinforces neural connections. Children in their first three years are so active and need so much stimulation because they are building their brains. Older people are frequently encouraged to tackle crosswords to avoid the onset of dementia. Brains also need to rest. Learning, like food, is most effective when it occurs in 'chunks' followed by periods of digestion. To continue the diet analogy, too much learning, especially a rich diet of learning, with no time to reflect and consolidate will lead to 'mental indigestion'. When planning and organising learning, teachers must ensure regular changes of activity and regular periods when the brain can have a break.

Increasingly, educators are looking to neuroscientific research for the latest developments in learning. Blakemore and Frith (2005) present an excellent overview of recent research on the brain's development at various stages of life. One of the key points they make is to do with the brain's plasticity, which means the brain's physical changes and adaptations to new circumstances and new learning. This brain plasticity is a factor right through our lives, an idea which has clear implications for lifelong learning in that everyone can learn at any stage of their lives. Blakemore and Frith use a very helpful gardening metaphor of learning and the brain. They say that:

> Education can be considered a kind of 'landscaping' of the brain and educators are, in a sense, like gardeners. Of course gardeners cannot grow roses without the right soil and roots in the first place, but a good gardener can do wonders with what is already there . . . individual gardens involve making the best of what is there and it is possible to make astonishing new and influential designs.
>
> (Blakemore and Frith 2005: 10)

Learning styles

There is no 'theory', at least not a coherent theory, of learning styles. Rather, there are a number of ideas about how people learn and their learning preferences loosely gathered under the general heading of learning styles.

Even a cursory observation of a learning group at work will confirm that learners have preferred ways of doing things. Raised eyebrows and muttered complaints frequently greet the instruction to write or take notes. Fear and trembling is apparent in those who do not like to speak in class. We know that some learners like to write; some like to talk; others like to make, do or create; many seem able to do several things at once.

A recent survey (Coffield et al. 2004) discovered at least 70 different learning styles inventories and systems. Clearly, a review of all these would be very tedious and not particularly helpful, so this chapter will round up and review a few of the 'usual suspects'. They are:

- VAK (visual, auditory, kinaesthetic);
- Kolb;
- Honey and Mumford;
- Gardner's Multiple Intelligences.

VAK

These categorise learners into three types and suggests that we should assess the preferred learning style of each learner so that we can employ appropriate techniques.

- *Visual learners* like to see and use diagrams, pictures. They are likely to respond well to advance organisers, particularly graphic organisers.
- *Auditory learners* like to listen to lectures, teacher inputs, recordings, hearing stories.
- *Kinaesthetic learners* like to move about and be active. It's good to move them around groups to get them coming up to the board – if you've got one.

To a great extent, these categories appear to be a statement of the obvious. The value of them for teachers is that they make us aware that a 'sit down and listen class' will not be effective for everyone. Given that many learners frequently use at least two of these in sessions, we should be wary of labelling individuals as exclusively visual, auditory or kinaesthetic.

Kolb

David Kolb (1976, 1984) devised a 4-part cycle of learning based around the ideas of reflection and learning by experience. We can also connect Kolb's learning cycle to constructivism and Bruner's spiral curriculum; as Harkin, Turner and Dawn (2001: 40) point out, 'Kolb . . . has been a key contributor to the theory that effective learning concerns the reinterpretation and reshaping of experience.'

Kolb's learning cycle is shown in Figure 3.4. At the risk of over-simplification the cycle could be summarised as:

- Do it
- Think about it
- Formulate a theory about it
- Do it again and see if it's any better.

No stage of the learning cycle, however, is effective on its own. The value of Kolb's theory is that we conceive of learning as a process of development. We

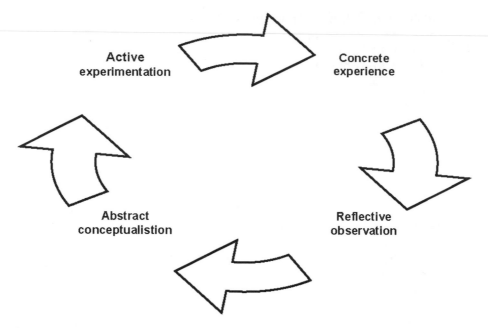

Figure 3.4 Kolb's learning cycle.

can easily apply it to our own experience, for example, learning to drive. Our first tentative attempts at clutch control will, most likely have ended in embarrassing kangaroo hops and stalling. Given a patient teacher we can reflect on the experience; consider ways to improve; try it again and observe the results. Through this cycle of experience, reflection, conceptualisation and experimentation our driving ability becomes natural; a process summarised by the move from 'unconscious incompetence' to 'unconscious competence' (see Chapter 1, 'The reflective teacher').

Honey and Mumford

Honey and Mumford (1986) drew on Kolb's ideas in the development of their four different learning styles (see Table 3.1), which are:

- activists;
- reflectors;
- theorists;
- pragmatists.

Learners have preferred styles. Some adult learners will have become accustomed to one style; others may be comfortable with all four. Teachers

Table 3.1 Activists, reflectors, theorists, pragmatists: preferred learning styles

Activists like	dislike
• New and challenging experiences • Working with others • Leading discussions	• Listening for long periods • Following instructions • Reading, writing, thinking alone
Reflectors like	dislike
• Observing • Reviewing • Doing tasks without tight deadlines	• Acting as leaders • No time to prepare • Being thrown in at the deep end
Theorists like	dislike
• Complex tasks where they can use their skills and knowledge • Structure and purpose • Questioning and probing ideas	• Emotions and feelings • Unstructured situations • Unclear instructions
Pragmatists like	dislike

• Links between theory and practice
• Useful techniques, e.g. time
  management
• Role models; examples of good
  practice
	• No obvious benefit to learning
	• No guidelines
	• No apparent purpose to the learning

in lifelong learning will have a preference for a particular style of learning; this will influence their choice of teaching and learning strategies. *Theorist* teachers may wish to spend the majority of the time questioning and probing ideas; the *non-theorist* learners, probably the majority of the group, will just want to get on with things.

Multiple intelligences

The final learning style we will consider is Howard Gardner's 'Multiple Intelligences theory' (1993). This was developed out of a concern that standard measures of intelligence have been based on linguistic and mathematical/logical abilities. This narrow definition of intelligence does not allow everyone to demonstrate what they are good at or to use different types of intelligence in their learning. Gardner originally proposed seven types of intelligence; an eighth, naturalistic intelligence, was added later. We should not make the mistake of assuming that an individual learner is a 'linguistic' learner or an 'interpersonal learner', in much the same way learners can be simplistically categorised as 'visual' or 'kinaesthetic'. Individual learners will have a certain level of intelligence in each category but will have a preference for one or more.

- *Linguistic preference*: these learners like language and words; reading and writing; speaking and listening.
- *Logical/mathematical*: learners with this preference like number activities, patterns, deduction, solving problems. They like scientific learning and making connections between pieces of information.
- *Visual/spatial*: these learners are good at visualising and creating and using mental images. They like graphic organisers and reading images.
- *Interpersonal*: these learners like working with others. They are good communicators and are empathic.
- *Intrapersonal*: these people are good at understanding themselves and their motivations and feelings. They tend to be reflective and use *metacognition* (thinking about thinking).
- *Bodily/kinaesthetic*: these learners tend to be 'sporty' types and have physical skill. They are good at coordinated body movement.
- *Musical*: these learners are good at composing, appreciating and performing musical patterns. They are not necessarily musicians but they do enjoy rhythm, pitch, tone and beat, as in poetry or rapping.
- *Naturalistic*: learners with this preference have knowledge and understanding of nature and the environment. They are good at working outside and observing nature.

Learning styles – just an educational fashion?

There has been a proliferation of learning style inventories, questionnaires and associated materials since the mid-1980s. Many of these are tied to expensive packages of materials and training, which cast doubts on their reliability and validity. The report *Should We be Using Learning Styles?* (Coffield et al. 2004) was based on extensive analysis of more than 70 different learning style models. Not only do the authors of the report criticise the varying quality of some learning style models, they also question the practicality and the utility of efforts to measure individual learning styles and to match them to teaching and learning activities. Moreover, the report suggests there is little to be gained from labelling learners – as in, 'I'm a reflector', 'I'm a kinaesthetic learner'.

Should we, then, abandon learning styles? Based on this report and subsequent writings, perhaps not. What we *do* need to do, however, is consider how we assess learning styles and, more importantly what we do with the results of such assessments. Learning styles are most valuable, it is suggested, as tools for learner self-development, rather than as a means of categorising learners as particular 'types'. 'A reliable and valid instrument which measures learning styles and approaches could be used as a tool to encourage self-development, not only by diagnosing how people learn, but by showing them how to *enhance* their learning (Coffield et al. 2004: 51, original emphasis).

The most valuable message teachers in the lifelong learning sector get from learning styles is that people learn in many different ways; consequently teachers should have a wide, and continually developing, range of techniques to draw on for long- and short-term planning. The various models of learning styles, particularly those described above, can serve as a useful *aide-memoire* of teaching and learning methods and techniques.

Adult learning – androgogy

Adult learners tend to have different motivations and learning preferences from those in compulsory education. This, basically, is the assumption on which Malcolm Knowles theory of *androgogy* is based. According to Knowles, education in schools is based on *pedagogy* and tends to be teacher-dominated with learners assigned a passive role having minimal control over their learning. The most obvious difference is that school education is compulsory whereas adult learning is, to a great extent, voluntary. Androgogy suggests a different model of learning in which adults are more self-directed and active. They see education as empowering and have high expectations of it and those who provide it. According to this theory adult learners are distinguished from younger learners in the following ways:

- Adult learners need to know why they are learning particular things.
- Adult self-concept – they need to perceive themselves as self-directed and responsible for their own decisions.
- Adult learners have a wide variety of experience which represents a rich resource for learners and teachers. They do, however, need to recognise bias and subjectivity in their opinions and experiences.
- Adults have readiness to learn those things which will help them to deal with real-life situations.
- Adults are motivated to learn things which are of interest or important to them. This, and their readiness to learn, implies that adults have intrinsic motivations for learning.

Knowles's ideas have been widely criticised, frequently because the distinction between adult and compulsory education seems too rigid. We probably know from our experience of adults who are not willing or motivated learners. In many schools the experiences of children are respected and included as part of the learning. Perhaps the best use we can make of Knowles and androgogy is that they give us more ideas about how we should treat our learners and facilitate their learning. Clearly, adults wish to be respected as individuals and not treated as children, but this is equally true of 14–19 learners.

Situated learning

My early memories of learning geography at school involved 'doing' Canada. An outline map of the country was rolled into my exercise book and I assiduously inked the outline and coloured in various parts of the map according to height or natural resources. My greatest achievement was the production of a bar chart showing the annual rainfall in Winnipeg. All of this effort, however, meant nothing because it wasn't connected to anything I knew or cared about at the time. A study of the weather and the local industries in the East Midlands would have been more relevant and I could have connected to it more easily and made it meaningful.

The reason for this anecdote is to illustrate that learning must be in a context which is relevant and meaningful to the learner. There are various names for this area of theory: *situated learning; situated cognition; socially situated learning.* I will stick to the term situated learning. There are two main principles in this theory. The first is that learning should be situated in an authentic and meaningful context and/or the learning activities should be relevant to the learners and authentic. The second is that learning takes place within a social situation; within 'communities of practice'.

My geography example suggests that I could not get interested in Canada or connect it to any previous knowledge. If the geography teaching had begun with a problem-based approach such as, 'Why is there this pattern of industries in Derby and Nottingham?', I could have related to it more, if only because I knew people who lived there and worked in those industries. It is equally true that maths learning becomes more meaningful and situated when it deals with ideas and concepts that the learners have some previous knowledge of.

The second element of this theory concerns the extent to which the learning takes in social settings where there are shared goals and activities, in other words 'communities of practice' (Lave and Wenger 1990). Much of our discussion so far has concerned psychological and brain-based theories of learning. Lave and Wenger contend that it is at least as important to consider learning as something which results largely from our experience of participating in daily life. Our workplaces are 'communities of practice', which are strange and unusual when we first enter them but learning involves moving from the periphery to the centre and becoming a 'professional'. As we shall see when we consider Skills for Life and Key Skills, learning which is meaningful and authentic, preferably in a work situation, will be deeper and more effective.

Without too much thought, we should all be able to identify communities of practice we are part of – work; hobbies or interests; voluntary work. The learning which takes place in these communities is so integrated and natural that the participants probably don't even realise they are learning at all. My sister started a history group in her village and in no time there was a community of practice in which the members, without a curriculum or a plan, learned about and acquired skills in research, team-working, using IT, fundraising, organising exhibitions and many more. Clearly, learning in post-compulsory settings cannot be quite so informal but situated learning theory makes us think about creating learning which is contextualised, authentic, meaningful and relevant.

What can we learn from theories of learning?

This chapter does not aim, and would not be able, to cover the full range and complexity of learning theories. Rather, it provides an overview of the main theories relevant to lifelong learning. If you wish to follow up these ideas and others in more depth, suggestions for further reading are provided at the end of the chapter.

Theory is of little use unless we apply it to practice. The following points summarise the practical relevance of the learning theories when planning, preparing and facilitating teaching and learning.

- Positive rewards and encouragement are more effective than negative responses.
- Active learning should be preferred to passive.
- Active learning must connect to and extend previous learning
- Learners need time to reflect on and practise learning.
- Learning is easier and more effective when a framework, or 'big picture', is provided. Advance organisers can help to do this.
- Learners need to construct their own learning. They need to construct mental maps.
- Learners need to 'play around' with ideas and concepts. They need to use learning and transfer it to other situations.
- Learning is a social process; we benefit from interaction with others.
- Learning is more effective when it is 'situated'; when it is relevant to the learners and authentic.
- Learners are motivated by challenges and problems to be solved.

- Teaching 'by asking' is as important as 'teaching by telling'.
- Scaffolding will help learners to reach the next level.
- Teachers should provide emotionally (and physically) safe and secure learning environments.
- Learners need to feel good about themselves and develop a positive self-concept. No one ever learned from feeling threatened, humiliated or anxious.
- Unconditional positive regard can seem difficult but is worth the effort.
- Teachers and learners must recognise the brain as a vital organ which needs water, nutrition, exercise and rest.
- The brain searches for structure and meaning.
- People learn in different ways, therefore teachers need a comprehensive toolkit of teaching and learning techniques.
- People learn by experience and by 'doing'. We need time to reflect on and learn from our experiences.
- All learners benefit from being respected and treated as adults.
- We should have high expectations of all our learners.
- Everyone can learn.

For your journal

Consider the extent to which you have consciously considered theories of teaching and learning in planning, preparing and delivering teaching and learning. For example, have you used a humanist approach to create a supportive learning environment? Have there been any examples of behaviourism in your sessions, particularly in relation to learner behaviour and motivation? To what extent has constructivism influenced the planning of learning methods and activities?

Activity

Read the following journal extract.

- Can you identify any elements of learning theory in this account?
- What conclusions can you draw about how people learn best?
- Describe the role of the teacher in this situation.
- What principles can you apply to your own teaching?

Journal extract: Russell, trained as a teacher of construction

I was feeling very confident this week. I experimented with a plastering session with _ _ _ _ _ using my theory that 'you learn more by making mistakes than doing it right first time'. They were to skim and finish the low wall that they undercoated last week. This was their first time and the conditions cramped and the light poor. I had taught them to work in a confined space last week so now we could concentrate on the mixing. I allowed them to do it as they wished the first time. The mix was horrible, dry and lumpy and would not stay on. We reviewed the situation and all agreed it was too dry. I then let them mix it too wet and wet the walls as it is much easier to work but far too messy. The students were covered with plaster and one of the senior lecturers was raising his eyebrows at the mess. Once the students had experienced using wet plaster and seen the finish they could achieve their confidence grew. We reviewed the 'too wet' method again and cleared up. I asked them to mix it 'just right' this time and showed them a wall that had been finished by an experienced plasterer. The students without hesitation made a good mix and got to work. Before long they were handling the skim like professionals and took pride in making a very good job of it.

Further reading and useful websites

Blakemore, S-J., and Frith, U. (2005) *The Learning Brain: Lessons for Education*. Oxford: Blackwell.

Curzon, L.B. (2004) *Teaching in Further Education*, 6th edn. London: Continuum.

Legge, K. and Harari, P. (2000) *Psychology and Education*. Oxford: Heinemann.

Pritchard, A. (2005) *Ways of Learning: Learning Theories and Learning Styles in the Classroom*. London: David Fulton Publishers.

www.doceo.co.uk This comprehensive and generous site is a 'must see' for all teachers.

www.support4learning.org.uk/education has a wide range of articles and links, particularly on theories of learning.

4 Planning for teaching and learning

There is a strong relationship between thorough planning and effective teaching. Syllabuses and programme requirements should be translated into clear and comprehensive schemes of work that are understood by learners. Individual lessons should be well planned, but lesson plans should not be so inflexible that they cannot be adapted to reflect the progress of learners.

(*Handbook for Inspecting Colleges*' Ofsted 2006, para. 182)

Many lessons are insufficiently planned. Students are not given clear aims and objectives. Teachers talk too much and pay too little attention to matching teaching to the learning needs of the students.

(Extract from a college inspection report quoted in *Why Colleges Fail*, Ofsted 2004, para. 17)

What this chapter is about

- Why is planning necessary?
- Planning a course
- What will I teach – where does the content come from?
- Planning a scheme of work
- Writing aims and objectives
- Producing session plans
- Using individual learning plans
- Differentiation and personalised learning

LLUK standards

This chapter covers, at least, the following standards:

AS 1; AK 1.1; AP 1.1

CS 2; CK 2.1; CP 2.1
DS 1; DK 1.1; DP 1.1; DK 1.2; DP 1.2; DK 1.3: DP 1.3
DS 2; DK 2.1; DP 2.1; DK 2.2; DP 2.2
DS 3; DK 3.1; DP 3.1; DK 3.2: DP 3.2

Why is planning necessary?

Consistently good teaching and learning doesn't just happen by accident; it is the result of thorough planning and preparation. Someone not involved in education might observe an impressive session where the teacher is performing at the top of her game: the learners are learning; the session flows effortlessly; it is clearly structured; there is a wide variety of active learning methods; there is an excellent working relationship between teacher and learners, in short, everyone is enjoying themselves. The observer might regard this is a matter of talent, natural teaching ability or luck, but appearances are deceptive. Much like the swan which appears to glide effortlessly on the water, there is considerable effort beneath the surface. Even the quality of the relationship between teacher and students is rarely a matter of good fortune, it has to be planned for and worked at.

Effective planning is a fundamental part of the process of being a reflective teacher; it is part of a cycle of PLAN – DO – REVIEW. In Chapter 1 we considered Donald Schön's concepts of 'reflection in action' and 'reflection on action' and suggested that continuing improvement comes from reflecting on and evaluating the effectiveness of teaching and learning sessions and drawing conclusions which will inform the planning of future sessions. In this sense planning for teaching and learning is part of your continuing professional development and improvement.

Effective teaching and successful learning are not possible without proper planning. In short you have to make a planning journey from the specifications or syllabus, or the competencies, or the content you have negotiated with learners, to the detailed planning of individual sessions and the subsequent evaluation of those sessions (evaluation of teaching and learning is discussed in Chapter 12, 'Synthesis and evaluation'). Figure 4.1 encapsulates this process.

There are three main elements to planning teaching and learning in post-compulsory education and training:

1 *Long-term planning.* This could be for a term, a year, a module, or a sequence of sessions – a module or a sequence of sessions could be regarded as medium or short-term planning. This is generally done as a *scheme of work* document. The purpose of this long-term planning is

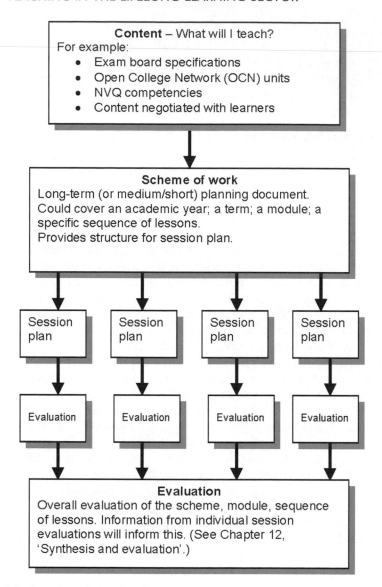

Figure 4.1 Overview of the planning process.

to provide a big picture for the teaching team, and the learners, showing when and in what order the content will be delivered. Schemes of work show less detail than session plans; their main function is to ensure that the necessary content is delivered in the time available and that the teacher and the learners don't get behind or ahead of schedule; to ensure a range of teaching, learning and assessment techniques, and to plan and provide resources.

2 *Session (or lesson) planning*. This is the planning and preparation of individual teaching and learning sessions. These are, usually, paper documents which the teacher uses to guide him/her through the session to achieve the aims and objectives. Particularly as a trainee, you are likely to meet teachers who say they don't bother with lesson plans, generally claiming that they don't have time to do them. Whilst it may be true that experienced teachers produce session plans which are fairly rudimentary, it is equally true that limited planning will result in limited and ineffective learning. Sessions can only be planned effectively one at a time using the session you have just delivered as a starting point.

3 *ILPs*. Increasingly learners and teachers will use ILPs – you will have produced one yourself if you are currently doing teacher training. ILPs are especially valuable in groups of learners who are working at different levels and progressing at different rates. Individual learning plans particularly in Skills for Life, are planned together with learners based on information gained from initial and diagnostic testing. They are regularly reviewed and amended by learners and teachers.

Planning the scheme of work

The first question a new teacher is likely to ask is 'what will I teach?' In most cases the content to be learned and assessed is provided by an examining authority (Assessment and Qualifications Alliance (AQA), OCR, Edexcel) or by some other national or regional awarding body, in the form of specifications, or a syllabus. The form of external assessment is usually prescribed, frequently in the form of national examinations. The Open College Network (OCN) provides units with specific learning outcomes at a variety of levels; these are widely used in access and adult education courses. In National Vocational Qualification (NVQ)-style courses vocational competences are prescribed stating what learners should be able to do. Occasionally, teachers will be able to negotiate content, to a greater or lesser extent, with their learners.

Even though the content and forms of assessment are largely prescribed, the specifications do not stipulate the order of delivery, the amount of time allowed for teaching and learning, specific details of content, resources and formative assessment. The teacher, frequently as part of a team, will need to plan the course delivery and produce the scheme of work. This can be one of the most challenging, yet creative, tasks teaching staff undertake. However, time spent thinking through and producing the scheme of work will make a significant difference to the success of the learning.

The scheme of work gives teachers the 'big picture' from which they can plan each of the sessions. A properly planned scheme of work is a working document – not a pristine document you keep in a file just in case of inspection. The scheme will probably be annotated and adjusted to some degree, although major changes to the structure and timings should not be necessary and should be avoided. Its purpose is to keep you on track and ensure that you have you have covered the content, met the aims, carried out assessments and kept to the schedule. You can't afford to dwell on one particular topic because it's your 'favourite bit; I've witnessed several occasions on which teachers have got halfway through but only covered 20 per cent of the scheme.

What factors influence planning the scheme of work?

Before you begin planning your scheme there are many factors you need to consider. For the sake of consistency, I will use the same model I set out in Chapter 2 based on the five key questions:

- Who? – the teacher;
- What? – the content;
- Whom? – the learners;
- How? – methods, strategies, resources;
- Why? – the aims and purpose of the learning.

Obviously, the five questions interlink and will have consequences one upon another. For example, a group of 14–16-year-olds attending a college one day a week will probably need a different approach from adult learners at an outreach centre or a group of A2 students studying physics. If you want learners to develop autonomy and thinking skills you will need to include teaching and learning methods which encourage active and deep learning. Teachers often feel that time is limited and they will have to use didactic, teacher-centred methods in order to cover all of the specification's content. This can be a mistake; limited time doesn't necessarily mean not using student-centred learning.

Who? – the teacher

This is an unconventional starting point for planning but it is useful to consider yourself – the teacher – in relation to what you are planning to teach.

We all have our specialist subjects but the reality of life in post-compulsory education and training is that we are frequently called upon to stretch our expertise to areas we have not previously taught or even considered teaching. During my time teaching in colleges I moved from teaching general and communications to day-release students to delivering A Level communication studies and, subsequently, media studies, English language, and teacher training.

You need first to consider how closely your knowledge and skills match those required in the specifications. This could be as a basic as an English literature teacher reading and researching the set text or IT lecturer familiarising herself with a new software package. You might need to develop your teaching and learning techniques to cope with new learners, for example, there has been a considerable growth recently in the number of 14–16-year-olds taught by college lecturers. Teachers need support in providing for these new learners and developing new teaching and learning strategies and coping with some young people who may have challenging behaviour and a history of underachievement. You will have to study the specifications closely to assess your own development needs. Is your subject knowledge current? Are you up to date with the latest initiatives and research? If you're delivering as a member of a team you will need to assess the strengths of the team members and allocate teaching and learning accordingly.

What? – are you going to teach?

If you are working from published specifications you must first make some decisions regarding the content. Are there any sections you can edit or omit and still meet the aims and assessment objectives? You may not need to include everything in the specifications or it may be possible to condense or edit some elements. Some elements of the required skills and knowledge shown in the specifications can be taught as integrated units of work.

The working arrangements of most teachers, particularly in FE colleges, are such that much planning has to be done before the first meeting with the learners but for others, perhaps in adult and community education, there will be opportunities to negotiate the content and the sequencing, possibly even the assessment, of the course with your learners. Clearly, this is desirable since it gives learners more 'ownership' of the course and offers the possibility of integrating their own learning and experience. You need to consider the order in which you will teach the specifications. Is there a particular order suggested or implied in the specifications or can you be creative in the sequencing of learning?

Finally, what level is the course? All courses (including A level, GCSE, NVQ, GNVQ, Skills for Life, Key Skills) are expressed in terms of the National Qualifications Framework (NQF; see Appendix 1). The level indicates the levels of assessment and attainment which are expected of learners at that particular stage and, as such, represents a key consideration in your planning and preparation.

Whom? – the learners

To risk stating the obvious – learning is for learners. Consequently we need to know as much as possible about them. The following overview is not comprehensive but provides some examples of things you should consider.

First, we should consider the needs of the learners. As we shall see when we consider planning for differentiation, it is inappropriate to consider any group of learners as an undifferentiated group who have more or less the same needs and characteristics. At a fundamental level, you might have learners who have special or particular needs, such as those with hearing or sight difficulties, or wheelchair users. All learners are individuals and will have different learning styles and preferences. Allowing for these different styles is difficult, especially if you are planning before you meet your learners, but you can at least ensure that your planning includes a variety of teaching, learning and assessment strategies.

Second, your new students will arrive with many different experiences of learning, and life and prior knowledge. You could possibly assume that learners starting an AS level course will have similar experiences, skills and knowledge from GCSE, but even then they will have had varying success.

A group of adult learners, however, will be extremely diverse, many having had negative experiences of previous learning and with a bewildering array of existing skills and knowledge.

Other factors include motivation and commitment to learning, confidence, social and communication skills. The key to effective planning is to know as much as you can about your learners as soon as possible.

How? – will learning happen?

The most important aspect of planning is deciding how learning will happen. Obviously this is related to who the learners are and why they are there. If their need, and your purpose, is to get them passing examinations in a limited amount of time you will probably tend towards more didactic, teacher-centred learning. However, as we have seen earlier such methods are not necessarily compatible with the development of confidence, deep learning and independent learning. You have to plan the optimum strategies to meet the needs of the institution for results but also the need to create a stimulating learning environment.

How much time is available for learning? The trend in FE colleges since the early 1990s has been towards fewer taught hours per course. How can you best accommodate the same, or more, content, in less time?

How many sessions per week will there be and how long is each one? When I taught media and film studies, learners were constantly frustrated by the need to watch films in two halves! Is it possible for some parts of the course to be given over to the students to learn for themselves? Geoff Petty (2004) suggests that elements which involve straightforward, factual learning can be run as independent learning units. Clearly, there are risks in such an arrangement because it requires student commitment and organisation, but there is also a bonus in terms of the development of learner autonomy and independent learning.

The range, suitability and availability of resources will affect your planning. Increasingly, teachers use ICT in their delivery extremely effectively, but learners often complain of, for example, 'death by PowerPoint'. Over-reliance on one particularly resource will become tiresome for learners and teachers alike. I am always rather suspicious of trainee, and experienced, teachers who begin their planning by designing a PowerPoint presentation.

Why? – the aims of the learning

There are many reasons why teachers provide courses and learners choose them – desire for success and achievement; to pass exams and gain qualifications; develop knowledge and skills or to develop confidence. An implicit, often explicit, aim of learning is to develop independence and responsibility in learners. All these factors will influence your planning and choice of methods.

Learners and teachers frequently have conflicting aims and purposes. Whilst many begin their learning programmes with enthusiasm and commitment, others will be less willing, possibly even hostile. It is often assumed that all learners in post-compulsory education and training are there because they have made an individual choice to learn – unfortunately this is not always the case. For example, a student in an FE college on a programme of 4 AS levels might have chosen yours as a last resort or because it's the only one that fits his timetable. It's part of your job to enthuse such learners and sell them your subject or area of expertise.

There will be other elements which you will have to include in your planning and delivery, such as:

- Skills for Life;
- Key Skills;
- information and learning technologies (ILT);
- differentiation;
- equality and diversity;
- Every Child Matters (ECM);
- developing thinking skills.

These will all be considered in detail in subsequent chapters.

From specifications to scheme of work

Preliminary activities

Find a copy of the specification/syllabus/competences for one of the courses you teach. If you haven't got one, ask a colleague or download one from the awarding body's website.

- What are the stated aims of this syllabus?
- What part/s of it are you teaching?
- What do you already know?
- What skills do you already have?
- What do you need to research?
- Take one section (a module, perhaps) and start to think about the order in which you would deliver it.

Because we can't teach everything at once, we need to break the specification content into *topics*, or 'chunks' of learning, each of which has a specific focus. These topics are assembled into an order which the teaching team thinks will provide the most effective learning experience. This ordering, or sequencing, of content can be difficult to decide and you will probably be familiar with colleagues in other establishments who deliver the same programmes as you do but in a very different way. For example, one team delivering an advanced vocational certificate of education (AVCE) media communication and production course might develop a scheme for each of the units – some more theoretical, some more practical – whilst a different team might deliver holistically through a series of integrated projects.

How is the scheme of work sequenced?

Your first task in planning a course or sequence of lessons is to translate the key elements of the specifications into a broad list of topics and to consider how they should be sequenced and how much time should be allotted to each. For example, an AS English language course might include the following topics in two modules:

Module 1 – Language framework
- grammar
- punctuation
- semantics

- phonology
- design/layout

Module 2 – Writing for specific/purposes and audiences
- audience
- the writer
- subject matter
- purpose – to inform, to persuade, to instruct, to entertain
- mode of writing

These are the topics prescribed by the examining body, but teachers can be creative in the ways in which they sequence and deliver these topics. One method would be to arrange them in more or less the way in which the specifications imply, one element following another. A more imaginative way might be to adopt a themed/problem-solving approach involving the examination and analysis of texts bringing in the various elements of the topics as required. The approach could begin with some 'big' questions, for example, 'Why and how is this article in *The Guardian* different from this article in *Hello* magazine?' 'In what ways are the audiences different?' 'What are these different texts aiming to do – amuse, inform, persuade?'

There are many different organising principles for producing a scheme of work. The following list is not exhaustive:

Easiest first. This seems the most obvious method and will probably be true of all schemes. It would be difficult to plan for students to make complex joints in wood occupations, if they hadn't previously been introduced to, and practised, using tools and basic techniques. Learners have to move from the 'known' to the 'unknown'; from the simple to the complex. This echoes the idea of the *spiral curriculum* (see Bruner in Chapter 3, pp. 64–5) in which the same area of work can be revisited but at successively higher levels and learners can become more independent and use higher order thinking skills.

Themed. As suggested above, it might be a more effective learning experience to integrate all the various topics into a project. This could even be developed as *problem-based learning* (see Chapter 5 methods). For example, a childcare problem-solving approach could begin with a 'big' question, such as 'Why do some children appear to be well behaved and others not?' There is much scope here for initial discussion to bring in learners' ideas and experiences and to introduce elements of theory to support or modify these inputs.

Assessment requirements. Assessments, particularly external, are a fact of educational life and need to be planned into schemes. Some learners will be taking exams quite soon; in AS courses students starting in September might take their first exam in the following January. Remember, however, that not all assessment is so formal; there are many ways of checking and developing understanding. As far as possible, you should use assessment *for* learning; that is, formative assessment based on developmental feedback to help learners' progress (see Chapter 7).

Most interesting topics and activities first. This can apply to teachers and learners. As a teacher you might feel most confident delivering what you know or like best first; this can be a trap because it might not be the most appropriate sequencing for the learners. However, doing interesting things first can be an important way of 'selling' your subject to the learners and getting them enthused and involved straight away, especially if it involves questions or problems to be solved which, like soap opera cliff-hangers, keep them coming back for more.

Writing the scheme of work

Having identified the main topics and considered the sequencing, your next step is to produce the actual document. Many larger learning organisations stipulate a particular format for the scheme, but if you need to design your own you should consider using the following columns on your grid:

- date/session number
- content/topics
- learning and teaching activities
- resources
- assessment
- key skill opportunities

Although the scheme of work is a planning document produced by teachers for teachers and learners, you should remember that managers and inspectors will ask to see it and will, often, make judgements about you planning based on a fairly cursory examination. Clearly, a wide range of learning and teaching activities and assessments is important for successful learning, but you need to make it obvious on the scheme. Figure 4.2 shows an example of a scheme of work.

Session planning

I have chosen to use the term 'session planning' rather than 'lesson planning' in this book mainly because 'lesson' planning has connotations of school-type learning in formal, classroom settings. 'Session planning' seems more appropriate to the wide range of provision and learners in PCET.

FAB
FE College
Further and Better

Scheme of work   Course: AS Media Studies

Module: Key Concepts   Year: 2006–7

Week	Topic/content	Learning/teaching activities	Assessment/checking learning	Resources	Key Skills
1	Representation • Age • Gender • Race/ethnicity	Teacher input – introduction to representation; Groupwork – analysis of advertisements; Discussion; Poster activity	• Question and answer • Poster display • Discussion	Handout - definitions; Advertisements – magazine and TV; Poster paper/scissors/ glue sticks	
2	FHM case study • Introduce case study	Teacher input; PowerPoint presentation on representation; Reading; Discussion; Note taking	• Question and answer • Discussion of examples • Reading and discussion	Case study; Readings; PowerPoint presentation	
3	FHM case study • Group workshops and preparing presentation	Small group activity preparing presentation; Learning centre research; Internet search; Prepare resources for presentation	• Teacher support • Discussion	Learning centre; Internet access	WWO 3.1; 3.2; 3.3 Comm 3.2 ICT 3.1; 3.2 3.3
4	FHM case study • Student presentations	• Student presentations	• Student presentations	Data projector; OHP	Comm 3.1a; 3.1b

Figure 4.2 Scheme of work example.

Session planning is the most fundamental and important of all the tasks which teachers are required to do. Inspection reports from Ofsted all make the same point that poor learning sessions are invariably badly planned sessions. Even given the wide range of learners and learning in post-compulsory education it is generally the case that all good sessions are good in similar ways and all ineffective sessions tend to have the same faults. Some of the most frequent criticisms of session planning are that the purpose, aims and objectives are not clear to learners; there is too much teacher talk and too little learner activity; learners are treated as an undifferentiated mass and there is little differentiation; there is lack of structure and poorly handled transitions; no clear conclusions and no 'rounding out' of sessions.

In this section we will consider the following:

- Why is session planning important?
- What is a session plan?
- How to plan;
- How to structure a learning session;
- What makes an effective learning session?

Why is session planning important?

For effective teaching and learning

Basically, session planning is important because without it the learning and teaching is likely to be poor and ineffective. Poorly planned lessons will be characterised by their lack of structure, vague transitions and teacher and learner uncertainty. Occasionally, teachers can take a session at short notice and 'fly by the seat of their pants', but generally it doesn't work.

So you and your learners know what you are doing

Clarity of purpose is vital to successful teaching. This begins with the teacher being clear about what they want learners to achieve; knowing the learners' starting point and previous learning; and knowing how best to achieve their aims ands objectives. If your students ask, 'What are we doing?' and 'Why are we doing it?' there's something wrong with your planning. The purpose should be made clear from the start of the session.

To provide structure

Poor sessions are, generally, poorly structured. In short, there should a clear beginning, middle and end with a variety of activities to mix teacher inputs and learner activities to suit a range of learning styles. One of the most difficult tasks for trainee teachers is judging how long each activity will last, this is why trainees spend so long on session planning, but without practice in planning they will not develop this vital skill. Each section should be introduced and explained to learners and learning summarised and checked before moving on.

Because learners' attention span is limited

In universities the traditional method of teaching has been, and in many cases continues to be, the formal lecture. The best examples of lectures are interesting, motivating and serve as a stimulus to further study. In post-compulsory education, however, the lecture is rarely used because even the most dedicated students can only listening attentively to a teacher for about twenty minutes. Excessive teacher talk nearly always produces feelings of frustration, boredom or annoyance – not the ideal conditions for learning. Unfortunately, some teachers still take the view that it is the learners' responsibility to be interested and maintain attention whatever inputs and teaching style they use. Thorough planning allows you to vary the teaching and learning activities to create and maintain learners' attention, interest and activity.

So you don't get lost or miss vital elements

Without a written plan there is a greater chance that you will lose your way, miss vital elements, or introduce new learning for which your students are not prepared. More importantly without a plan you are more likely to repeat things you've done previously – learners get particularly frustrated when this happens.

To build up a bank of materials and resources

Developing a regular planning habit will help you to build up a bank of resources and materials for future use and development. Like many other teachers, I still keep a teaching file which contains the session plans and copies of printed resources I have used in each session. Rarely have I been able to take a previous session and use it unmodified for a subsequent one, but previous plans do provide starting points and the basis for continual improvement. These files are the most valuable resources you will create. I feel reassured by physical files full of paper but increasingly teachers will store these electronically which further facilitates their modification and improvement. Electronic files can be kept as shared resources used by other teachers and by learners.

What is a session plan?

Many experienced and long-serving teachers will tell you that they don't have or do session plans, often claiming that they don't have time to produce them. This is not good advice and there are several things wrong with such assertions. Generally these people mean that they don't produce a detailed, written plan for every session. Further questioning would be likely to reveal that they do some form of planning, even if only of the most rudimentary kind. As you become more experienced your own session plans will probably become more concise but they will remain the key to your planning and to continuing improvement.

Session plans vary considerably in their format and style. Many teachers design their own formats, whilst others are obliged to use a standard format supplied at their workplace. Standard plans at least provide some consistency and are frequently well designed to encourage teachers to consider aspects of planning which they might otherwise overlook. However, it is questionable whether a standard lesson plan can be designed to cover all learning in a particular institution from tree surgery to A-level physics. One should be prepared to modify and adapt them according to need. If they are provided as word-processed templates it shouldn't be too difficult to adjust the layout and the size of the boxes to suit individual needs. The Ofsted *Handbook for Inspecting Colleges* states that inspectors 'will not be prescriptive' and that, 'Colleges should not assume, for example, that lesson plans must be in a particular format' (2006, para. 182).

In the prevailing atmosphere of increased accountability, session plans are key documents expected by managers, auditors and inspectors – this is an entirely reasonable and legitimate expectation. However, it is important to state that session plans are produced *by* teachers *for* teachers; they are not management tools to ensure compliance.

A session plan must be a written document, which you can store in a file or electronically. However, the aim of session planning is not merely the production of this written document; it is the act of thinking and working out what you want to do and how you will achieve it. As Michael Marland says: 'The key to this planning, however, is not the writing down ... [it] is the ability to think through a lesson in advance, as it were, to preview rapidly the entire stretch of time' (Marland 2002: 120).

So, what is a session plan? I would define it as follows:

> A session plan is a written guide which shows you the teaching and learning strategies, resources, assessment techniques and other key information you need to use with a particular learning group to achieve specified aims and objectives in an effective, structured and enjoyable way.

Minton (2005) refers to session plans as 'cue sheets'. This is a useful definition since it reminds us that a lesson plan is there to keep us on track and to remind us when and in what order we have planned to do things. An effective session plan means we don't have to keep all the details in our heads and allows us to concentrate on the immediate matters in hand. Bourdillon and Storey (2002) describe session plans as 'mental maps' because they are the physical result of imagining our way through the session.

Trainee teachers are frequently worried that they are expected to stick rigidly to their session plans and to achieve all the aims and objectives they have set. A session plan, however, is not a straitjacket; it is a guide which can be adapted and adjusted as the session develops. Inspectors will not be impressed by teachers who push their plans through relentlessly but ignore opportunities for discussion and interesting diversions which contribute to learning, especially if they relate to learners' experiences. If you regularly need to make changes and adaptations you should reconsider your planning in general. However, minor changes and adjustments should be immediately recorded on the session plan. This not only provides vital information for planning subsequent sessions, but also provides evidence of evaluation and 'reflection-in-action' as you monitor the session's development.

Clearly, lesson plans will vary in their format and style, but they should all have similar basic elements, including:

- basic information: date, time, course, level, number of learners;
- aims and objectives;
- key topics/content;
- learner activities;
- teacher activities;
- timings and structure;
- assessment/checks on learning;
- resources;
- evidence of differentiation;
- space for comments, evaluation, notes and reminders for the next session;
- other possible elements:
  - reference to Key Skills and Skills for Life;
  - details of units, elements and competences.

How do I plan sessions?

Essentially, planning can be reduced to three questions:

- Who are the learners and what is their starting point?
- What do you want to do/learn/achieve?

- How will you facilitate and assess the learning?

Before we consider these questions it must be stressed that session planning is an activity which can only be done satisfactorily one session in advance. I have met a numbers of teachers who have written, or have been instructed to write, batches of lesson plans in advance of delivery. One teacher proudly proclaimed that he had written a scheme of work and all the session plans for an entire year ahead. This is not session planning; it is merely the production of a very detailed scheme of work. Each learning session must be planned using the previous session as the starting point of the next. If this is not done teachers cannot truly claim to be meeting the needs of their learners or reflecting on and adapting to learning as it progresses.

The starting point of planning is recalling and reviewing what was done in the previous session. Were all the objectives of that session met? Did the learners achieve? Were there any points which need to be reinforced or covered again? In addition, we need to consider the session in relation to the scheme of work and to confirm what has already been covered and what learners already know or can do. Once you've ascertained where you and the learners are now, the next part of the process is to plan what will happen this session and what you want the learners to achieve. This takes us to aims and objectives.

Aims and objectives

There is considerable debate in more academic texts concerning the precise meaning and use of learning aims and objectives; the differences between them and other concepts such as learning outcomes or general and specific objectives. Some educationalists argue that teaching by aims and objectives is mechanistic and based on behaviourist theories of learning. As part of your continuing professional development you should engage with these debates and reach your own conclusions. Despite these debates, however, aims and objectives are still widely used to provide clarity and structure to learning sessions. The next section provides a simple introduction and guide to their use.

Aims

Aims are general statements of what the teacher wants to achieve with the learners. They provide a 'big picture' which shows the destination of the course or of individual sessions. They are usually descriptive in that they state where learners are going, but don't describe how they will get there or what they will do on the journey. Aims can be expressed at two levels:

- course, module or unit aims;
- session aims.

Course aims – indicate a very general, overall destination. They encapsulate the whole of what a student is intended to learn and are sometimes used in marketing and promoting courses. For example, a counselling skills programme's aims could be stated as: 'To introduce participants to the principles and practice of counselling, active listening, reflection and empathy'. Course aims are frequently prescribed by examining and assessment boards.

Session aims – are not used by all teachers but they can be useful to put into a nutshell the purpose and direction of a session for teachers and learners. Examples of session aims could be: 'To understand and develop the use of the apostrophe and the comma'; 'To be familiar with the main types of sports injuries'; 'To introduce the concept of socialisation and identify the main agencies of socialisation'; 'To examine strategies for motivation and control with 14–16-year-old learners in further education colleges'.

In summary, course planning requires teachers to adopt prescribed aims or to create their own to describe the key purposes and destination of the course. At session level, the aims describe the purpose and destination of each particular session. Having established session aims, the next part of the process is to decide the learning objectives.

Objectives

Whilst aims tend to be descriptive, objectives are prescriptive, that is, they prescribe precisely what the learners will know or be able to do at the end of the session.

Objectives should be measurable or observable so that the learning can be assessed. My trainee teachers, in their early planning attempts, tend to use the word 'understand' when writing objectives, for example, 'learners will understand photosynthesis'. 'Understand' might be useful for a session's aims but it doesn't state what it is that learners will do or produce which demonstrates their understanding. To assist in writing precise objectives it can be useful to use the SMART acronym to check them. SMART encapsulates the key requirements of learning objectives. They are:

- **S**pecific. Objectives relate to a specific learning activity and state clearly what learners will do.
- **M**easurable. The objectives can be measured, observed or assessed in some way. Thus, *list, define, analyse* and *evaluate* are measurable; *understand* isn't.

- **A**chievable. There's no point setting objectives which learners cannot achieve at their current level. Students need objectives which give them opportunities for achievement.
- **R**ealistic. Objectives should be realistic in terms of students' level of development, the resources available and the aims.
- **T**ime-bound. Objectives should be achievable within a specified time. Students are motivated by series of relatively short-term objectives which give small, cumulative steps to achievement.

Bloom's taxonomy

Learning objectives have to relate to levels of learning. There will differences between what your students at entry level 3 will be able to do and to work towards as opposed to those at level 3.

A taxonomy is a system of classifying general principles. Benjamin Bloom developed his taxonomies of educational objectives using three domains of learning:

- the *cognitive* domain: concerned mainly with thought processes;
- the *psychomotor* domain: concerned mainly with manual skills and practical skills;
- the *affective* domain: concerned mainly with emotions, attitudes and feelings.

Using objectives based on Bloom's taxonomy will help you when writing schemes of work, producing lesson plans, writing assessments and giving feedback to learners. We will be concerned here mainly with the cognitive domain – defining and describing each level, providing a range of active verbs to use in writing objectives for each level, and examples of objectives at each level.

The cognitive domain

In the cognitive domain, Bloom identified and described six levels of learning from the simple to complex:

1 knowledge
2 comprehension
3 application
4 analysis
5 synthesis
6 evaluation

(*Note*: the verbs provided at each level are not necessarily restricted to that level alone. Neither are the lists complete, they are intended simply to illustrate examples at each level.)

1 *Knowledge.* This is the base level and refers to, for example, the observation and recall of information; knowledge of dates, places, names; knowledge of facts and ideas.

   When writing learning objectives and/or assessment objectives at this level, the following verbs may be useful.

list	define	describe
identify	show	label
quote	name	repeat
reproduce	recognise	write
collect	measure	match
select		

   Example: Media studies – learners will define Uses and Gratifications theory.

2 *Comprehension.* This level is to do with understanding information and ideas; comprehending meaning; interpreting, ordering and grouping.

   Examples of verbs for writing objectives and assessments at this level include:

summarise	interpret	explain
estimate	comprehend	clarify
give examples	report	rewrite
present	illustrate	restate
convert	classify	extend

   Examples: Media studies – learners will explain Uses and Gratifications theory.

3 *Application.* At this level learning objectives are concerned with, for example, the use and application of learning; using theories, concepts and methods; solving problems

   Verbs for writing objectives at this level include:

apply	demonstrate	calculate
solve	examine	modify
change	classify	discover
construct	operate	predict
produce	prepare	practise
adapt	derive	use

Example: Media studies – learners will apply Uses and Gratifications theory to the study of soap opera.

4 *Analysis*. This refers to recognising and explaining relationships between components and elements; seeing patterns and organisation; recognising and understanding parts and wholes

Examples of useful verbs at this level include:

analyse	separate	order
connect	classify	deconstruct
arrange	divide	relate
infer	distinguish	contrast
categorise	diagnose	break down

Example: Textual analysis in Media studies – learners will analyse a magazine cover in relation to audience, purpose and effect.

5 *Synthesis*. This refers to the combination of knowledge, skills and ideas to create new understandings; to relate knowledge from several areas; to draw conclusions and develop new ideas, practices and artefacts.

Examples of verbs for objectives and assessment at this level include:

combine	integrate	rearrange
create	invent	design
prepare	produce	propose
generate	organise	compose
adapt	synthesise	modify
plan	implement	reconstruct

Examples: In media studies – learners will combine skills in video production with knowledge of film techniques to create a short pop video.

In IT – learners will combine knowledge of and skills in the use of word-processing; spreadsheets; scanners and digital cameras and publishing packages to create a community magazine.

6 *Evaluation*. This level is concerned, for example, with developing and using criteria to make critical and aesthetic judgements; comparing ideas and discriminating between them; evaluating effectiveness; assessing the value of different theories; the valuation of evidence and the recognition of subjectivity.

Examples of verbs used at this level include:

assess	decide	test
recommend	judge	discriminate
evaluate	determine	conclude
appraise	criticise	critique
value	question	discuss

Examples: In media studies – learners will evaluate the validity and effectiveness of Uses and Gratifications theory in explaining media effects on audience.

In IT – learners will assess and evaluate the suitability of the community magazine they have produced in relation to its audience and purpose.

The psychomotor domain

This learning domain is concerned with manual tasks and physical movement. The taxonomy starts from copying from others and goes to the learning becoming automatic. It is similar to the journey from unconscious incompetence to conscious competence (see Chapter 1). In, for example, craft, engineering or construction it could be used when learners are acquiring skills in tools and processes. It could also be related to sports coaching and other physical activities.

Imitation
The learner observes a skill demonstrated by another and tries to repeat or replicate it. The learners will be able to, for example – *copy; repeat; replicate*.

Manipulation
The learner is able to perform the skill from instruction or memory. The learners will be able to, for example – *build; recreate; perform*.

Precision
The learner can carry out or reproduce the skill reliably, usually independent of help. The learners will be able to, for example – *demonstrate; show; control*.

Articulation
Learners can adapt, combine or integrate skills consistently and with expertise. The learners will be able to, for example – *construct; combine; coordinate*.

Naturalisation
Learners demonstrate automatic, unconscious mastery of one or more skills at strategic level. The learners will be able to, for example – *design; manage; invent*.

The affective domain

This domain is concerned with feelings, attitudes, emotions and behaviour. It could be used, for example, in the field of personal and social skills development. The development rises from becoming aware of attitudes, feelings and behaviour and moves towards increasing internalisation of them as core values. This domain might also be about encouraging learners to acquire and internalise safe working practices or health messages or, at a more fundamental level, challenging and modifying stereotypical attitudes towards, for example, gender, ethnicity, disability and culture.

Receive
Learners become aware of, or are willing to hear, a particular message. The learners will be able to, for example – *listen; ask; read; acknowledge.*

Respond
At this stage learners begin to react and participate to particular ideas or messages. The learners will be able to, for example – *respond; contribute; write.*

Value
Learners start to adopt ideas and values voluntarily. The learners will be able to, for example – *argue; persuade; criticise.*

Organise
At this stage learners are starting to organise ideas and beliefs and to develop value system. The learners will be able to, for example – *defend; contrast; compare.*

Characterise
Learners adopt and internalise values and ideas and behave consistently with them. The learners will be able to, for example – *display; influence; practise.*

How to structure a learning session

> 'Lesson plans need to be varied to take into account pupils' interests as well as their emotional and intellectual needs' (Bourdillon and Storey 2002: 100).

The next stages in lesson planning relate to structure and timings, choice of learning activities, forms of assessment and checking of learning and the planning and use of resources. The last three of these will be considered in detail in subsequent chapters. Here I will concentrate on session structure and timings.

People, learners in particular, like structure. Feedback from learners in schools, colleges and universities indicates that they do not like teachers who are unprepared and whose learning sessions are unstructured and vague. A clear structure helps learners to see where they are going and how they are going to get there, and to reinforce their learning and connect it to existing knowledge and experience. This applies both at course and module level where learners need handbooks and maps to provide them with the 'big picture', but also at session level.

Michael Marland refers to the rhythm of a lesson. This is a good metaphor which we can usefully extend. Like an enjoyable piece of music, a good session has rhythm and, to develop the musical theme, structure; variations in pace, loudness and softness, periods of reflection and periods of activity. In your sessions, as in music, there should be smooth transition from, and links between, one passage and the next. When you are producing a session plan, you are, in a sense, composing a piece to suit your learners and their needs. At session level, there are three basic elements: beginning, middle and end, or introduction, development and conclusion. We will examine the important elements at each stage.

Introduction

Like a good salesperson, a good teacher hooks her audience immediately. First impressions count and a well planned and well delivered introduction will set the tone for the whole session. The opening of a session, particularly the first time you meet a group of learners, may be referred to as the 'establishment phase'. The following points are general guidelines but you should make a point of thinking them through and allowing time in your plan for them.

First, do not turn up late for the session; it makes you look unprofessional and your learners will feel that you don't respect them. Turning up late with disorganised materials and without prepared resources will not inspire your learners with confidence in your organisation and ability. Whenever possible, arrive before you learners. Get your resources sorted – laptop set up, board pens ready, printed resources to hand – so that you can make an immediate start.

Begin the session promptly and don't wait for latecomers; other students will resent it when they've made the effort to be on time. Lateness should be challenged appropriately. Don't grill people in front of the whole group; they might have a genuine reason for the delay. In some learning situations, perhaps in adult and community learning, you will not need to be so disciplined regarding arrival times, especially if learners have personal or domestic constraints. Remember adults want to be treated as adults. Equally, however, they will expect a rigorous and structured approach to the organisation of learning.

Make a firm and decisive start to your session. Speak clearly and loudly to gain everyone's attention and explain what the aims and objectives of the session are. It might be appropriate to share your objectives, exactly as you have written them, with the group. This is acceptable provided the objectives have meaning for the learners, but it can look somewhat sterile and mechanistic. However you introduce the session you must make clear what it is about; what people are going to do; why they are doing it, and how it fits with previous learning. There should always be an introduction to the session. Even if it's a workshop or practical session it's useful to 'touch base' with the whole group to review progress and see if there are any issues which concern all the learners. If you have regular practical sessions based on individual work, it's advisable to ensure that you schedule time on the session plan for learners to record what they've done and what they need to do next time. This makes a starting point for subsequent session.

Effective learning requires continuity between sessions. As a general rule, the introductory phase should include a review and recap of the previous session. This can be done in several different ways:

- Ask learners to tell you what you and they did.
- Use lower order questions to recall content and check learning.
- Use higher order questions to extend learning and, possibly, use this as a way into the current session.
- It might be appropriate to ask if anyone has been able to apply their learning since last time or if they have any examples or experiences which illustrate any of the things they covered.
- A brief activity such as a gapped handout or a wordsearch can be used for revision.
- Try to include a stimulating activity to enliven and enthuse your learners. Using brain gyms can work with adult learners just as effectively as with younger learners.

Development – the main body of the session

This is where the content is delivered, the objectives met and, most importantly, the learners learn. Effective learning uses a variety of teaching and learning techniques which are clearly structured and timed with smooth and seamless transitions between them. It is important to estimate and plan the length of time needed for activities and inputs and share this with the group. They will lose focus and motivation if activities are not timed and just seem to drift to a vague conclusion. Estimating timings is a significant challenge for trainee teachers requiring some experimentation and risk-taking.

In general for a whole group session there should be a change approximately every twenty minutes. This will vary according to the learners and isn't a formula which has to be rigidly adhered to – if all the learners seem to be involved and interested then it's acceptable to continue with that activity or input. Reflective teachers recognise the signs which indicate when it's time for a something different. Careful planning helps you to manage transitions smoothly without any gaps or periods of inactivity. Research suggests that learners enjoy being kept busy and don't appreciate inactivity. Some learners who present with challenging behaviour and poor motivation might exploit any gaps in the session to behave inappropriately.

Your planning should ensure that the main body of the session allows for regular checks on learning and opportunities for people to show what they've learned. Remember, assessment doesn't necessarily mean a formal test; it can be a discussion, a series of questions or asking for student examples which demonstrate learning.

A typical session could involve the following elements in the structure:

- introduction and recap
- begin by asking rather than telling. (Asking retail students to tell you what they think are the key elements of good customer service is more effective than telling them.)
- teacher talk/input
- student activity
- feedback and discussion of activity and conclusions drawn
- another, different activity
- feedback
- students recording activity/completing journals
- conclusions
- summary of learning.

The session plan example later in this section will indicate a structure of activities in more detail.

Ending

The ending should round out the whole session and bring it to a clear, crisp conclusion. Some sessions just fade away without any real review of the learning or indication of what will happen next; others just suddenly stop unannounced, rather like falling off a cliff.

The elements of good ending include:

- a clear statement or signal that the session is moving into its final phase;
- a review of the learning;
- a summary of the main learning points;
- final checks on learning;
- possibly a plenary activity;
- asking if learners have any final questions;
- linking forward to the next session with a brief statement of content. Inform learners of anything they need to do in preparation;
- a prompt finish on time. You might wish to thank the learners for their attention and effort.

Activity

Initial planning

Your initial planning will probably involve several scraps of paper on which you start to list topics, their possible order and begin to estimate timings, for example:

- 9.00   Introduction
- Content overview/aims and objectives
- Recap previous session
- 9.40   Student input/activity – What is customer service?
- 9.50   Discussion and examples
- 10.05   Video
- Viewing (10 minutes)
- Discussion (10 minutes)
- 10.25   Consequences of behaviour (Groupwork?)
- 10.50   Summarise main points
- 11.00   Conclusion

Do you use this method in your initial planning? If not, what, if any, methods do you use?

Figure 4.3 shows an example of a session plan. It indicates the main elements of style and layout, but is intended for guidance only. You will be probably be asked to use a standard format.

Individual learning plans

> Inspectors will consider the extent to which teachers and trainers ... work with learners to develop individual learning plans that are informed by initial assessment and which are reviewed and updated regularly. Handbook for Inspecting Colleges.
>
> (Ofsted 2006, para. 180)

Colleges and other providers of post-compulsory education and training have been using individual learning plans (ILPs) with their learners for several

FAB
FE College
Further and Better

Session Plan   Course _____

Date _____   Time _____   Site/room _____

AIM/S

- To introduce learners to the purpose and use of the phonetic alphabet in the study of language

OBJECTIVES: At the end of this session learners will be able to:

- Define phonemes
- State the need for the phonetic alphabet
- Recognise some of the main symbols in the phonetic alphabet
- Express simple words in written form using the phonetic alphabet

RESOURCES/MATERIALS

- Introductory handout
- Word list handouts
- Worksheets

Time	Content	Teaching and learning activities	Assessment/checking learning	Resources
9.00	Introduction and aims of session	• Teacher input		
9.05	How do you pronounce these words?	• Student activity • Discussion of problems of writing the sound	Discussion Questions	
9.15	Phonemes – definition	• Teacher input • Discussion • Student notes		Definition handout
9.25	Phonemes – relation to linguistics	• Teacher input	Discussion Questions	Module booklet

9.35	Problems with standard alphabet	• Student activity Work out some problems of using standard alphabet to indicate pronunciation	Student activity Feedback and discussion	Word list
9.45	Phonetic alphabet	• Teacher input – worked examples	Discussion Questions	Explanatory handout
10.00	Student practice	• Groupwork • Practice • Feedback – response to activity	Student practice Discussion and correction	Word list
10.30	Summary	• Teacher input – review objectives – summarise main points		
10.40	Conclusion	• Set problem for next session • Overview of next session		Worksheet for next session

Evaluation notes

Next session

Figure 4.3 Sample session plan.

years. ILPs were originally developed for use with learners on Skills for Life, ESOL and 14–19 programmes but they are increasingly seen a useful tool in managing and improving learning for all students. This trend will continue as learning providers move towards systems of 'personalised learning' (see below). If you are training to teach in post-compulsory education and training you will have agreed an ILP with your course tutors. This ILP forms the basis of your CPD whilst working in the lifelong learning sector.

What is an ILP?

An ILP is a plan which is drawn up as a result of initial and diagnostic assessment of learners and negotiation between them and teachers to set goals and objectives for individual achievement and progression. They are regularly reviewed and discussed between teacher and learner and feedback is provided to aid learning and development. ILPs are an integral part of what has become known as the 'learning journey', that is, the recognition by an individual of the need or desire to learn; the identification of long-term goals and the development of targets to reach those goals.

The steps in the planning and management of an ILP would generally look something like this:

Life or career goals

This might be that a learner wants to work in construction, more specifically in bricklaying. Other goals might be, for example, to achieve independent living. Support for learners begins at this stage with initial advice and guidance.

Long-term goal

These goals are what the learner wants to achieve by the completion of his time in college or in training. This goal could be stated as a specific qualification such as, 'achieve level 3 in bricklaying.' Other goals might include learning to drive and some basic elements of running a business. For some learners these goals include working towards target grades based on analysis of their entry profile. This can be a useful motivational device, but many learners will be de-motivated by them because they have negative experiences of being graded and expectations placed on them.

Short-term goals (or targets)

These are the small, achievable steps, agreed with teachers and trainers, which learners take to achieve their goals. They could include qualification-specific targets such as completing a specific building project or acquiring a particular skill. Others might include working on literacy, numeracy or IT targets or personal skills like time management or budgeting skills. These targets are reviewed at each meeting with the teacher.

ILPs and Key Skills

I have long been of the opinion that Improving Own Learning and Performance is the *key* Key Skill because it requires learners to take responsibility for their learning and development – this is at the heart of the ILP philosophy. The Qualifications and Curriculum Authority (QCA) *Key Skills Standards: Improving Own Learning and Performance* (2004) say that learners should:

> *'Confirm your targets and plan how to meet these'*
> Work with an appropriate person, such as your tutor, supervisor or adviser to:
> * make sure you understand what is meant by targets, action points and deadlines, and the importance of reviewing your targets and trying different ways of learning;
> * develop an individual learning plan that includes:
>   ○ targets that clearly show what you want to achieve in your learning, work or personal life, and how you will know if you have met these
>   ○ the actions you will take (action points) and dates for completing them (deadlines) to help you meet each target
>   ○ how to get the support you need, including who will review your progress and where and when this will take place.
>
> (QCA 2004)

ILPs: advantages and disadvantages

There is little doubt that ILPs contribute to effective and successful learning. The advantages of their use include:

* being used as a key organising document to support the Improving Own Performance Key Skill;
* encouraging learners to take responsibility for learning and helping them become more effective learners;
* motivating learners by agreeing achievable steps related to their individual context and progress so far (developmental feedback is an essential part of this process);
* working as a means of differentiation and formally recognising that all learners are individuals;

- providing structure for reviews and tutorials;
- helping colleges and providers to plan their provision.

However, it is important to remember that we are primarily concerned with the process and development of learning rather than the production, monitoring and auditing of paper and electronic documents. The documentation is there to support learning. As John Callaghan (2004: 8), writing in the context of using ILPs in ESOL, opines 'formal procedures for identifying learners' needs – including ILPs – are consuming amounts of time disproportionate to their value, as well as distorting the process of goal-setting and reducing possibilities for other kinds of activity'. The challenge, therefore, is to create ILP systems which are meaningful and useful to learners whilst being efficient and avoiding unnecessary bureaucracy.

Planning for differentiation

Differentiation worries some teachers. Frequently, this is because they are exhorted to do it but without support and training in the best ways of achieving it. However, in many ways the concept of differentiation reminds me of something which really is obvious and doesn't need research to prove. We know that people of all ages outside of educational institutions do things differently and learn at different rates and in different ways. However, when people are put into learning groups, in schools, colleges or any other setting, there seems to be an expectation that they will progress at roughly the same rate whilst covering the same content and using a fairly limited range of teaching, learning and assessment methods.

What is differentiation?

> When we plan for differentiation in the classroom we are attempting to meet the individual needs of each student while providing a challenging learning experience for all students in the class.
>
> (Le Versha and Nicholls 2003: 96)

Differentiation means enabling and ensuring that learners from a wide range of backgrounds and varying experiences of education and with different abilities and different learning styles can achieve. Differentiation aims to reduce the frustration and lack of self-esteem which many learners experience when the teaching and learning doesn't suit them. Differentiation is closely allied to motivation and behaviour. Two motivational states which affect learning are anxiety and boredom. Anxiety occurs when teachers expect too much of their students; boredom when they expect too little.

How do teachers differentiate learning?

In common with all aspects of effective teaching, the key to differentiation is knowing your students, being alert to feedback on their progress and recognising problems or different levels of progress. At first you will know them through initial testing and assessment, but increasingly you will build a more comprehensive picture of each learner's style, preferences and abilities as you work with them.

Some lesson plan formats require teachers to indicate differentiation by showing:

- what *all* learners must do/achieve;
- what *most* learners should do/achieve;
- what *some* learners could achieve.

This system could be amended by reference to:

- core activities;
- support (similar to the notion of 'scaffolding');
- extension – having extra materials available at a higher level, often as independent activities.

Stradling and Saunders (1993: 129) suggest there are five types of differentiation:

1 *Differentiation by task*. learners cover the same content but are set different tasks at different levels of difficulty.
2 *Differentiation by outcome*. Learners are given the same tasks but different outcomes and a range of responses are anticipated from learners at different levels.
3 *Differentiation by learning activity*. Resources and materials cover the same content but are differentiated according to learners' needs. For learners with communication difficulties, resources can be provided in a different form – for example, large print for those with sight difficulties. Extension activities could be available for learners who complete tasks early or are working at a higher level. This links to the next point.
4 *Differentiation by pace*. Learners cover the same content at the same level but take more, or less, time to achieve.
5 *Differentiation by dialogue*. This refers to the interaction and discussions between learners and teachers in which their progress is monitored and varying levels of support provided. A useful method here is to consider the use of 'peer teaching' in which learners developing at a

faster rate can help and support others, an added consequence being that one of the most effective methods of learning is to teach someone else.

Differentiation can only be achieved successfully if the teacher plans and uses a variety of teaching and learning techniques to meet the learning styles and preferences of all members of the group. You will find it useful to revisit the section on learning styles (Chapter 3, 'Learning theories').

Activity

List as many ways as you can think of in which learners are different. For example, age, previous achievement.

For each of these, consider what strategies and methods you would use to meet their differing needs and abilities.

Personalised learning

At the time of writing the government has made further announcements on their plans to develop 'personalised learning' in schools. Clearly such a system would need to extend into lifelong learning, indeed, it could be argued that this sector has been more receptive to individual and personalised learning than schools have been. The Department for Education and Skills (DfES) issued a consultation document in 2006, *Personalising Further Education: Developing a Vision*, which sets out its plans to introduce 'a range of changes to strengthen personalisation in FE and make a reality of the 14–19 Skills Strategies'. In summary, personalisation is defined thus: 'In an educational setting, personalisation means working in partnership with the learner and employer – to tailor their learning experience and pathways, according to their needs and personal objectives – in a way which delivers success' (DfES 2006: 7). The development and use of initial and diagnostic testing and ILPs provides a firm foundation for the introduction of personalised learning, but, as in so many educational developments, the key beneficiary of all this activity should be the learners. It is important to remember that personalised learning, like all effective learning, involves the learners; it is something that is done *with* them, not *to* them.

For your journal

- Provide examples of how you have planned for differentiation.
- State differentiation strategies you have used.
- Evaluate the effectiveness of these strategies.
- Follow-up and research further on differentiation; note, and consider for use any strategies which are new to you.

Journal extract: Lisa, training to teach music and drama

I feel that the students benefited from having a structure of the aims and objectives in front of them on the board. The discussion at the beginning and the end of the session showed that the students were able to write their own targets for the session ahead, and during the end of the session they could evaluate and assess each other's learning. The discussion allowed the students to be interactive with each other, and it also brought them together as a community. The students were able to experiment with learner autonomy, by allowing themselves to be more independent.

Journal extract: Jasvir, training to teach IT

There was a time when I never followed my session plans; I just thought they were there for managers or observers to look at. I used to be a little disorganised with my paperwork for the course and the resources, I did not know whether I was coming or going. I now realise the importance of having a session plan and how it helps the structure of my lesson, assessment and meets the criteria for the course within the timescale. I now always make sure I follow the session plan and that learners have met the aims and objectives of the session.

5 Teaching and learning methods

What this chapter is about

- Key elements of a range of teaching and learning methods
- Guidelines for using these methods in the lifelong learning sector

---

LLUK standards

This chapter covers the following standards:

BK 2.1; BP 2.1; BK 2.2; BP 2.2; BK 2.3; BP 2.3; BK 2.5; BP 2.5; BK 2.7; BP 2.7
CK 3.1; CP 3.1; CK 3.2; CP 3.2; CK 3.5; CP 3.5
DK 1.2; DP 1.2

Introduction

To be an effective teacher in the lifelong learning sector you will need to have a repertoire of teaching and learning methods to meet the demands of a wide range of learners. As you develop you will probably prefer a regular suite of methods, but remember it's not just about what suits you but what suits your learners. You should always be prepared to try something new and to expand your repertoire. You will become able to merge several different methods into one session and even develop hybrids of methods which are unique to you. (This is the kind of 'theory in practice' you can record and reflect on in your journal.)

Teaching and learning methods are often categorised according to whether they are teacher dominated or student centred or tend to be active or passive, surface or deep. I'm not going to classify but will provide guidance and comments in each case. The best thing is to try out various techniques and see if they work. If they don't work, reflect and try to work out why. Do you need to modify or adapt the technique, do you need to keep practising it, or is it just not right for these learners for this purpose? Once again reflection is the key.

As you consider the range of techniques I have suggested, some of them might seem similar. Case studies, projects, discovery learning and problem-based learning overlap to some extent. This doesn't matter. Categorisation is not really important and you will be able to draw certain aspects from each to develop your own methods.

We will consider the following methods in this book, but there are many others you can follow up elsewhere:

- lecture
- case study
- discussion
- student presentations
- demonstration
- brainstorming
- buzz groups

- projects
- role play
- concept mapping
- games and quizzes
- discovery learning
- problem-based learning
- coaching

Lecture

Formal lectures, in which teachers address groups of students who listen and take notes, are rarely used in post-compulsory education. Traditionalists might deplore the demise of the lecture and consider it symptomatic of 'dumbing down' and minuscule attention spans, but we have to do what works and use whatever gets results in terms of learning. Even in the best universities, students will frequently preface the word 'lecture' with the word 'boring', and the old maxim that 'a lecture involves the transference of the notes of the lecturer to the notes of the student without passing through the minds of either', still applies in a few cases. However, given the expansion of students in universities, lecturers are developing a wider range of strategies, particularly those which encourage active learning and deep learning (see Biggs 2003).

However, let's not reject the lecture completely. There may be times when it is appropriate for you to use one, especially as an introduction to a new course or module for degree students studying their first year in a further education college.

Guidelines for preparing and delivering lectures

- A lecture should be enjoyable, stimulating and thought-provoking. Think of it as a 'scene-setter' in which you set out the big picture and outline the main issues. Students should leave it wanting to find out more.

- Students need a clear structure to help them navigate their way through the lecture and to identify the key elements.
- A clear structure begins with an introduction which states the purpose and key objectives and provides an organising framework for the students, for example, 'It is generally agreed that there are three main industries on which the Industrial Revolution was based – coal, cotton and iron. We will examine each in turn.'
- As the lecture develops the main headings – in this case, coal, cotton and iron – form the basic skeleton of the lecture. Each of these will have subsidiary elements to guide the students.
- You can support the students by supplying printed diagrams showing the structure, possibly linked to a visual presentation.
- Use visual presentations, especially PowerPoint, sparingly.
- Be aware of your voice; an extended presentation requires the careful employment of pace, pause, volume and variety. Use some humour; we learn more effectively when we laugh.

However, it's fair to say that most teachers in PCET have never used, and probably never will use, a formal lecture.

Case study

Case studies can vary to such a great extent that it's difficult to offer one simple definition. Case studies are generally student-centred learning activities which are based on real-life scenarios, events or problems with contextual information which provide learners with an opportunity to apply learning, develop higher-order skills, and to diagnose and solve problems.

Case studies are frequently used in business courses to study particular businesses or business sectors, and to analyse and evaluate their success or failure. Learners could, for example, study and analyse a real or fictional failing business and develop ideas for organisation, products and marketing to revitalise it. In engineering, learners could examine specific engineering problems and develop innovative ideas and solutions.

Case studies have a number of educational benefits including the following:

- They are invaluable in developing higher-order skills (see Bloom's taxonomy) and thinking skills such as analysis, evaluation, synthesis, decision-making and problem-solving.
- They can be integrating activities in that they bring together a number of skills and learning around a theme. For example, in a business case study learners can use knowledge of economics, marketing, human resources and finance in the analysis of a business.

- Case studies, particularly extended ones, encourage the development of cooperation, team-working and role specialisation thus developing group-working and team-building skills.
- Larger case studies might require learners to use a range of resources and information sources to support their work thus developing research and information–gathering skills.
- They help develop time management. To be realistic, learners could be required to work within deadlines to produce responses to the case study. The conclusion to the case study could be a presentation.
- Case studies provide ideal opportunities to prepare and give presentations which will help students develop skills they are likely to need in employment.
- Case studies can be both formative and summative methods of assessment.

There are many websites and textbooks which provide case studies you can use with your learners, but it's much more rewarding and relevant to develop you own. They can be detailed, long-term activities which require the production of reports and presentations or shorter ones based around specific issues with some specific questions to be answered or tasks undertaken.

Activity

A learning group case study

Choose a group of learners you work with on a regular basis and use them for a case study. You can use the group as a 'laboratory' for trying out new ideas and analyse and evaluate them.

This is an opportunity for you to integrate a range of knowledge and skills and to try out theory in practice. Here you can explore, for example, learning theories, communication and learning and teaching methods. You can study group dynamics and observe the effects of different sub-groups and experiment with room settings.

If you are training to teach you might already be doing this as part of your PDJ, but you could choose one class for a more in-depth study. You will find it useful to present your ongoing study to trainee colleagues and discuss and develop ideas with them.

An example of a brief, focused case study used to introduce the use of discussion in teaching and learning can be found in the following section.

Discussion

In order to demonstrate the use of a case study, this section on using discussion starts with a case study of a sociology teacher attempting to use discussion in his class. You should use this scenario to analyse and evaluate the teacher's use of discussion and to recommend guidelines for him to improve his technique. You will also find it useful to apply your guidelines to your own teaching practice.

Activity

An introductory case study

Ron is a very keen 28-year-old teacher recently appointed as a part-time sociology lecturer in a further education college in an inner city. The college has a wide ethnic and cultural mix. He has been asked to deliver a sociology input on a BTEC Health and Social Care course. The subject he is dealing with is the family. He has provided some inputs on types of family and the functions of the family. Ron has been told that discussion is a valuable teaching method and is keen to have a go.

There are eleven people in the class. Their motivations vary from very keen to a couple who are on the course because they couldn't really think of anything else to do. There are three mature students (30+) and one male student. It is September and only their third week in college.

The class runs from 11.00–12.30 on a Friday morning. At 12.10 the eager Ron says, 'Right. Let's have a discussion. What do you think about the family?' No response. Several students look at their notes or gaze out of the window. Some look at Ron as if wanting to help him out. Ron aims a question at an individual,

'Chantelle, what are your views on the family?' Chantelle blushes and mumbles, 'Well ... it's OK for some people,' an enigmatic response.

Dawn, a mature student previously a shop steward in a garment factory, says, 'The nuclear family is another example of Western cultural imperialism, isn't it?' Ron looks pleased. Exactly his opinion.

'Any responses to Dawn's point?' There are none.

Darren says, 'It's like on *EastEnders*, isn't it?'

'Eh?' replies the temporarily baffled Ron, 'What do you mean?' His tone is not hostile but Darren declines further comment.

'Don't matter,' he mutters.

In a last act of desperation, Ron aims a question at Zeinab, who is normally keen to speak. 'What do you think, Zeinab? Do you agree with the functionalist view?'

'No,' says Zeinab.

After a period of silence Ron says, 'Well, you don't seem to have any opinions, do you?'

The class is set out like this:

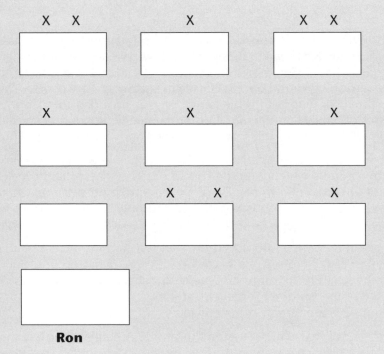

Ron

1 Analyse Ron's use of discussion and his use of questions.

2 What should he do to have a better chance of success with discussion as a learning and teaching technique?

3 Produce a set of guidelines for effective use of discussion.

Discussion is something we take for granted, often regarding it as just 'having a chat' with learners or, worse still, it is derided as not 'proper teaching'. Discussion deserves serious consideration as a learning and teaching method, particularly in the development of active, constructivist learning and thinking skills.

The essence of discussion is dialogue and the exchange and expression of ideas, opinions and knowledge. Discussions might range from a structured and planned learning experience to the unplanned but welcome opportunity to air some ideas. Inspectors are keen to see that sessions are not so rigidly planned that opportunities for discussion are missed. Discussion is an excellent way of developing thinking skills and higher-order learning. You should refer to Chapter 6 on questioning and explaining and examine the use of Socratic questions to extend discussion and develop ideas. Discussions are important when exploring opinions, beliefs and attitudes and encouraging learners to appreciate other points of view, but be careful because people can have strong views and may find it difficult to be objective (including teachers!).

Discussion is often considered to be a method more suited to the arts, humanities and social sciences which, it is mistakenly assumed, have more 'issues' to discuss, rather than science or mathematics which might be considered more in the realm of facts. Science is based on theories and debates, many of them controversial, and they need to be discussed. One of my trainee teachers recently described a session in which she introduced students to genetics through a discussion of ethical issues based around transgenic animals. This seems to me to be an excellent way to introduce a topic; make it relevant to real life and to remind learners that science is not neutral but has social, moral, religious and ethical implications.

Mathematics might seem to many teachers and learners not the place for discussion – what is there to discuss, they might ask? Research by Malcolm Swan, based on GCSE maths retake students in FE colleges, suggests there is considerable benefit to be gained from using discussion in maths sessions. Students retaking maths tend to improve by one grade on average, if at all, and much of the teaching is teacher-centred and 'transmission-based'. These methods have already failed the learners and merely repeating them does little to boost their confidence and motivation. But, as Swan says of the discussion-based resources which were developed:

> ... there is evidence here to suggest that learning is enhanced, particularly when they are used in student-centred ways. In particular, this means students' existing knowledge and misunderstandings are brought to the surface and discussed in the lessons. The greatest gains (approximately one standard deviation) were made in the group that used many lessons in student-centred ways. The more student-centred approaches seem to have prevented a general decline in confidence and motivation that may occur when traditional didactic approaches are used in FE classrooms.
>
> (Swan 2006: 240)

Guidelines for using discussion

In the case study above, Ron did very little to plan for the use of discussion as part of learning about the family. If you are going to plan discussion into a session, here are few things to consider:

- Do you need some stimulus material or something to start the discussion? Ron could have provided an article about families, perhaps something which related family to adolescent behaviour. He could have used some statistics about the family or even an extract from a soap opera.
- Encourage learners and give them opportunities to explore ideas. Darren, in the case study, with support from Ron might have developed his thoughts about *EastEnders* into a useful vehicle for exploring issues about the family.
- Teachers shouldn't dominate discussion or force their ideas and opinions on the group; like good chat-show hosts their role is to encourage and facilitate inputs from others.
- As a teacher you will sometimes need to take the role of chair and to keep things under control and to keep the discussion focused on the main point. Occasionally, you will need to thank contributors for their input but ask them to hold back a bit so that others can join in.
- It's a good idea to establish some rules – only one person can speak at a time; no interrupting; no offensive or inappropriate statements or actions; listening to each other.
- The important thing is to make sure that everyone is involved, and willing to be involved, in the conversation. I've observed a number of sessions in which teachers are really enjoying an in-depth discussion with a few like-minded learners about an item of mutual interest whilst the majority of the group are showing clear signs of boredom.
- Don't let a discussion ramble on. When it's reached the end of its useful life, bring it to an end but don't forget to summarise the key points and relate them to the learning topic – better still, get the learners to summarise.
- Consider the room layout. Everyone needs to be able to see each other, so old school-style rows with people looking at the backs of heads is not appropriate.

Student presentations

Student presentations are valuable learning experiences which develop a wide range of generic skills as well furthering subject knowledge.

Unfortunately many students dread them; however, this is no reason to avoid them. If we create the right atmosphere and provide support and guidelines for learners they can gain considerable benefit in terms of planning, organisation and confidence. Presentations are very effective in the development and claiming of Key Skills. A group presentation with the necessary research and preparation, accompanied by a PowerPoint presentation and followed by discussion and questions can easily cover several performance criteria in Communication; IT; Working with Others and Improving Own Learning.

Presentations could be based around the idea of a seminar in which individuals or small groups of learners research a specified topic, or part of a topic, and present their findings to their colleagues. Presentations may also be the final part of a case study or a report on projects students are currently working on.

A disadvantage of presentations is that they are time-consuming in both their preparation and delivery. A class of 15–20 learners working towards an AS level might find the benefits are outweighed by the disadvantages resulting from time 'lost'.

Guidelines for using presentations

- Ensure that learners know what they are doing, why and how. You will find it useful to prepare an assignment brief stating exactly what is expected and how long the presentation should last.
- If the presentation is part of an assessment make clear to the learners what they are being assessed on; is it the development of subject-specific knowledge and skills or their presentation skills, or both?
- If possible provide guidelines to the learners about preparing and delivering a presentation. In colleges, there may be study skills workshops or resources to help them. There is a wealth of support in books and on websites about how to overcome nerves and anxiety related to presentations.
- In particular, stress that structure is important and that they should consider tried and tested methods such as cue cards; PowerPoint slides can provide a similar structure. Remind them not to write out a script and give a reading.
- Allow time for practice, or recommend they practise at home.
- Make learners aware of the importance of being a good audience as well being good presenters. Presenters need to know that their audience is interested in them and is going to support them. Create a classroom climate of low threat but high challenge.

Demonstration

At its simplest, a demonstration involves showing other people how to do something; it is the display and explanation of a skill. The demonstration may be of practical/physical skills or of cognitive/intellectual skills. Examples in post-compulsory education might include:

Practical/physical
- hairdressing techniques
- first aid demonstrations
- science experiment
- computer file management
- sport routine/exercise
- bricklaying

Cognitive/intellectual
- mathematical calculation
- poetry analysis
- writing a business letter
- analysing a media text
- using apostrophes

Some teaching, particularly of practical skills, is not possible without using demonstrations – it would be difficult, for example, to teach bricklaying without demonstrating. Demonstrations allow the linking of theory to practice. Continuing the bricklaying example, learners will have been given information about the components of a mortar mix, the proportions in which they are combined and some general points regarding how the procedure is carried out. However, the teaching is only effectively done by demonstration, with the teacher explaining each step of the process. A good demonstration, especially if the end-product is impressive, will leave the learners keen to have a go to see how well they can carry out the skill.

Practical demonstrations are nearly always followed by sessions in which the learners practise the skill, observed by the teacher who encourages and motivates learners by recognising correct practice but also patiently pointing out incorrect practice and reinforcing that particular element of the demonstration (see the journal extract by Russell in Chapter 3).

Teaching intellectual and cognitive skills is, like practical skill teaching, based on modelling a skill or procedure to learners followed by observed and corrected practice. An English teacher demonstrating the use of apostrophes explains the theory and the use of this punctuation mark, states the general categories of their use, and then demonstrates some worked examples using the board or a clearly visible medium. The same English teacher carrying out an analysis of a magazine advertisement in relation to audience and purpose, uses a worked example, then sets individuals or groups the task of applying the analytical process to another example.

Guidelines for using demonstration

- Preparation: ensure that all materials are available and ready for use. It's embarrassing for you and unimpressive to students if you have to nip out and collect something you have forgotten.
- Preparation will involve breaking the procedure down into a series of connected key points. These will provide a framework for the learners.
- Practice: a good demonstration is like putting on a show. The first time you do it should not be in the class or the workshop. Try it out beforehand; you could even video yourself and analyse the result. If you are demonstrating a mathematical calculation, make sure you've checked it and can do it with confidence.
- Ensure that all health and safety requirements are in place. If it's a science experiment, does everyone need lab coats and eye protection?
- Arrange the room and ask learners to move so that they can all see clearly. You might need to find ways of making things more visible; in a demonstration of computer file management it's difficult to get everyone around one computer so you will need to consider using a data projector.
- Consider the following. Does the demonstration link to previous learning and knowledge? Have you prepared the ground so that learners can see the demonstration as part of a continuum of learning?
- Consider the pace of the demonstration. Don't rush it; you can even slow it down to an unnaturally slow pace and observe learners' reactions to see if you need to speed up.
- Allow time for questions, particularly if they are for clarification or repetition of something missed, but also be prepared to deal with some questions later if they interfere with the flow of the demonstration.
- Avoid unnecessary jargon or terms which learners haven't previously encountered. The use of acronyms and abbreviations can be particularly annoying when people aren't familiar with them.
- To check learning, try a second demonstration in which the learners tell you what to do. After demonstrating the application of a sling, a First Aid trainer could repeat the demonstration and ask the learners to tell her what to do at each stage.
- Don't make the demonstration too long otherwise you'll start to lose your audience. Can it be broken down into two or more demonstrations with student practice in between each? You will want to consider the level and previous experience of your learners when making these decisions.

Activity

Identify links and explain the connections between:

- demonstrations;
- Kolb's learning cycle;
- communication;
- active learning;
- explaining.

Brainstorming (thought showers or word showers)

This is a technique which can be used to generate quickly a large number of ideas or possible solutions to a problem. It can also be used to introduce a topic and get people thinking. When I taught communication studies, I began the course by asking learners to brainstorm as many different methods of communication as they could think of.

A brainstorming session should, ideally, last between 5 and 15 minutes. You will need to set clear rules and guidelines – no shouting all at once; no obviously silly or offensive ideas – and keep a brisk pace going. You, the teacher, will write the ideas onto the board or flipchart or you could ask a member of the group to do it. Sometimes you might want to use the brainstorming session as a warm-up exercise where the topic and the solutions are less important than getting the group active and participating. Try, for example, brainstorming the possible uses of a brick.

It's a good idea to use brainstorming with a concept map or spider diagram to organise key ideas round a central theme. Figure 5.1 shows an example.

Buzz groups

The 'buzz' is the noise that results from this activity. This method entails breaking a large group of learners into several smaller groups (ideally 3 or 4) and giving them a question to answer or a problem to work on for about 5–10 minutes. For example, I recently set a large group of trainee teachers into buzz groups to consider some of the causes of behavioural problems in classes of young learners. The time limitation is important because it increases the urgency to get the job done and heightens the 'buzz'. When the time is up, it's usual to ask each buzz group to feed back their ideas to the whole group.

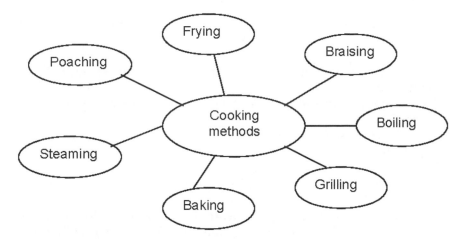

Figure 5.1 Concept map as part of brainstorming activity.

It's a good idea to ask for one or two ideas from each group in rotation; if you go round the groups asking each one to report all their ideas the final group might find all their suggestions have already been covered.

When you set up this activity be clear about what the task or question is and state specifically how much time is available. You might find it useful to appoint a leader or spokesperson for each group. Tell the groups how you want the feedback – just an oral response or do you want them to produce flipchart diagrams or come up and use the board?

Buzz groups are ideally for adding variety to learning sessions and getting the learners involved and thinking. A wise teacher will know from observing her learners when she has been talking for too long and needs to have a change. Buzz groups are an easy activity to introduce unplanned.

Projects

What is a project? You will probably have memories of doing project work at some stage in your educational career, at school, college or university. In the lifelong learning sector a project could include, for example: an art and design project; an engineering project; an extended essay or report in English or psychology; a magazine project; a research project; a family history research project or making and/or marketing a product.

What, if anything, do all these different examples have in common? The term 'project' can be very vague and covers a wide range of endeavour in so many curriculum areas. Jane Henry (1994: 12) suggests six main points which define a project:

- The topic is usually selected by the learner. There may be limitations on the choice introduced by the teacher or the examining or awarding body.
- The learner finds their own source material and carries out their own research.
- The learner presents an end-product (a written report, a presentation, an artefact).
- The project is usually independent. (Group projects may sometimes be appropriate.)
- The project covers an extended period.
- The teacher acts as a facilitator/adviser/'critical friend'.

Using projects has many advantages for learners, the most obvious being that they are examples of independent learning which the learner has some control over in terms of content and activity. This can be highly motivating, especially if they can synthesise skills and knowledge across a curriculum area or areas. For example, a magazine or web design project in IT gives learners the opportunity to combine word-processing, digital photography, desk-top publishing or web design, not to mention further links into market research and design. Projects, it is clear, provide significant opportunities for Key Skills development, including Working with Others if it is a group project.

Guidelines for developing and using student projects

- Projects need to have a proper focus and be clearly structured. Given that projects are essentially student-centred this may seem a contradiction. Students need a project or assignment sheet which tells them clearly what they are expected to achieve and the time in which they have to do it. Timing is very important; too little time will be discouraging for learners and they will feel they can do nothing more than a cursory piece of work; too much time can lead to a leisurely approach, frequently followed by furious last-minute activity. As C. Northcote Parkinson suggested in his famous 'law', 'work expands so as to fill the time available for its completion'.
- Ideally, the project or assignment brief should indicate the assessment criteria and state clearly what learners have to do and/or produce.
- The teacher is the facilitator. This means that they have an active involvement and should not use project work as an opportunity to let students get on alone while they nip back to the staffroom to do some marking. The first use of projects and the initial stages of any project require close observance and support from teachers.
- During the early stages of the project it is essential to get learners to develop a clear statement of intent or a learning contract. This might

be adapted or modified according to suggestions from the teacher concerning feasibility and practicality. These learning contracts can become part of the regular review process.

- To facilitate and support project work it will be necessary to have regular meetings and tutorials with learners to help them assess their progress, review their work and consider the next stages. It is advisable to draw up a tutorial or meetings schedule and ensure that learners turn up for them and bring the necessary materials. Get the students to put these dates in their diaries; better still develop a project logbook. Logbooks and diaries also provide good evidence for Key Skills. Long-term projects could include presentations of work in progress to fellow learners with discussion and criticism sessions.
- Extended practical projects may need to be supported by extra skill development workshops in, for example, IT or using digital cameras. This requires advance planning and liaison with colleagues.
- Resources will need to be booked according to need and availability. Schedules need to be negotiated and agreed with learners and resource providers.
- Some projects will require support for the development of study skills, such as: using library and Internet, report writing and finding and interpreting information. Some projects require learners to undertake primary research for which they will need help with research methods, for example, questionnaire design.
- Group projects can be especially difficult to manage, particularly when members of the group are assigned to specific roles. As a media studies teacher I well recall group video projects, involving script-writing, filming, sound and editing, sometimes lasting a term or more. It is vital that students know their role and are committed to fulfilling it. In group projects individual logbooks are necessary to record the activities and progress of each learner, together with their own evaluations.

In short, project work is a valuable learning experience which, at its best, encourages the development of independent and motivated learners, but without firm management and clear guidelines learners can lose focus and interest.

Role play

Role play is a popular technique with many teachers. In some curriculum areas, particularly health, nursing and counselling, it is a staple of the teaching and learning process. Used well it can be a fruitful and illuminating activity, particularly in the development of emotional intelligence, rapport and empathy. Used less well it has little value and can even be upsetting for learners.

In essence, a role play involves the creation of a situation in which learners act out particular roles, followed by discussion and analysis. A simple example would be the use of role play in retail to explore dealing with difficult customers. Participants in counselling courses frequently use role play to develop their listening skills. In human resources and trades union training role play can be used to simulate negotiations on pay and conditions or the resolution of disputes.

Role play has the advantage that it can simulate 'real world' situations for learners to explore without the threats of a real situation. It provides opportunities for learners to 'get into role' and experience how it feels and the emotions involved. Used well it is a valuable way of developing confidence and reflective skills. Role plays, however, can feel very uncomfortable for many learners and some will even refuse to take part; no one should ever be pressured to take part in role play if they don't wish to. At the other extreme will be those who relish being in the limelight and will use the role play as an excuse to perform to an audience, especially if it gets laughs. The danger here is that the participants and the audience miss the whole point of the exercise and learn little or nothing from it. We should remember humanist principles of learning which suggest that learners thrive in an emotionally safe environment; for many, role play is not an emotionally safe activity.

Guidelines for using role play

- You should first consider why, indeed whether, you need to use role play. The retail students acting out the awkward customer and sales assistant scenario could probably learn as much from a training video made by professional actors.
- If role play is right for the learners and the learning need you need to set it up and prepare it carefully. There's nothing to be gained from suddenly springing a role play on to an unsuspecting group.
- This preparation could involve the writing of 'role cards' or information sheets giving the players all the information they need about the situation and their roles.
- It will be necessary to simulate the physical elements of the situation in some way, even if it's simply moving the furniture to represent a shop or a hospital ward. More advanced role plays can include props, for example, phones, computers, office equipment.
- Teachers must monitor role plays carefully and be prepared to step in or to intervene if students get so deeply into their role that they act out inappropriate behaviour. It may be necessary to tell some groups

that, however authentic the role play is aiming to be, some kinds of behaviour and language are not acceptable.

- Following the role play, it is essential to debrief the participants, and the audience, to get them out of role and to defuse and discuss all the emotional elements.
- The discussion will include the analysis and evaluation of the role play; summarising key learning points and relating practice to theory; this part is the real value of role play.

Concept mapping

Concept mapping is the most widely used term to describe this kind of activity; other terms include 'mind-mapping', 'spider diagrams', 'tree diagrams' or simply 'mapping'. Concept mapping was developed by Joseph Novak of Cornell University in 1972 from the work of the educational psychologist David Ausubel. Concept maps combine several key ideas in teaching and learning – active learning, constructivism, advance organisers and visual learning.

Concept maps are attempts to represent schemas. As you might recall from Chapter 3 on learning theories, schemas are mental models which each of us build to represent, organise and understand our world. You will be developing your own schema relating to teaching and learning which will be adapted and modified as you assimilate new information and ideas. Concept maps are constructivist in that they help learners to organise, process and represent schema, make connections and fit new information into their existing knowledge. Concept maps are particularly useful for people who have a visual learning preference and for dyslexic learners. They allow fleeting ideas represented by spoken or written words to be held static so that connections can be seen and new information assimilated. Information presented visually in this way can lead to improved retention and creativity.

Concept maps have a wide range of uses in teaching and learning, as well as business and many other areas of work. They can be used for:

- creativity;
- brainstorming;
- memory;
- revision;
- critical thinking;
- problem-solving;
- summarising (e.g. an article);
- planning a report, essay, project or assignment;

- assessment;
- communicating complex ideas.

Guidelines for using concept mapping

- Start with a central idea, such as cooking methods as shown in Figure 5.1 (p. 133). Write the idea or key concept in a box or an oval.
- Start putting in secondary ideas which spring from the central idea. Connect them to the main idea with lines.
- Each secondary idea can lead to several further (tertiary) ideas.
- Do it as quickly as you can. You can refine it later.
- Introduce your own symbols and ways of representing ideas using, for example, different colours or shapes.
- You can start to link some of the primary and secondary ideas on the map where you see connections.

For an example, see the concept map of the Industrial Revolution, Figure 3.1 in Chapter 3 (p. 63). English teachers often find it useful to get students to produce concept maps of, for example, plays. They can introduce pictures of the main players and start to connect them and use them to show relationships and work out causes and consequences. I have also seen a concept map which provides an overview of the origins of the First World War – it's a very crowded map!

There are several concept mapping IT packages which you can use. If you work in a large college or other institution ask your IT people what's available. These packages are particularly effective when used with an interactive whiteboard so that you can expand and collapse the diagram as part of an explanation.

Tony Buzan has developed a related technique known as mind-mapping which uses visual and graphical elements and colour in their production. He has produced several books which you might find useful to refer to (see the bibliography).

Activity

Concept maps are useful tools when you are planning courses or teaching sessions. They can help you discover relationships between different areas of your teaching. In addition, these maps can be used to give students a visual overview (advance organiser of the course).

Take a course you currently teach and work out key topic areas, or use the ones provided in the specifications to make a concept map. Extend the map as much as you like as long as it remains helpful to do so.

Mapping and using visual or graphic organisers is an extremely fruitful area to consider for your teaching and for your students' learning. You can follow this up by searching the internet for 'graphic organisers'; you will find a bewildering array of ideas including tree diagrams, hierarchies, organisation charts, cause and effect diagrams, maps and many others.

Games and quizzes

It's OK to have some fun and have a laugh once in a while; indeed, many educationalists believe that laughing is positively beneficial to learning. Using games and quizzes not only provides opportunities for enjoyment but also for active and experiential learning. There is such a wide variety of educational games in textbooks, on the Internet and commercially available that this section is only intended to alert you to the possibilities of using games and to find and develop your own.

Educational games usually involve competition and or cooperation and can be based on individuals competing or teams competing. Games will help to develop a range of skills in learners, including team-building and cooperation, problem-solving and communication skills. They can be used as icebreakers to help groups relax and get to know each other. Games need to be chosen and deployed carefully to match the needs and the level of learners. A game which seems too simple or childish might offend or patronise some; a game which is too competitive will not suit those who don't like competition – or are poor losers!

Some examples of educational games

Broken information exercises

These involve a situation or a problem being broken down into a series of printed cards so that each learner has some information but nobody has all of it. The group has to cooperate to piece together the information. 'Murder Hunt' (Ginnis 2002: 179) provides clues which learners have to put together to solve a murder case, and explain the circumstances of it.

Decision-making games

These involve learners having to work together to make, and justify, decisions the whole group agrees on. Classic examples are the desert survival exercise in which learners imagine their plane has crash-landed in the desert. They have to rank in order of importance to their survival a number of items saved from the wreckage. A further example is the lifeboat game in which learners have to make decisions about which people to throw overboard because there is insufficient food and water. This game is good for examining attitudes, emotions and prejudices, but needs to be handled carefully.

Bingo

This can be played straight for developing numeracy skills or adapted to revise and practice words and concepts (Ginnis 2002: 73).

Quizzes

Learners at most levels generally enjoy a quiz now and then. They provide an element of competition which is a motivating factor for most of them. Quizzes are also a useful method of assessment, particularly of more fact-based rote-learning, for example: history dates and events, the periodic table, characters in literature.

You can be as inventive as you like with games, provided your students enjoy them; there is some educational benefit and there are no health and safety issues. Think of family games you play at Christmas – use and adapt them as appropriate. Many numeracy teachers use cards and dice to develop number skills; some even use darts!

Discovery learning

Discovery learning, at least in schools, has had a very bad press. Many educationalists, politicians and journalists decry discovery as just another example of 'trendy teaching' or, worse still, not teaching at all. Such thinking is often founded on the notion of education as a form of social control, with the emphasis on discipline and rote learning. This is a shame because discovery is how most of us have been learning for most of our lives.

Lefrancois (2000: 209) defines discovery learning as: 'The learning that takes place when students are not presented with subject matter in its final form but rather are required to organise it themselves. This requires learners to discover for themselves relationships among items of information.' Discovery learning is not about telling learners to go away and find out. It requires structure and guidance for learners. The essence of discovery is finding out, working things out and making connections. Discovery links to several other key themes and methods in this book: active learning, deep learning, thinking skills and using questions as part of teaching by asking.

Working with trainee teachers, I have used an example of discovery learning based on Greek and Latin word roots. Students are provided with word roots, prefixes and suffixes and invited to make and explain the meaning of as many words as they can make. This method also works well to develop specific vocabularies; some of my trainee teachers in the ambulance service used it to help trainees learn medical terms and vocabulary.

Briefly, here, in no particular order, are a few examples. See what you can make with them. (Some classical scholars will criticise my definitions!)

- *geo = earth*
- *morph = shape*
- *ology = study of*
- *a, -ab, abs, = away from*
- *bio = life*
- *graph(y) = writing/writing about*
- *auto = self*
- *poly = many*
- *psyche = the mind*
- *tele = from afar*
- *skopos (scope) = to see*

You've probably come up with words such as *geology*, *telescope*, *autobiography*. The trick, of course, is that once you have learned the meanings of the parts you can work out the meaning of previously unencountered words.

Most things – language, art, music, engineering, numbers, film, fashion – are made up of a range of basic elements which are combined together in a variety of different ways. Whatever you're teaching, try to identify some of the basic elements and let people play with them – rather like children playing with bricks – and see what they can discover or create.

Problem-based learning

Most learning begins with learning something particular (knowledge and skills) and then, hopefully, using it to solve problems. Problem-based learning (PBL) works the other way round; it begins with the problem and asks learners to identify what knowledge and skills they already have but also what additional learning they need in order to solve the problem.

John Biggs (2003: 232) believes that: 'PBL reflects the way people learn in real life; they simply get on with solving the problems life puts before them with whatever resources are to hand. They do not stop to wonder the relevance of what they are doing or at their motivation for doing it'.

This sounds remarkably similar to discovery learning but while discovery learning involves finding things out around a theme or topic, PBL is more focused around finding the solution to a specific problem.

Problem-based learning began in medical and health education as a response to the situation in which some health professionals had a wealth of knowledge but fewer problem-solving skills. If you think about it, turning up at the doctor's or at the hospital with a complaint is about asking a health professional to make a diagnosis and solve your medical problem. Similarly, turning up at a garage with a spluttering, under-performing car is about asking a motor vehicle technician to solve your car's problem. Much of our working lives is concerned with solving problems; it doesn't take too much thought to extend the above examples to include business, engineering, science, design, construction, health and social care and social work training.

PBL, as far as I am aware, has not been widely used in post-compulsory education and lifelong learning. In FE colleges, in particular, teachers feel that they do not have sufficient course time to indulge in PBL and similar strategies. This is a real concern, but sometimes it's necessary to take risks. John Biggs states that PBL 'is not so much a method as a total approach to teaching, which could embody several possible TLAs [teaching/learning activities] and assessment methods' (Biggs 2003: 231). In this respect, PBL provides an ideal integrating focus on BTEC, the new Specialised Diplomas and similar vocational courses, but might be less viable for A-level students.

PBL has a number of advantages. First, it recognises that learning is a process of construction by the learners, not just reception of information. Because it is constructivist PBL develops greater knowledge retention and recall skills, as well as higher-order skills. It provides an integrating focus for learning which can bring together skills and knowledge from within a particular subject or across the curriculum. PBL also develops subject-specific skills; for example, in business studies learners might draw on but also develop accounting, budgeting, marketing. A case study of a failing business could easily be the basis for a problem-based learning activity. In addition to subject-specific skills; PBL develops general, or transferable skills, such as teamwork, time management, decision taking and communication.

The kind of PBL practised in universities might be too large-scale for use in lifelong learning but we can use the principle and adapt to some smaller scale activities. Let's consider a few possible problems:

- problems with a car;
- problems with behavioural difficulties in children;
- problems in IT or electrical equipment;
- problems of accessibility and mobility in a building;
- problems with the profitability of a company (this might have begun life as a case study).

Guidelines for using problem-based learning

- The most obvious first step is to state clearly what the problem is.
- As a teacher, you need to decide on the time frame for completion and the time available within the course as a whole.
- You might also want to decide what degree of autonomy you will give to your learners in organising the work and providing a solution.
- Connected to the above point, you might suggest that learners work as a formal group with meetings, agendas and minutes.
- The group will probably want to break into sub-groups working on specific smaller tasks and report back to the whole group.
- You might want to build in some taught sessions as part of the programme which will act as a stimulus for further learning and application of learning.
- On completion of the exercise, it's important to ask learners not only how they have solved the problem but also to evaluate their acquisition of subject-specific and transferable skills and knowledge.

Coaching

Coaching is frequently associated with sport, in particular the development of specific skills such as serving in tennis. Increasingly coaching is used in the lifelong learning sector as well as in training for business and human resources.

- Coaching is a one-to-one technique.
- It usually lasts for short periods.
- It focuses on improving performance and the development of specific goals and skills.
- It helps people to evaluate how well they are doing and what they need to learn.
- It is essentially non-directive: it doesn't tell people what to do but supports them in their own improvement and development.
- The basis of coaching is giving and receiving feedback.

Coaching can be difficult to distinguish from mentoring. A mentor is generally considered to be a person who has more experience, skills and knowledge than the learner or trainee; people learn *from* mentors. A coach doesn't necessarily have to be higher status or more experienced person. MacLennan (1995) makes the distinction between a mentor as someone we learn *from* and a coach as someone we learn *with*. He defines a coach as:

someone for the performer to work WITH. Coaching is the process whereby one individual helps another; to unlock their natural ability; to perform, to learn, and achieve; to increase awareness of the factors that determine performance; to increase their sense of self-responsibility and ownership of their performance; to self-coach to identify and remove barriers to achievement.

(MacLennan 1995: 4)

Coaching is based on a dialogue between learner and teacher. It requires the teacher to use her skills of non-directive support and questioning techniques to help learners assess, evaluate and develop their work. So rather than saying, 'I can see what your problem is' or 'What you should have done is . . .', the teacher uses questions such as, 'Tell me what you think is going on' or 'What do you think went wrong and how could you improve it?'; 'What do you think you need to do next?'

The GROW model of coaching is used in training and development as a means of developing coaching skills. It is based on a cycle of four elements:

- Setting **G**oals
- Assessing current **R**eality
- Generating **O**ptions
- Setting a **W**ay forward.

The model is shown in Figure 5.2 and can be expanded thus:

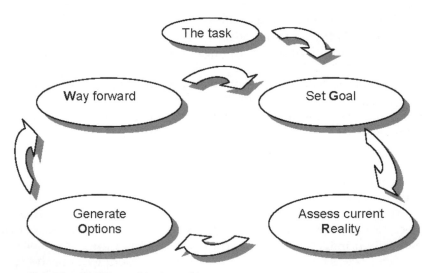

Figure 5.2 The GROW model of coaching

1 The **G**oal: what do you want to do or achieve?
- What is your goal? What do you want to achieve?
- How will you know when you have achieved it?
- What is the aim of today's discussion?

2 Current **R**eality: what is happening now?
- What is happening? What are you doing at present?
- What difficulties are you encountering?
- What's holding you back?
- What have you achieved so far?
- What have you done so far?
- What results have your actions produced?

3 **O**ptions – what could you do?
- What options or courses of action do you have?
- What else could you do? What alternatives are there?
- What if . . .?
- What would be the benefits/advantages of these options?

4 **W**ay forward: what will you do?
- What options or strategies have you chosen?
- Will they meet your objectives?
- What do you need to make this happen? What steps will you take?
- Can you foresee any difficulties?
- What resources do you need?
- Do you need to develop new skills/knowledge to achieve this?
- Do you need any support?

The self-coach

You may have noticed similarities between the GROW model of coaching and the experiential learning cycle. All of these models are based on a cycle of improvement which is essential for effective learning but also for reflection and continuing professional development. The GROW model can be used by more experienced learners as a form of self-coaching in which they ask themselves the questions and explore the options. Clearly, self-coaching is another form of reflective practice and, as such, can form part of your PDJ.

Activity

A coaching role play

Working in groups of three, assign the roles of coach, coachee and observer.

Decide a topic from your teaching area which involves a task or a project to be completed.

Using the techniques and skills mentioned above, the coach should focus on the coachee and help them to develop their goals.

The observer can use the examples of questions shown above to analyse and evaluate the coaching process.

Coach and coachee can discuss their experiences of the roles.

In summary, the range of techniques discussed above is only intended to be a representative sample. You should research and develop others, particularly those which are suited to subject specialism.

For your journal

1   As part of your ILP you might have carried out an audit of the range of methods you use. What methods have you tried and added to your repertoire since then?
2   Consider a method/s you have tried recently.
    •   Why did you choose this method?
    •   How was this choice related to the level and characteristics of the learners and the learning task?
    •   How successful was it? In what ways would you modify or develop it?

Journal extract: Becca

Project work is a series of studies/tasks that can be drawn together for assessment. It gives the student more responsibility for their own learning and encourages the learner to make relevant discoveries. The projects are usually guided by some kind of criteria backed up by a project brief, which states the required learning outcomes and keeps the learners on track. Unfortunately there were no project briefs with this series of lessons as the learners were not taking on any projects as such. Being their first term in print the students were simply learning and practising the various approaches to printmaking so they could incorporate them into projects later in the course. When reflecting, my thoughts were that learning could be improved by introducing briefs. The brief could have stated what approach we were practising and how the learners were expected to experiment with it. Then there could have been a specified requirement for how much work was to be submitted and what it should show. Although there was no main project a brief could have been customised, this would have been a clear guide for the students and perhaps a more sufficient method of directing the learners.

Further reading and useful websites

Clow, R. (2007) Using role-play, in R. Clow and T. Dawn (eds) *The Ultimate FE Lecturer's Handbook*. London: Continuum.

Ginnis, P. (2002) *The Teacher's Toolkit*. Camarthen: Crown House Publishing Ltd.

http://ferl.qia.org.uk Further Education Resources for Learning (FERL).

www.doceo.co.uk This comprehensive and generous site is a 'must see' for all teachers.

www.goldust.org.uk Learning and teaching resources developed by the Standards Unit at the DfES.

6 Questioning and explaining

What this chapter is about

- What is a question?
- Why do teachers use questions?
- Levels of questioning
- Types of questions
  o closed
  o open
  o linked (or Socratic) questions
- Questioning skills
- What is an explanation?
- Different types of explanation
- How to provide good explanations

LLUK standards

This chapter covers the following standards:

AK 4.1; AP 4.1
BK 1.3; BP 1.3; BK 2.1; BP 2.1; BK 2.2; BP 2.2; BK 2.5; BP 2.5 BK 3.2: BP 3.2;
BK 3.3; BP 3.3
CK 2.1; CP 2.1
ES 4; EK 4.1; EP 4.1; EK 4.2; EP 4.2

Introduction

Questioning and explaining are the two most important skills in teaching and learning. Effective questioning and explaining help learners to develop a fuller understanding of what they are learning and to promote deep and lasting learning. They are fundamental to creating an active learning environment, for connecting learning, for checking learning and above all in developing interaction between teachers and learners.

Given the importance of questioning and explaining it is surprising that much teacher training in post-compulsory education treats these vital skills in a cursory manner. Like many other skills they can be taken for granted, assuming they are such everyday skills that people can just do them naturally. However, there is considerable evidence to suggest that learners at all levels find teachers ineffective explainers and poor users of questions. Reflective practitioners are aware of their use of explaining and questioning and constantly seek to improve them.

Questioning

Good learning starts with questions, not answers.
Asking good questions is the basis for becoming a successful learner. If children [and adults] aren't asking questions they're being spoon-fed. That might be effective in terms of getting results, but it won't turn out curious, flexible learners suited to the 21st century.

(Claxton 1990: 78)

The importance of using questions in teaching and learning

Ted Wragg's research (1984) suggests that teachers in schools ask up to 400 questions a day, which represents about 30 per cent of their total teaching time. However, only about 8 per cent of these could be considered as higher-order questions, that is, questions which stimulate, for example, thought, analysis and evaluation. The majority of questions by far were concerned with management and control issues ('are you listening?') or recall of information ('who was Juliet's boyfriend?'). In lifelong learning, we could assume that there will be fewer issues relating to management and control of discipline and behaviour, although in some further education colleges there are increasing numbers of 14–16-year-olds, some of whom might exhibit challenging behaviour. Can the same assumption be made about the use of higher-order questions in the lifelong learning sector?

The skilled and appropriate use of questions is frequently taken for granted, yet it should be a key element in the continuing professional development of teachers and a regular feature in the reflections and evaluations of trainee teachers. One of the underlying assumptions of this book is that learning is best when it is active, enquiring and involves the learners in discussion and higher-order thinking. 'Teaching by asking' is at least as important as 'teaching by telling'.

What is a question?

This seems a disarmingly simple question in itself. We could argue that anything which, when written down, ends in a question mark, is a question. Our lives, not just as teachers, are dominated by the asking and answering of questions, from the simple ('what time is it?' or 'is my tea ready?') to the complex.

As teachers we may ask our students:

'How are you getting on?'
'Can you finish this by lunchtime?'
'Have you watched *Titanic*?'

Such simple questions have their place and can be important in establishing communications and rapport. Some utterances, however, are not recognised as questions.

We can indicate questions by intonation, as in:

'*Wordsworth* said "to be or not to be"?'
'You are *sure* that this will alter the size of font?'

Other questions are rhetorical and not necessarily intended to be answered:

'Can you believe it? What is the world coming to?'
'And so, what was Newton's response to this problem?'

Given the range and variety of questions teachers ask, it might be useful to adopt Ted Wragg's definition of a question in teaching and learning as, 'any statement intended to evoke a verbal response' (Wragg 1984). Our main goal is to become more aware of our use of questions, analyse and evaluate them, and to consider how we can ask better and more effective questions.

Why do teachers ask questions?

There are many reasons why teachers use questions. Some are used consciously and purposefully, such as checking learning or encouraging discussion; others may be less apparent, such as developing learners' confidence. However, research and observation suggest that teachers frequently use questions merely as a matter of course without being clear about their purpose or effect. The following categories suggest and explore some reasons for using questions.

1 To gain attention or check that learners are paying attention

Even the most well-behaved groups will sometimes need to be brought back on track or kept focused by an appropriate question. Questions can be used to simultaneously keep people on task and check understanding, for example, rather than merely asking, 'How are you getting on?', it might be more appropriate to ask, 'Can you show me what you've discovered so far?' A question can be used to signal the end of groupwork activities and to summarise findings, for example, 'So, what suggestions have you come up with?'

2 To reinforce and revise learning

Sometimes teaching by repetition and reinforcement – such as learning dates, formulas, procedures, lines from poems or plays – is necessary and appropriate. We will want learners to repeat or reinforce knowledge and ideas, particularly those which are used regularly. Bloom's taxonomy (see Chapter 4) provides a very useful framework for asking questions at the appropriate level. At the base of Bloom's taxonomy are knowledge and comprehension and questions at this level would, for example, ask learners to name parts of the human body; to identify the key components of a computer; to repeat a formula, or recall a line from a poem. After recalling the line from the poem, learners might subsequently be asked higher-level questions regarding the meaning or interpretation of the poem or why the poet used that particular combination of language, metre and rhyme. Questions at this level are generally referred to as recall questions.

3 To check on student learning and understanding

Effective teaching and learning always include checks on learning and understanding. It's no good just ploughing on with your session plan unless you have ascertained whether or not learners have grasped particular points. Questions to check learning need to be specific and to assess specific points which have been covered. Vague questions such as 'Did everybody get that?', or, worse still, 'Alright?' or 'OK?' will often be met with silence and averted eyes. Even 'Are there any questions?' is unlikely to get a helpful response, if any, because it's too easy just to answer yes or no, and many learners will not want to put their heads above the parapet and admit that they don't understand. Questions to check learning need to be more specific, such as, 'So, can you tell me what is the main ingredient of hollandaise sauce?', or, 'Can you give me an example of a metaphor in this passage?'

4 To diagnose learners' difficulties and adjust and re-present as necessary

This develops from the above point. Sometimes it becomes clear from learners' responses to questions that the level of the knowledge, ideas and material is wrong and the teacher will need to reflect and adjust the content and, or, the delivery. This kind of thinking on your feet is to be expected of a reflective practitioner and relates to Schön's idea of 'reflection in action', hopefully followed by 'reflection on action' in which the lesson is evaluated and conclusions drawn for subsequent planning.

5 To check the level of previous learning and introduce new topics

Verbal questioning is one of the most effective methods of ascertaining learners' prior knowledge, either at the first meeting of a new group or at the introduction of a new module or unit. It's generally more interesting, as well as more active, for learners to be asked to discuss what they already know rather than for the teacher to just tell them things. For example, instead of starting a sociology module on the family with some rather dry information and theory, it would be far more effective to ask learners, 'Why do most people tend to live in families?' 'In what ways are families different?' Such discussion, if skilfully handled will almost inevitably raise some of the key issues of the module.

Alan Pritchard makes the point that 'learning is a process of interaction between what is known and what is to be learnt' and that it is important to activate prior knowledge. In a passage which applies equally to adult learners as to children, he suggests that:

> effective approaches involve what is sometimes referred to as 'elicitation'. This is the process of drawing out from the children [and learners of all ages] what they already know, even if they do not realise that they know it. By careful questioning, a teacher can draw out from individual children, or even large groups of children, ideas, facts, and notions which can be of direct relevance to the topic the teacher wishes to introduce and develop.
>
> (Pritchard 2005: 96)

6 To create a communication climate in which learners know that asking questions is encouraged and expected

As we saw in Chapter 2, 'Communication and the teacher', one of the main determinants of successful learning is the establishment of a positive communications climate. One way we can develop such a climate is by the skilful and encouraging use of questions in our learning sessions. Questions which confuse, humiliate, discourage or fail to challenge learners will contribute to a climate in which they will switch off and not want to contribute to the sessions. This kind of climate is more likely to produce a passive learning situation where learners are not encouraged to discuss ideas and knowledge or to create their own meanings. For many adult learners such passive, teacher-centred learning was the norm in school and asking questions was not encouraged – possibly even discouraged. It is vital that we create an atmosphere in which learners feel that it is acceptable, indeed desirable, to ask questions, whether it's for information and ideas to be repeated or clarified, or whether it's to stimulate discussion and enquiry, or to promote thinking skills and deep learning.

7 To develop learners' confidence

Post-compulsory education – especially further and adult education – has a tradition of giving second chances to people who have 'failed' in their previous encounters with education and, consequently, had their self-esteem and confidence knocked. Many learners need help in developing their confidence in speaking, suggesting and testing ideas, giving examples and, above all, asking questions. You can help to break the cycle of failure and flagging self-esteem by the ways in which you ask and respond to questions. Adjust the level of questions to suit the abilities and level of your learners; give them opportunities to answer and have their answers valued. Make sure that you acknowledge every learner's answers positively and, wherever possible, build on them by extending and developing with further questions and answers. Even when answers are wrong, let people down gently and don't humiliate them.

Increasing confidence provides motivation, hence the next point.

8 To provide motivation

All learners, whatever level they are working at, need to be motivated and the best way to do this is by giving them regular opportunities to demonstrate their learning and feel a sense of achievement. Questions give learners the opportunity to succeed, demonstrate learning and get the positive feelings that go with it. However, it is important to get the level of questioning right and to avoid too many closed questions (see below) or too many recall questions. The sense of achievement is heightened when learners have successfully responded to higher-order questioning particularly when they have solved a problem or reached a conclusion.

9 To develop discussion

Discussion is a technique widely favoured by learners at all ages and levels. The initiation and development of discussion requires the use of well-structured and considered questions. We shall see later how the use of linked questions can be used to develop discussion and draw ideas from learners and help them develop thinking skills.

10 To contextualise and connect learning

Questions give learners opportunities to put their learning into context and to connect it to existing learning. In a music class learners can put music theory into practice by relating it to their favourite music by asking, for example, 'What's the chord sequence in that song? How can I develop something similar in my composition?' Similarly, in a health and social care group learners might be asked questions to relate their learning to their own experience or to items in the news.

11 To develop higher-level thinking skills and encourage a problem-solving approach to learning

Questioning is one of the main methods of developing thinking skills. The use of higher-order questions, as opposed to simple recall and comprehension, makes learners apply, analyse and evaluate their learning. We will develop this point further when we look at Socratic questioning. Thinking skills are not only for learners. Kerry (2002a) refers to the 'thinking teacher', that is one that has, 'a curious mind; one that investigates problems rather than accepts the solutions of others,' in other words, a 'questioning teacher'. Kerry also refers to questions being used to 'think aloud and make the intuitive leap'. Learners can be encouraged to suggest ideas and hypothesise, particularly in relation to problem-solving. However, they need to feel confident that they can ask questions or provide answers which seem initially to be incorrect or even 'off the wall'. Such thinking frequently turns out to be original and creative.

Levels of questions

The level of a question can be located anywhere on a range from lower-order, which requires learners to *remember*, to higher-order questions, which require learners to *think*. Bloom's taxonomy of educational objectives (cognitive domain) is useful not only for writing learning objectives but also for framing questions.

Some examples of questions at each of Bloom's levels are as follows:

Knowledge:	What are the main components of a computer?
	In what year was the Russian Revolution?
Comprehension:	Can you explain what a modem does?
	Can you describe that in a different way?
Application:	What happens when you put salt on ice?
	How does physical exertion affect blood sugar levels?
Analysis:	What do the results of your experiment tell you?
	How has this poet used metaphor to affect the reader?

Synthesis:	How can we use our analysis of film in making this video?
	How can we combine these ideas?
Evaluation:	In what ways could you improve this piece of work?
	How effectively does Hardy use language to evoke nature?

Effective questioning requires teachers to consider the level of questioning in relation to the learners' abilities and prior learning; their confidence and motivation; level of learning; and the session objectives. It would be wrong to assume that higher-order questions can only be put to higher-level learners; all learners can respond to higher-order questions if they are expressed unambiguously and develop clearly from previous recall and lower-order questions.

Types of questions

We can distinguish between three basic types of question:

- closed
- open
- linked (or Socratic).

Closed questions

These generally only have one correct answer or can be answered with a simple 'yes' or 'no'. Closed questions don't require the answerer to develop the response or take the discussion any further; they put the initiative back on to the questioner. At a simple, light-hearted level, an example of a closed question would be, 'Do you come here often?' A simple yes or no answer is sufficient and nothing further needs to be said – end of encounter!

In teaching and learning, closed questions have their place, for example in checking learning and understanding. 'Who developed penicillin?' is a useful question to check knowledge, but without further questions it's not going very far.

Too many closed questions are likely to switch learners off because they feel unchallenged and not able to engage with the learning at a higher level.

Open questions

These may have several possible answers, rather than one correct answer. They require the answerer to provide more than just a one word or phrase response. Open questions are generally higher-order questions which require learners to think and to develop deep, rather than surface learning, and discussion. If we develop the penicillin example further, we could ask learners questions such as, 'What were the effects of penicillin?' or 'To what extent is penicillin still effective today?' or 'Why is penicillin becoming less effective?' Research suggests that effective teachers use more open questions than less effective teachers. Open questions are the key to building linked sequences of questions, sometimes known as Socratic questions.

Linked or (Socratic) questioning

2500 years ago, Socrates practised his philosophy by engaging participants in a series of questions to test their assumptions and to extend their thinking. He believed that people already knew a great deal and that his task was to draw the knowledge from them by rigorous and linked questioning. Socrates never wrote anything down but his dialogues were recreated by Plato, his pupil, who featured Socrates as a character in works such as *The Republic*. In our learning sessions we may not necessarily be discussing the big questions which concerned Socrates and his pupils, such as virtue and democracy, but we can still use Socratic questioning to get students thinking through ideas and testing their assumptions and their reasoning.

An example of a series of linked questions might look something like this example from a media studies class:

Teacher	Jason, why is there a cliffhanger at the end of a soap opera?
Jason	To make sure people keep watching.
Teacher	Good. Zaheera, why is it important that people keep watching?
Zaheera	To maintain high viewing figures.
Teacher	Yes, right. So, Kylie, why do TV companies need high viewing figures?
Kylie	To attract advertisers.
Teacher	So, why is it important to attract advertisers?
Kylie	Because they pay to advertise.
Teacher	Precisely, income. Sean, what do the TV companies do with the income?
Sean	Make more programmes.

Activity

Write a script similar to the above, using a series of linked questions which could happen in one of your classes.

Clearly, the success of these linked questions depends on learners giving the 'right' answers or answers which will generate further questions. Using open questions will help to generate a dialogue.

Robert Fisher is one of the leading figures in developing philosophy for children. Fisher's key work, *Teaching Thinking* (2003) is based on the belief that philosophy is an active, questioning process which is open to all and is concerned with real, everyday issues of life, as opposed to the academic tradition, in which philosophy is the preserve of the educated few. The Philosophy for Children movement was originally developed by Matthew Lipman at Montclair University (USA). Fisher quotes Lipman's opinion regarding the 'decline' of children's natural desire to learn: 'Why is it that children of four, five and six are full of curiosity, creativity and interest, and never stop asking for further explanations, by the time they are eighteen they are passive, uncritical and bored with learning?' (Lipman 1982: 27). Clearly, Lipman is expressing an opinion, but he does underline a widely-held belief that as children grow and mature they lose their natural desire to question, explore and play with ideas. Whether this change is the result of maturation, teenage angst or the supposed deadening effects of formal education, we cannot be sure. However, in lifelong learning we have the opportunity to use, or to reawaken, adult learners' desire to enquire and explore ideas by the ways in which we, as teachers, use questions.

Trainee teachers frequently acknowledge the difficulties they have in developing open and linked questions and, I am sure most experienced teachers would agree, it is a skill which needs conscious reflection and practice supported by examples and role models. Fisher (2003) gives examples of the types of questions which, he believes, are 'invitations to better thinking' (see Table 6.1).

Table 6.1 Examples of questions to develop higher-order skills

Questions that seek clarification

Can you explain that ...?	*Explaining*
What do you mean by ...?	*Defining*
Can you give me an example of ...?	*Giving examples*
How does that help ...?	*Supporting*
Does anyone have a question to ask ...?	*Enquiring*

Questions that probe reasons and evidence

Why do you think that ...?	*Forming an argument*
How do we know that ...?	*Assumptions*
What are your reasons ...?	*Reasons*
Do you have evidence ...?	*Evidence*
Can you give me an example/counter-example ...?	*Counter-examples*

Question that explore alternative views

Can you put it another way ...?	*Re-stating a view*
Is there another point of view ...?	*Speculation*
What if someone were to suggest that ...?	*Alternative views*
What would someone who disagreed with you say?	*Counter-argument*
What's the difference between those views/ideas?	*Distinctions*

Questions that test implications and consequences

What follows from what you say ...?	*Implications*
Does it agree with what was said earlier ...?	*Consistency*
What would be the consequences of ...?	*Consequences*
Is there a general rule for that ...?	*Generalising rules*
How could you test to see if it was true ...?	*Testing for truth*

Questions about the question/discussion

Do you have a question about that ...?	*Questioning*
What kind of question is that ...?	*Analysing*
How does what was said/the question help us ...?	*Connecting*
What have we got so far/can we summarise ...?	*Summarising*
Are we any closer to answering the question ...?	*Concluding*

Source: Fisher (2003).

Questioning skills

Questioning in teaching and learning is frequently taken for granted, but it is a skill which needs conscious development if we are to become effective teachers. The following summary outlines some of the most important questioning skills:

- Create an appropriate climate in which learners will want to ask questions.
- Express questions clearly. Avoid over-long and complex structures; try not to use two-part questions.
- Use appropriate volume and speed of speech – ensure that learners can hear you.
- Ensure that the content and language of questions are appropriate to the learners. This entails knowing your learners; one way we get to know our learners is by questioning them.
- Avoid questions which are too easy or too difficult for that group. Be

prepared to ask differentiated questions with learners of different abilities in the same group.

- Put questions into context and provide necessary background information.
- Make sure you pause and allow learners thinking time – teachers can get nervous if answers don't come immediately. You could consider using collaboration in which pairs of learners work together to provide an answer.
- Use prompts and provide clues to help learners get to the answers. Questions can be part of the 'scaffolding' process which provides initial support for learners to reach new heights in their learning (see Chapter 3, 'Learning theories').
- Use follow-up questions to extend thinking and make greater cognitive demands on learners. Encourage learners' thinking skills by using higher-order questions. Develop linked questions.
- Involve the whole group not just a 'favoured few'. Distribute questions around the group and use people's names to invite them in. When a learner asks a question, ensure the whole group is listening.
- Acknowledge and give praise to learners' answers, even if they are not what you were looking for or expected.
- Never make light of or disregard learners' responses. Make them feel that their contributions are valued.
- Remember the importance of NVC – especially smiles, eye contact, tone of voice – in encouraging learners.

Activity

What's wrong with these questions?

- 'What did I just say?'
- 'Don't you think you ought to know this?'
- 'Did everyone get that?'
- 'Can you have this done before Easter?'
- 'In what ways is the situation in Iraq a disaster?'
- 'Why is daytime television so poor?'
- 'How many of you know the answer to this?'
- 'What are the government's reasons for the introduction of 90-day detention for terrorist suspects and how have people argued against them?'

Explaining

Activity

Your task is to explain to a group of new learners on an 'Introduction to computers' course the basic elements of a computer, what they do and how they relate to each other. The learners have little or no previous knowledge of computers. On completion of the task, you should consider:

- How did you explain the computer?

- What methods and resources did you use?

- What difficulties did you have in explaining?

- What conclusions can you draw about effective explanations?

Explaining and questioning are the skills most widely used by all teachers. But explaining is something we take for granted. It's easy to assume that explaining is just a matter of telling people things that we understand and following this, somehow, *they* will understand them. We don't generally consider explaining to be a skill, neither do we consider how we can improve the clarity and effectiveness of our explanations. As teachers and as students you will certainly have experienced the feelings of frustration, bordering on annoyance, when trying to explain something and people don't understand. Poor teachers will blame their learners for failing to understand them – good teachers will reflect on the process and content of their explanations and consider how they can make them more effective.

Having sound subject knowledge can be seen as the key to giving good explanations and there is research to support this assertion. However, it can equally be the case that those with expert knowledge are not good explainers – this can be a problem, for example, in the health service when doctors try to explain their diagnoses to patients. In addition to sound knowledge, good explanations are clearly structured, related to learners' existing knowledge, relevant to the learners and interesting.

The purpose of this section, then, is to identify ways in which we can analyse and improve our explaining skills.

Activity

Read the following poem by Craig Raine. Clearly the Martian is trying to explain things he has observed to the folks back home. Can you identify the things he is trying to explain (e.g. what is a 'Caxton')?

What method is he using to explain the things he has seen?

A Martian sends a postcard home

Caxtons are mechanical birds with many wings
and some are treasured for their markings –

they cause the eyes to melt
or the body to shriek without pain.

I have never seen one fly, but
sometimes they perch on the hand.

Mist is when the sky is tired of flight
and rests its soft machine on ground:

then the world is dim and bookish
like engravings under tissue paper.

Rain is when the earth is television.
It has the property of making colours darker.

Model T is a room with the lock inside –
a key is turned to free the world

for movement, so quick there is a film
to watch for anything missed.

But time is tied to the wrist
or kept in a box, ticking with impatience.

In homes, a haunted apparatus sleeps,
that snores when you pick it up.

If the ghost cries, they carry it
to their lips and soothe it to sleep

with sounds. And yet, they wake it up
deliberately, by tickling with a finger.

Only the young are allowed to suffer
openly. Adults go to a punishment room

with water but nothing to eat.

> They lock the door and suffer the noises
>
> alone. No one is exempt
> and everyone's pain has a different smell.
>
> At night, when all the colours die,
> they hide in pairs
>
> and read about themselves –
> in colour, with their eyelids shut.
>
> **Craig Raine** (Copyright Craig Raine 1979)

Your analysis of the poem will have yielded a number of different interpretations – as will the postcard's Martian recipients. You might have concluded, perhaps, that he is comparing mist to a cloud which has fallen from the sky. In each case, he is trying to explain what he sees by reference to something else and this provides a valuable insight for us – we can only successfully explain anything by reference to what people already know. In other words, all explanations must be built on existing knowledge. Our attempts at analysis of the poem also remind us of the fundamental goal of explaining – that is, to produce understanding.

What is an explanation?

explain: to make plain or intelligible; to unfold and illustrate the meaning of.

explanation: the act of explaining or clearing from obscurity; that which explains or clears up. (Chambers Dictionary)

The root of the word 'explain' comes from Latin and means 'to make plain'.

Brown (1978) tells us, quite simply, that, 'explaining is giving understanding to someone else'. Some of you might question this definition by pointing out that we can't simply *give* learning and knowledge to people, as if in a package which they can open to reveal the meaning; they have to construct it for themselves from the inputs we provide. From these inputs we hope that our learners will understand and that their understanding will match ours as closely as possible. Therefore, a discussion of explaining is incomplete if we don't include discussion of understanding. Brown and Atkins (1997) suggest that, 'understanding involves seeing connections which were hitherto not seen'. When we understand something we make connections; we 'make sense' of things. Two important points follow from this; first, we can see that explaining and understanding are clearly linked to cognitive and constructive learning theories; second, in order to be meaningful learning and understanding must connect to, and extend, existing learning.

Types of explanation

Brown (1978) suggests that there are three types of explanation:

- What? (interpretive)
- How? (descriptive)
- Why? (reason-giving)

The DfES (2004b) offers additional types, including:

- explaining purposes and objectives of sessions
- explaining concepts (often abstract).

Explaining the purpose and objectives of learning sessions

It is pointless explaining definitions, procedures or concepts if students don't know why they are being asked to understand them. The first step to good explanations is to provide a context, usually by telling learners the aims and objectives of the session and why they need to do what they're going to do. For example,

> 'Today we are going to look at the differences between diesel engines and petrol engines. The reason for this is that you will have to service both kinds of engine in your work.'

or,

> 'Today we're going to start our study of Seamus Heaney's poetry by looking at his choice of words and his use of rhyme. This will help us to analyse the meanings of his poems and evaluate their effectiveness in later lessons.'

Clear opening statements of the session's purpose are vital for effective explanation and understanding. They can be supplemented by, or take the form of, advance organisers which help learners to get the 'big picture', for example, an organisation chart of a business as an introduction to a session on the structure of businesses.

What (interpretive) explanations

These kinds of explanations involve the definition of terms, the meaning or interpretation of a statement or the clarification of issues. For example, What is a chromosome? What is a poem? What is the four-stroke cycle? What is a spreadsheet?

How (descriptive) explanations

These involve the description of structures, processes or procedures; they explain how things work. These kinds of explanations are generally based on sequences of key points leading from one to another which link to make a complete understanding. This kind of explanation can be, or may be accompanied by, a demonstration. They will include words such as 'first', 'next' and 'finally'. Examples would be: 'How does the poet use language?'; 'How does the four-stroke cycle operate?'; 'How is a spreadsheet set up?'

Why (reason-giving) explanations

These kinds of explanations are intended to develop understanding of why things happen or work. Like descriptive explanations they are generally based on sequences, but they explain why one thing follows from another; they will feature phrases such as 'because' and 'this causes'.

Explaining concepts

In my teaching career, one of the most difficult things I ever had to explain was 'ideology' to media and communications studies students. There are several reasons why it was so difficult to explain. First, ideology is an abstract concept – you can't see, hear, touch, smell or taste it. Second, it was an abstract concept unfamiliar to most of my students. Other abstract ideas such as God, anger or democracy can be problematic but at least they were familiar with them. Third, it was difficult for me to connect the concept of ideology to the students' experience, largely because it required some political and sociological knowledge. They were all ideological, in various ways, and affected by ideology, but very few of them knew it. What I was trying to explain to them was the *concept* of ideology. Concepts, particularly unfamiliar ones, can be difficult to explain, although much interesting and useful discussion can be had along the way. A concept is an idea or a general notion; some are abstract, some are concrete. A useful illustration of concepts is shown in Table 6.2.

To explain ideology I generally resorted to the use of diagrams to show simple representations of class and power and by examples from language. To show the ideological bias of language I asked students to list the number and variety of derogatory terms for women as opposed to those for men – this can be a very revealing exercise. The DfES document *Explaining* (2004) provides

Table 6.2 Concepts

	Concrete	Abstract
Familiar	Terms in everyday use and observable: e.g. wave (sea), trench, reptile, metal, paragraph	Terms in everyday use but not easily observable: e.g. design, democracy, health, flow (in dance), pace (in writing), erosion
Not familiar (often technical)	Terms used by specialists but observable: e.g. thermosetting plastic, gradient, ellipsis (in writing)	Terms used by specialists but not observable: e.g. urbanisation, atom, choreography, irony (in literature)

Source: DfES (2004b).

examples of 'using layers of modelling clay to represent layers of sedimentary rock, and using a school hierarchy to help understand the political and social hierarchy of a particular Shakespeare play'.

> **Activity**
>
> Using the grid in Table 6.2, identify concepts you need to explain to your learners.
>
> Which are familiar or unfamiliar; which are concrete or abstract?
>
> Consider a concept which is both abstract and unfamiliar to your learners.
>
> How will you explain it to them?

How to provide good explanations

Effective explanations have similar common elements. Some explanations will be planned and prepared prior to the learning session; others might be impromptu and require teachers to think on their feet. Good teachers will be aware of these characteristics of good explanations; they will choose appropriate techniques and adjust them to suit their learners and the purposes of the session. The most common elements are shown here as a set of guidelines.

Make sure you understand it yourself

Before you begin to explain something to your learners, make sure you fully understand it yourself. Have a run-through; practise it on a partner. I've observed trainee teachers demonstrating mathematical calculations which haven't worked out because they didn't rehearse them. Do you need to do any research? Have you got the latest information? Work out ideas and concepts using diagrams or some kind of visual structure; make this part of your planning.

Provide a clear structure

A frequent criticism of explanations is that they are not logical and clearly sequenced from point to point. Explanations should proceed step by step and you need to link each step clearly. A good explanation provides a clear framework for learners (you could make links here with 'scaffolding' and the zone of proximal development) and an effective way of doing this is by using 'keys'.

Use keys to 'unlock' understanding

Brown (1978) proposed the concept of keys in explaining. Keys are a series of linked statements which form the framework of the explanation. A key could be a statement, a principle, an example or an illustration. For example, explaining a complex, abstract concept such as 'socialisation' in sociology might begin with an illustration of a child with a series of labelled arrows showing the various agencies of socialisation, such as education, family and the media – these then act as verbal subheadings and their role in the socialisation process can be introduced. The diagram acts as an advance organiser to which subsequent elements of the explanation can be added and connected.

Keep the explanation as simple as possible

Keys need to be adapted in style, content and level to meet the needs of different learners. Some learners might feel patronised by the use of the labelled diagram to explain socialisation. However, a good general rule is to keep the explanation and the keys as simple as possible using just the basic minimum of information to develop initial understanding. *Romeo and Juliet* is fairly simply explained by a simple formula – 'boy meets girl; boy loses girl; boy tries to get girl back again; boy dies; girl dies'. Don't be afraid to start too simply and exclude any unnecessary information; even things you consider vital to understanding might not be needed by your learners in the early stages. Provide the framework first; details can be added later. It's better to start off with simplicity rather than complexity. You can always step things up a gear in response to feedback from your learners.

Providing a clear and engaging introduction

You should clearly signal to your learners that you are about to explain something and state what it is. If possible give an interesting and engaging introduction to 'hook' them in. For example, an explanation to hairdressing students about the structure of hair could be, 'Why is it difficult to do anything with your hair when you've just washed it?'

Link to existing learning and learners' experience

As we already know, it is essential to link new learning to existing learning. We need to ensure we don't make assumptions about what students know or have already learned with us. There's no point giving an explanation of inflation that involves understanding of economics that learners don't already have. Teachers frequently miss opportunities to explain concepts by using examples from the learners' own experience. For example, in customer service modules, many learners will have part-time jobs working with the public which can provide examples – there is even the possibility of developing them into case studies. Like so many other aspects of teaching, the key is to know your learners and to provide hooks to engage them and ways to connect new learning to old.

Avoid 'information overload'

'Information overload' is a phrase which has crept into everyday parlance. It means precisely what it says. If you give your learners too much information in one go without breaking it down into manageable chunks, they will react in a number of possible ways – hostility; incomprehension; disengagement; boredom. Explanations which introduce several new concepts and new terminology should be 'chunked' and delivered in clearly segregated stages, each followed by some form of checking the learning.

Checking understanding during and at the end of the explanation

Given that understanding is the goal of explanation, teachers must ensure that they provide regular checks on learning and opportunities for learners to demonstrate their understanding or request clarification if they don't. Clearly, there is a link here between explaining and questioning. During an explanation, a closed question might be appropriate, for example 'What links the piston to the crankshaft?' Open questions will allow learners to apply and analyse their learning. Make sure that you leave spaces in your explanation for questions and clarification.

Use appropriate language

By 'appropriate', I mean language which is appropriate to the learners at this level and at this stage. Avoid the unnecessary use of jargon; make sure that new technical terms are introduced and defined. Learners particularly dislike the use of acronyms and initialisations which teachers assume they are familiar with, e.g. ICT; LSC; QTLS; QCA and QIA.

Use connecting words

Connecting words provide structure and indicate how the elements of the explanation are linked. They can indicate sequences by using words such as 'first', 'next', 'second', 'after this' and 'finally'. They can also be used in explanations of reasoning or cause and effect; 'because', 'this causes', 'this produces'. A well-planned explanation uses connecting words with appropriate resources to provide both visual and auditory input for learners.

Use examples and non-examples

Examples are essential for effective explanations. They should be appropriate and relevant to learners and linked to their experience. When discussing genre, a media studies teacher might suggest *Unforgiven* as an example of a western and *Love, Actually* as an example of a 'romcom' (romantic comedy). If students have previously studied the conventions of different genres they can classify other films by comparing with known examples. They can explain different genres by saying what they are like but also by what they are not like, in other words by using non-examples. Non-examples are useful in explaining because they allow us to say, 'It's like this, but not like that.' Learners can then demonstrate understanding of rules and categories by explaining why one thing is like another but different from a third, for example, what two liquids have in common as opposed to a gas.

Use resources

A variety of resources can be used to explain and to support explanations. Physical models can be used, for example in geology to show strata; in motor vehicle engineering to demonstrate various working parts of vehicles; in biology or health and social care to explain and demonstrate anatomy and physical processes. Printed resources may be used to provide supplementary information – readings, statistics, diagrams, references – for learners to build on after the explanation. A handout showing the key points or the framework of an explanation can help to keep learners focused and to scaffold their learning. A visual handout which requires learners to add terms and definitions is a useful way of reinforcing learning. For example, hairdressing students could be given an unlabelled diagram showing the structure of a hair and the scalp which they complete as the explanation progresses. These printed resources could be accompanied by a visual presentation.

ICT increasingly provides versatile tools for explaining. Word-processing packages contain quite sophisticated drawing programmes to make diagrams and models. PowerPoint presentations, with animation techniques used imaginatively, can reveal information or build up sequences more effectively than the old method of overlaying acetates on an overhead projector. There are several ICT packages which are designed to produce concept maps and other graphic organisers; these are particularly helpful in getting learners to see and discover connections in their learning. The PowerPoint slide shown in Figure 6.1 is one I used with trainee teachers in response to the task set at the beginning of this section – explaining the main elements of a computer. Starting with just the central processing unit each subsequent component is added, using custom animation, as that part of the explanation is reached.

Remember nonverbal communication

Explanations are enhanced by the positive and encouraging use of NVC – both voice and body language. Think about how a monotonous voice affects you; about how the unvarying drone of a teacher, colleague or relative tends to annoy or distract you. Well, it's the same for your learners.

When you are explaining it's important to vary the pitch, tone and speed of your voice to create interest and to engage your learners. You can use your voice as a kind of verbal punctuation; pauses and emphasis can act as verbal underlining of important words or phrases. Deliberate pacing, use of pauses and sequencing can represent verbal bullet points. Effective use of body language connects you with your learners and encourages them to be involved. Eye contact should be shared around all members of the group, but you can allow your gaze to rest on individuals for a couple of seconds at a time. Pausing and briefly surveying all your learners signals that they can ask questions or seek

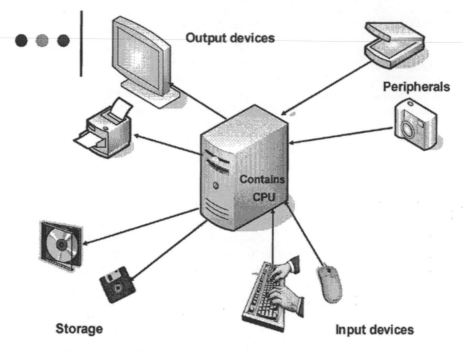

Figure 6.1 Explaining the basics of a computer.

clarification of particular points. All learners, whatever age, dislike teachers who deliver explanations to the space just above their heads and simply plough on, heedless of the quizzical or enquiring looks on the faces of their audience.

Summarise

There's a well-worn teacher's adage: 'tell them what you're going to tell them; tell them; then tell them what you've told them'. As a general principle of effective teaching and learning this is rather dubious advice. However, it can usefully be applied to explanations since it reminds us of the need for clear introductions and summaries. A good summary does precisely what the word implies – it reviews and connects the main points. Thus, a summary of the four-stroke cycle of the internal combustion engine could be something like this:

> And so we have seen that on the first stroke of the cycle a mixture of fuel and air, from the carburettor, is sucked into the cylinder through the inlet valve. This is called induction. The piston then moves up the cylinder and squeezes the mixture. This is called compression. Then the spark-plug ignites the mixture, which drives the piston back down the cylinder. This is

called ignition. As the piston comes back up the cylinder, the exhaust valve opens and the burnt gases are expelled. This is called exhaust. In short, the whole cycle can be summarised by four words – suck, squeeze, bang, blow.

Activity

The key idea to remember is that just because you understand something doesn't mean you can explain it to someone else. The opposite side to this, as many lecturers will testify, is that you don't *really* understand something until you *can* explain it to someone else (Exley and Dennick 2004).

To what extent do you agree with the assertion that if you can't explain something, you don't understand it?

Activity

Teachers, because they are generally experts in their subjects, can find it difficult to simplify.

Consider something you have to explain to learners.

Reduce and simplify it to a few basic steps. What elements did you find difficult to omit? Can you represent these steps in a visual form?

For your journal

As you develop your journal pay particular attention to your use of questions and explanations in teaching and learning.

Reflect on the explanations you provide and consider ways in which you can improve; you might find it useful to get feedback from your learners.

Consider, for example:
- structure;
- use of language;
- use of comparisons, analogy and metaphor;
- use of visual elements or models.

Reflect on your use of questions and consider your strengths and weakness. Consider particularly your use of open questions and the ways in which you use higher-order questions to develop thinking skills and deep learning.

Ask your learners by inviting formal or informal feedback on your questioning and explaining skills. You could even formalise this feedback by using questionnaires. Ask them for examples of things they had difficulty in understanding; ask them why and see if they have ideas for explaining it.

If you are using the two-page approach to journal writing, you can return to your record of events and amend it by adding new ideas and noting references to theory.

Journal extract: Zaheera

It was difficult getting them to speak about the poem as we went through it line by line, so as well as doing group work I used different levels of questions that got the students to think about what they had read and explain it to me. For example, 'Why is so and so saying this?' 'What is this an example of?' 'What is the effect of the technique?' 'Why does the poet do this?'

Further reading

Brown, G. (1978) *Lecturing and Explaining*. London: Methuen.

DfES (Department for Education and Skills) (2004) Key Stage 3 National Strategy *Pedagogy in Practice; Unit 7 Questioning*. London: DfES.

DfES (Department for Education and Skills) (2004) Key Stage 3 National Strategy *Pedagogy in Practice; Unit 8 Explaining*. London: DfES.

Kerry, T. (2002) *Explaining and Questioning*. Cheltenham: Nelson Thornes.

7 Assessment for learning

What this chapter is about

- What is assessment?
- Why and how do we assess?
- Types of assessment: initial, diagnostic, formative, summative, ipsative
- Norm referencing and criterion referencing
- Principles of assessment
- Competence-based assessment and assessing NVQs
- Assessment methods
- Convergent and divergent assessment
- Giving feedback
- The emotional impact of assessment

LLUK standards

This chapter covers the following standards:

BS 1; BK 1.1; BP 1.1; BK 1.3; BP 1.3; BK 2.1; BP 2.1; BK 2.2; BP 2.2; BK 2.5; BP 2.5
DK 1.1; DP 1.1; DK 2.2; DP 2.2
ES 1; EK 1.1; EP 1.1; EK 1.2; EP 1.2; EK 1.3; EP 1.3; EK 2.1; EP 2.1; EK 2.2; EP 2.2;
EK 2.3; EP 2.3; EK 3.1; EP 3.1; EK 3.2; EP 3.2 EK 4.1; EP 4.1

Introduction

As an experiment I'm going to start this chapter with some 'teaching by asking' rather than 'teaching by telling'. This is a challenge in a textbook because, to be effective, this technique requires a two-way dialogue using Socratic-style questioning. However, let's give it a go. Consider each of the questions as fully as you can – it's probably best done as a group activity – and see what conclusions you can draw and what connections you can make about assessment. Other questions of your own might arise; include them in your discussions.

Activity

Consider the entirety of your learning experiences in a variety of settings: school, college, university, training at work and discuss the following:

- What are your memories of assessment/being assessed?

- What kinds of assessment did you experience – tests, examinations, coursework assignments? Others?

- How important was the assessment to you and to others?

- How did you feel and what was your emotional state during and after the assessment
  - if you were successful?
  - if you were unsuccessful?

- If you were successful, did you feel you had learned something or just passed a test?

- What, if any, were the consequences of the assessment
  - if you were successful?
  - if you were unsuccessful?

- Do you recall making judgements about your colleagues or fellow students based on their performance in assessment? What kinds of judgement did you make?

- Did assessment help you to learn? If so, what forms of assessment worked best for you?

- Did you understand why and how you were being assessed?

- Describe the quantity, quality and usefulness of the feedback you received.

- Did you find assessment motivating? Did you look forward to it or dread it?

- Did you at any time, as a result of assessment, feel like a failure?

- If you felt like a failure, what were the effects on your subsequent learning?

As a result of your thinking and discussion you will, inevitably, have brought up some of the key issues relating to assessment, for example its uses and purposes, or its emotional impact. These issues will, most likely, reflect the main questions of this chapter, which are:

- What is assessment?
- Why do we assess?
- How do we assess?
- How does it affect learners?

From the outset, I want to express a fundamental belief about assessment. The principal purpose of assessment is to help people to learn; it should not be about testing people to see at what point they will fail. We must remember, however, that although assessment is primarily *for* learning we also live in the real world and learners will, in most instances, want assessment *of* their learning. Assessment information and data will also be required by you, your managers, learning providers, governors, funding bodies, LSC, Ofsted, potential learners, employers, marketing and publicity teams. The trick is to get the balance right and to use assessment primarily *for* learners and learning.

Why do we assess learners?

There are many reasons why we assess learners and their learning. These reasons could be grouped under the following headings.

Because we are required to

Much of the teaching and learning delivered in the lifelong learning sector is assessed by external agencies, such as examination boards, and the assessment information and data is made publicly available. Generally, our learners come to us to undertake courses which lead to formal, summative assessment by external bodies and the attainment of a grade or statement of achievement.

As indicated above, we are required to measure our learners' and our own performance and if it is unsatisfactory we may lose funding and, in the worst-case scenario, be closed down. We are in receipt of public money and it seems reasonable that we should be asked to provide evidence that this money is well spent; this evidence comes, in part, in the form of assessment results and grades. An over-reliance on summative assessment and grading, however, can be counter-productive and lead to an 'examination culture' in which results become an end in themselves and the wider aspects of learning are neglected. In schools and colleges teachers may feel under pressure to 'teach to the test'.

For grading, selection and progression

In a pub quiz we compete against others by trying to answer more questions correctly than they do; we are then ranked in winning order and receive prizes and congratulations, or commiserations, accordingly. In short we are graded. We do this for fun and the consequences are of little importance. We might not like the idea of grading in educational settings but it is a fact of life and its consequences are considerable. Success in gaining employment or entry to university is based on being assessed and graded. Some of you may be delivering on courses where you are regularly required to grade your learners as they go through the course and to report estimated grades to examination boards.

   Adult learners over a certain age will have memories of a significant grading and selection exercise – the 11-plus examination. Many of these people will still feel that they are 'failures', not just in their education but as people.

To find out if learning has taken place

We use assessment to find out if and to what extent our students have learned and how they have developed. Without some form of assessment it would be impossible to ascertain whether progress has been made by all or just some of our learners. This can be done by informal methods, such as questioning and discussion, or by more formal methods such as essays or phase tests. Much of this assessment is used to check learning and understanding regularly prior to moving on to the next sections. Reflective teachers use checks on learning and understanding to adjust and adapt teaching as necessary. Without some form of assessment we can't give feedback to learners; we now know that positive and structured feedback is the most effective form of teaching and assessment. Effective feedback is motivating which leads us to the next point.

To motivate and encourage learners

Learners and teachers tend not to consider assessment motivating, but for some students it is. Many learners will like to be tested and will find assessment, particularly tests and examinations, to be both stimulating and rewarding. Unfortunately, there are at least as many who find such assessments to be fear-inducing. Learners who are usually confident and able can be stricken by 'performance anxiety' when it comes to testing. Unfortunately, most 'high stakes' assessments are, to a greater or lesser extent, based on tests and examinations. So, if only in the interest of equality and inclusivity, there should a range of assessment techniques in your teaching and learning toolkit.

Assessment can discourage learners by giving them the impression that they have not performed well enough or that they are simply not clever enough. Effective assessment is an aid to learning and helps learners and teachers to recognise achievement but also to identify areas for improving or extending learning. We should use assessment to motivate learners, not demotivate.

To diagnose learners' needs

If learners are to be successful there needs to be an assessment of their starting points. We need to know what learning, skills and experience they arrive with when they come to us. Initial and diagnostic testing helps us to plan the learning for groups and individuals and to provide support and meet individual needs and learning styles. The information from these tests can form the basis of ILPs which are regularly reviewed in consultation with the learners.

To evaluate and develop learning programmes

To use a shopping analogy, learning providers must deliver courses which meet learners' needs; are useful and enjoyable; help them to progress; and provide good value. We need to be accountable to our learners. When we buy unsatisfactory goods we should complain and ask for our money back. There is no reason for us to expect that learners will accept unsatisfactory learning products. There are many ways in which learning is evaluated; one of them is assessment of learning which feeds into a continuing drive for improvement. (Many of you will want to pick holes in my shopping analogy – rightly so.)

Activity

Consider two or three assessments you have recently carried out with your learners.

- Why did you use them?
- Did your learners know why they were being assessed?
- To what extent do you think they valued the assessment?
- Could you have assessed them differently?
- How did the assessment contribute to their learning?

The main purposes of assessment

Having considered the general reasons for and aims of assessment, we can now examine the main purposes of assessment. These are:

- initial assessment;
- diagnostic assessment/testing;
- formative assessment;
- summative assessment;
- ipsative assessment.

Initial assessment

As the name suggests, this type of assessment happens at the beginning of a course of learning, or even before the learning starts if we include activities such as pre-entry advice and guidance, application and enrolment. Initial assessment will be a key part of the induction process for new learners and, as such, should be handled sensitively to welcome learners in rather than scare with formal testing and assessment procedures. Initial assessment has developed mainly in the realms of Skills for Life, work-based and vocational learning, but increasingly it is valued as part of the learning journey for all students.

Initial assessment may include diagnostic assessment (see below) but it comprises a much wider range of assessment and information gathering, including, for example: career intentions and suitability; qualifications and achievements; prior learning and experience; key skills; and basic skills. Learning styles inventories are often used at this initial stage but all too often learners and teachers do not know why they do them or what they are used for. Information on students' learning styles is pointless unless it's used to inform planning and delivery of learning. Initial assessment is also used to identify any particular requirements learners might have. Wheelchair users will expect access to buildings and facilities; people who have hearing difficulties may require rooms with induction loops or perhaps a communicator. We have legal obligations to anticipate and to meet the needs of all learners.

Muriel Green, writing about initial assessment in work-based post-16 provision states that initial assessment is:

> A staged process that helps the learner cross the threshold to the most appropriate post-16 provision … It is really important to 'get it right', so that the learning and support opportunities offered are the best possible match with the interests, abilities, aptitudes, aspirations and needs of the individual.
>
> (Green 2003: 5)

Given the emphasis on retention and achievement of learners, it will be apparent that initial assessment is designed to benefit not only the learners but also the learning provider. The formula is quite simple: get the right learners on the right courses; help them to stay on programme and to achieve; help them progress to the next stage. Initial assessment is crucial to the first stage in this formula.

Diagnostic assessment

Diagnostic assessments or tests are used to discover how current performance or abilities differ from the expected or required level of performance. It can be used to identify specific problems that a learner may be experiencing and to provide appropriate learning support. As part of the initial assessment process diagnostic testing can be used to assess learners' abilities in Key Skills or Skills for Life, particularly literacy and numeracy. As we noted earlier, the temptation to sit new students in front of a literacy or numeracy test on their first day should be avoided.

Formative assessment

The main developments and debates in assessment practice revolve around the issues of formative assessment and summative assessment. Formative assessment is an integral part of the teaching and learning process and its aim is to promote learning and to motivate learners; it is assessment *for* learning. Summative assessment is the summing up or checking of learning at particular stages by, for example, testing or some kind of formal assessment. Such testing may involve making judgements about learners against national standards as, for example, in a GCSE or A-level examination: it is assessment *of* learning.

Formative assessment, used properly, is such an integral part of the teaching and learning process that one could argue that it shouldn't even be called assessment. When we consider teaching and learning methods, many of them – questioning, case studies, projects – are also assessment methods.

Some of the most significant work on formative assessment has been carried out by Black and William (1998); the influence of their work is evident in the QCA's guidelines on *Assessment for Learning* (2001). Black and William provide some basic premises to support the use of formative assessment, which are worth quoting in full. Their work is the result of research in schools but the conclusions are equally valid for learners of all ages, particularly adult returners who have basic skills needs, consequently, I have substituted the word 'learner' for 'pupil' in the following:

[T]he research indicates that improving learning through assessment depends on five, deceptively simple, key factors:

- the provision of effective feedback to learners;
- the active involvement of learners in their own learning;
- adjusting teaching to take account of the results of assessment;
- a recognition of the profound influence assessment has on the motivation and self-esteem of learners, both of which are crucial influences on learning;
- the need for learners to be able assess themselves and understand how to improve.

At the same time, several inhibiting factors were identified. Among these are:

- a tendency for teachers to assess the quantity of work and presentation rather than the quality of learning;
- greater attention given to marking and grading, much of it tending to lower the self-esteem of learners, rather than to providing advice for improvement;
- teachers not knowing enough about their learners' needs.

(Black and William 1998: 17)

Assessment for learning is based on the belief that everyone can learn and that formative assessment is a key strategy to help learners improve and develop.

It can be contrasted with summative assessment which, historically, was based on the notion that there was a limited pool of talent with innate ability which had to be identified and selected. Assessment for learning does not involve comparison with other learners.

Assessment for learning is an essential element of planning and delivering teaching and learning. Teachers should plan a range of activities and methods to allow all learners to know the what, how and why of assessment and to give them opportunities to progress towards their goals. The planning requires that feedback, the most powerful tool to improve learning, is central to learning. Planning should allow for interaction between teacher and learners so that the pace and delivery of the session can be adjusted to match the learners' progress.

Interaction between teachers and learners means that much assessment for learning is carried out informally by using activities such as listening; observing learners' work and their NVC; questioning, particularly higher-order questions; discussions; dialogue and reflection. Assessment for learning is closely linked to notions of active learning and deep learning.

Assessment for learning should also develop the use of ILPs, Improving Own Learning and Performance Key Skills, and personalised learning to encourage learners to reflect on their own performance, identify areas for development and take steps to carry them out. It should employ self-assessment methods which can empower and motivate learners.

Feedback is the most important aspect of formative assessment. Teachers can receive and give feedback in a variety of ways (you will find it useful here to link back to Chapter 2, 'Communication and the teacher'). Research suggests that immediate oral feedback is the most effective, provided it is developmental and makes learners extend their thinking and learning to a higher level. In this respect, the use of feedback is very much like the ideas of 'scaffolding' and the ZPD we discussed in Chapter 3. Learners, in dialogue with teachers, can see where they want to get to but initially may need help in the form of questions, prompts and pointers to get there. Black and William's research suggests that formative assessment based on high quality feedback has the greatest effect (i.e. effect on improvement) size of any techniques used in education.

Questioning is a vital skill for teachers to develop. Whilst lower-order, recall type questions might be useful for checking learning, higher-order questions which require learners to think are much more effective as part of formative assessment. You should refer to the use of Socratic questions outlined in Chapter 6.

Summative assessment

Summative assessment is the assessment *of* learning. It is usually carried out at the end of a course of learning or at specific points in a learning programme, such as at the end of a module or unit, or phase test. Summative assessments are nearly always formal – test, examination, oral, essay, assignment – and are used to see if learners have acquired the skills and knowledge required by the specifications or at that particular stage. Summative assessments may be used to decide whether a learner can or should go on to the next stage.

Summative assessments are important, as discussed earlier, because they lead to the production of grades and the gaining, or otherwise, of qualifications. We know that this process of qualification and grading is important for learners and many other interested parties. However, we need to remember the emotional aspects of assessment and the design of assessment, particularly to do with validity and reliability – all these aspects will be examined shortly.

Weeden et al. (2002: 19) suggest that:

> Summative assessment is a snapshot judgement that records what a [learner] can do at a particular time. It is concerned with providing information about a [learner] in a simple summary form which can be used to review progress, can be passed to a new teacher or school [or

university or employer] or can certificate achievement in a formal way. This function probably dominates most teachers' views of assessment.

It would be wrong, however, to suggest that formative and summative assessment are opposites – A-level candidates, for example, will be judged and graded by summative assessment, but their success and the quality of their learning is likely to be improved if formative assessment is the basis of the teaching and learning.

Ipsative assessment

Ipsative assessment is a form of self-assessment which allows learners to measure their own progress without comparing themselves to others or reference to standards set by external bodies. As a trainee teacher you will probably have carried out an initial audit of your skills, knowledge and attributes and produced a personal action plan with self-defined targets. When you review your targets you can assess the distance you have travelled and develop new targets as appropriate. For our own learners, particularly those who have not been successful in their previous education, ipsative assessment can be a powerful method of increasing self-esteem and confidence because it emphasises success rather than failure. This form of assessment works best when based on thorough initial assessment and identification of clear learning goals and targets supported by an ILP.

Norm referencing and criterion referencing

Norm referencing

When discussing forms of assessment, the word 'referencing' means what is the referent of the learner; in other words what is he or she compared to. In the case of ipsative assessment (see above) learners are compared to and judged against their own previous performance. Given that norm referencing has traditionally been, and to some extent continues to be, the main method of assessing and grading learners, you will almost certainly have experienced it at some point in your education. The most obvious example of this type of assessment is a formal, externally marked examination such as A level, the results of which will have been published and have had significant consequences for your continued learning and your career prospects.

In a system of norm referencing, judgements – and grades – about an individual's performance in an assessment are made by referring to, or comparing against, another group of learners. This other group could be the class, the school or college, or the whole cohort entered for that assessment. It is based on the notion that in any given group of learners there will always be some who are very able and will get the highest marks, some who are not able and would fail, and a range of people in the middle. The examination system would have grade boundaries and a pass/fail boundary and, consistently, roughly the same numbers of students would be allocated within each grade. This system encourages learners, and employers and universities, to perceive themselves as a 'pass' or a 'fail'.

Norm-referenced systems are relatively simple systems which are competitive and, implicitly or explicitly, suggest that the pool of talent is fixed and will not vary greatly in any given cohort of learners. The main function of the assessment in this system is to identify the high-fliers and to grade all the entrants. Such systems are still popular with governments because they can produce statistics and league tables, and with employers and further and higher education institutions because they facilitate selection. Given that schools and colleges are competing for learners, grades based on norm-referenced systems are an essential part of their marketing, recruitment and funding.

Criterion referencing

Criterion referencing grew, in part, from a desire to move away from norm referencing and ranking, with their connotations of passing or failing, to an emphasis on what students can actually do. In criterion referencing, learners are assessed against predetermined standards not with reference to their competitors. The standards prescribe the knowledge, skills and understanding that learners need in that subject or vocation. Criterion referencing assumed a more specialised form in competence-based assessment, as we shall see later.

A comparison with the driving test is often used to explain criterion-referenced assessment. All candidates for the driving test know what the criteria for success are and they are judged against them; if they fail they can work to improve and retake the test to see if they have met the criteria. If a norm referencing system was used to assess drivers, a certain percentage of the population would never be able to pass the test. Criterion referencing is generally considered to be fairer since it removes the competitive element and the assumption that there will always be roughly the same proportion at each grade. To ensure fairness and equal opportunities, criteria should be written in a clear and unambiguous manner so that all learners can understand them. In BTEC courses, criteria clearly state what learners must be able to do or produce in order to gain a pass, merit or distinction. It would be mistaken, however, to suggest that all assessments are either purely norm referenced or criterion referenced. Even A-level examinations have some criteria built in to them and the GCSE when it was introduced was said to be a criterion-referenced system which would motivate learners. Neither should we assume there is any system which is completely objective and without bias from the assessor or some other influence. As James Atherton points out: 'All assessment is ultimately subjective: there is no such thing as an "objective test". Even when there is a high degree of standardisation, the judgement of what things are tested and what constitutes a criterion of satisfactory performance is in the hands of the assessor' (Atherton 2005).

Some principles of assessment

Validity

When we set assessments for our learners we, and they, need to be sure about what we are actually assessing or measuring. An assessment can be said to be valid if it measures what it actually sets out to measure. For example, does a task assess the quality of a learner's written skills when (unless specified in the assessment criteria) it's an assessment in engineering?

'Face validity' is concerned with the extent to which an assessment looks like an assessment in that subject or vocational area. In examinations, for example, we expect clear, error-free papers in accessible and unambiguous language. Other aspects of validity relate to the extent to which the assessment reflects what is set out in the specifications and the extent to which the assessment measures the range of skills, knowledge and understanding outlined in the specification.

Reliability

Reliability is closely is linked to validity but the emphasis is more on the accuracy and consistency of its application. Would the assessment produce roughly the same results if used at a different time and a different place with a similar group of learners? One way in which we can ensure reliability is by a process of moderation or cross-marking based on all assessors using the same standards and criteria.

Transparency

Transparency is essentially about the extent to which learners understand the assessment and to which it matches the learning outcomes. Learners don't like to be taken by surprise by being assessed on something they didn't expect, don't understand or they just haven't covered. When designing assessments we must be sure that the task is aligned with the learning outcomes and the assessment criteria. Learning outcomes should be presented clearly and unambiguously to the learners and the links between the outcomes and the assessment criteria should be made plain to them, markers and internal and external verifiers.

Torrance et al. (2005) warn, particularly in the area of vocational assessment, that too much transparency can lead to a situation which goes beyond assessment *for* learning to a situation of assessment *as* learning. In other words, there is a danger that we can provide learners with so much clarity, explanation and assistance that they will succeed, but succeed at what? A balance needs to be struck between providing clarity of task and criteria with the possibility of challenge and discovery.

Authenticity

Authenticity in assessment has two meanings. First, it is concerned with how closely the assessment mirrors the real world, particularly in relation to vocational assessment. If we are assessing students in catering, is the assessment in an authentic catering setting using the latest equipment and techniques? Ideally, the assessment should be undertaken in a workplace using a work-based assessor.

The second aspect of authenticity refers to the originality of the work produced by the student. Is it their own? Have they had any help with it, or have they copied it? Given the ubiquity of the Internet and its access by learners, can we be sure that work has not been plagiarised? Plagiarism is most likely to be presented in written work, so perhaps we need to consider whether a written piece is always the most appropriate form of assessment.

Sufficiency

Here we are concerned with whether the quantity and the coverage of the assessment tasks and activities are sufficient to provide evidence that the learning outcomes have been met. Sufficiency is particularly important in the assessment of competence-based courses such as NVQs and General National Vocational Qualifications (GNVQs). In such programmes the emphasis is on learners collecting evidence and assembling portfolios which are judged by assessors and assessment decisions made. You may have seen portfolios which comprise small mountains of material lovingly indexed and cross-referenced by the candidate as evidence of their competence. Whilst we would wish to applaud candidates' organisational and presentational skills, there is always a danger that the collection of evidence and portfolio-building becomes an end in itself. The question is, 'do we need all this?' Is the evidence the minimum necessary to demonstrate competence and to ensure coverage of all the units and the performance criteria?

Competence-based assessment

The background to competence-based assessment

Competence-based assessment could be described as a more specialised and vocationally related sibling of criterion-referenced assessment. Wolf (1995) outlines the development of competence-based assessment from its mainly American origins, through its development in the 1980s and the establishment of the National Council for Vocational Qualifications. National Vocational Qualifications are based on a system whereby each vocational area is broken down into outcomes or units of competences, within which there are elements and performance criteria which describe specifically what a learner must be able to do. The process involves learners (or candidates) generating and collecting evidence, usually in a portfolio, which is then judged by an assessor against the outcomes.

There are several advantages to this form of assessment. First, given that it is a criterion-referenced system anyone who is able and meets the criteria successfully can achieve the qualification. Second, being vocational qualifications they are assessed in the workplace, hopefully with the latest technology and equipment, by assessors who are experts in the field. Finally, they are based on specific and transparent learning outcomes.

There are some downsides, however, not least the sheer bulk of portfolios and consequent difficulty of assessing them. In addition, the procedure involving assessors, internal and external verifiers and auditable evidence can be extremely onerous and bureaucratic. Others have argued that it is not realistic to disaggregate all work into a set of overarching competences. As Wolf (1995: 17) points out, NVQs are based on:

> the fundamental assumption that, for each industry, there exists a single identifiable model of what 'competent' performance entails. The idea that, for each role, there exists such an agreed notion of competence, which can be elicited and command consensus, is fundamental to any assessment system of this type.

Given these caveats, however, we must accept that competence-based assessment, like summative assessment, is a reality and that we have to design and implement it in the most efficient way and to encourage learning rather than merely collecting things.

Assessing NVQ: practical considerations

Underpinning knowledge

Early critics of NVQs claimed that there was little in the way of teaching and learning and that the process merely accredited skills people were already using. Hence the question, 'do we teach on NVQs?' The answer is, obviously, yes. If we expect candidates to demonstrate, for example, knowledge and practice of health and safety in a working environment, they have to learn about it first – legislation, safe working procedures – and then be observed and assessed doing it in the workplace. In short, they need the 'underpinning knowledge'.

Generating evidence

Evidence to support competent performance can come from a number of sources:

- *Accreditation of Prior Learning and Experiential Learning (APEL)*. A system of APEL recognises that a learner might not have a specific qualification in a skill or subject but they have gained experience from previous work or life experience. This might take the form of references, letters of commendation, a diary or a logbook from a previous workplace signed by a line manager.
- *Accreditation of Prior Learning (APL)*. This term and APEL are often confused and used interchangeably. A claim for APL is based on the accreditation and certification of prior learning. So, for example, in previous post-compulsory teacher training courses someone with a City and Guilds 7407 Stage 2 could claim APL and join the second year of a Certificate in Education.
- *Naturally occurring evidence and direct observation*. This kind of evidence is based on candidate's performance in the workplace; the things that they naturally do as part of their working routines. Some of this will be the result of acquiring, then applying, the underpinning knowledge. This might also include the production and collection of products or artefacts, for example, a letter produced by a candidate on a business administration course.
- *Performance on assignments*. Assignments and projects may be partly or wholly related to the candidate's type and place of work. The best kinds of projects are those which integrate theory and practice and provide opportunities to apply learning in the workplace. In addition, they should integrate key skill development. An example, would be in business administration where a candidate has been studying the Data

Protection Act and is able to research the ways in which the employer complies with the Act. Giving a presentation on this could also entail the development of Key Skills in communication and IT.

- *Photographic, video, audio or other electronic recording.* Learners, trainers and assessors are encouraged to use a range of assessment and evidence. Photographs of things produced by the candidate, candidates working with customers, receiving awards, can all be offered as evidence. Similarly, video and audio recordings may be provided. This is much easier than it was a decade ago because of the development of digital technology, although it's also easier to edit out the 'bad' bits!
- *Questioning.* Questioning is a useful method for assessors to check underpinning knowledge and to authenticate the validity and authenticity of evidence. Higher-order questions allow candidates to demonstrate their thinking skills and ways in which they have applied and adapted theory in practice.
- *Indirect evidence.* This includes items such as witness statements attesting to a candidate's performance and skill development in the workplace, certificates, awards, references.

As mentioned earlier, NVQ portfolios can become unwieldy and be very time-consuming to assess. Qualifications and Curriculum Authority guidelines on generating and collecting evidence emphasise that portfolios should, 'minimise bureaucracy and reduce the burden of assessment without compromising quality' (QCA nd). In addition, the guidelines urge candidates and assessors to use a range of assessment techniques and, wherever possible to develop 'evidence-rich' integrated projects and activities which avoid an 'element by element or pc (performance criteria) by pc approach to collecting evidence' and also reduce the overall amount of evidence collected.

The final point is important because competence-based assessment can be extremely reductionist and lead to performance criteria being 'ticked off' without recognising the connections between them or understanding the framework into which all the elements fit. All forms of work are holistic, connected activities, not just a collection of competences. Major, integrated projects follow best practice in teaching and learning in that they require learners to make connections and see the 'big picture'. It is important that candidates and assessors develop a 'helicopter vision' of the elements and performance criteria for each unit and are aware that the working day or the assignment can provide a range of valuable evidence.

Assessment methods

Is has been said that education is built on three pillars – what is taught (curriculum), how it is taught (pedagogy) and how it is assessed (assessment). For learning and teaching these three elements must be aligned and kept in balance. Many have argued that our education system is distorted by an overemphasis on assessment and that, to a great extent, what we teach is what we test.

When considering assessment methods we must decide what is the most appropriate method (or methods) for our learners in order to meet the aims and the learning outcomes of the course and the needs, abilities and styles of our learners. There is evidence to suggest that we are still too reliant on the use of written forms of assessment; this doesn't suit all people and there are equal opportunities issues for those who have dyslexia or sight problems. Equally the type of assessment might affect learners' perceptions of particular courses. Torrance et al. (2005) carried out significant research in the assessment of learning in the learning and skills sector and vocational learning. In one of their conclusions they point out that:

> Assessment methods *per se* do not directly affect learners' choice of award or likelihood of success, but the association of certain awards with methods which employ extensive writing (coursework assignments, exam essays) does. Thus for example, practical tests and/or multiple choice tests are seen as acceptable – and indeed unavoidable – across most groups of learners in the sector, especially younger trainees, but extensive written work is disliked and largely avoided except by A-level takers. Even in school and college-based AVCEs, the view is emerging that these are becoming too based on writing about the vocational field being studied, rather than engaging in the practical development of competence.
>
> (Torrance et al. 2005: 83)

It seems reasonable to suggest, therefore, that a significant task for professional development in lifelong learning is to widen our range and use of assessment methods.

The following overview of some assessment methods, indicating advantages and disadvantages in each case, is neither comprehensive nor detailed, but should serve as an introduction which you can follow up by further research and record and discuss in your journal. You will also see that many of these could also be described as teaching and learning methods and some of them are discussed in more detail in Chapter 5.

Examinations

Examinations, especially externally set and marked, still form a significant proportion of assessment in post-compulsory education. Variations can include 'open book' or 'open notes' examinations in which students can rely less on memory.

Advantages

Exams can help to focus learners because they know they have to work towards a specific goal. Externally marked exams don't provide any marking work for the teachers. Examinations are simple, summative form of assessment which produce grades and statistics.

Disadvantages

The most obvious criticism of exams is that they are fear-inducing for many learners and lead to grading based solely on the exam rather than a bigger picture of an individual's learning. I recently observed a group of students collecting their marked exam scripts and listened to their comments. Every student looked first at the grade, then read the limited feedback in a couple of seconds; one remarked that he'd done well enough considering that he didn't like this module and had only revised the night before! I found myself wondering what benefit they had derived from the experience. Apart from the limited feedback, exams can lead to a surface approach to learning in which both teachers and learners are geared mainly towards the exam and what's needed to pass it.

Essays

Many learners are assessed by essays because that form of assessment will be the basis of their final examination; so, in effect, the summative assessment structures the form of their ongoing assessment. Many are assessed by essays merely because they always have been.

Advantages

Like exams, essays can be a very useful form of focusing learners and getting them to produce a snapshot summary of their learning at a particular stage. A written essay can also be a useful method to assess a learner's written skills and their ability to identify and summarise key points, to present arguments, to analyse and evaluate. Timed essays set in class are useful as preparation for exams and are easy to administer, although they create a marking burden.

Essay performance gives a simple way to report predicted grades to exam boards.

Disadvantages

Essays are a symptom of our reliance on written forms of assessment. Whilst part of our job is to improve learners' ability to express themselves in writing, we do well to remember that in no situation other than an educational setting are people asked to write essays. Some people excel at essays and find it relatively easy to structure them and express themselves clearly; the danger here, of course, is that we might, even unconsciously, be marking learners on their essay writing skills rather than assessing their learning. Paradoxically, study skills support for essay writing may unwittingly reinforce the perception that the form is more important than the content. Equally, there is a possibility of a 'halo' effect by which the learners' achievements in previous essays will positively, or negatively, affect the marking of the current one. If I'm honest, I can recall looking at students' previous essay grades before marking the latest batch. Planned well and used judiciously, essays are a valuable element in an assessment package; used uncritically, they indicate teaching which is 'assessment-oriented' rather than 'learning-oriented.'

Reports

Advantages

Reports have the advantage that they are more 'real world' and likely to be part of learners' working lives. Reports can be clearly focused by providing guidelines as to their headings and style. Reports seem a natural follow-up to case study work or experiments and the learning and skills can be extended by summarising and presenting the key findings to colleagues.

Disadvantages

Like all written forms, reports have the disadvantage that they are time-consuming for learners and teachers, so we need to ensure that the effort is equal to the value of them. Often learners are asked to write reports without a clear understanding of their form and purpose and the ways in which they are different from other written forms.

Portfolios

You may have encountered the term portfolio in connection with NVQ, GNVQ or similar criterion-referenced systems. However, the term has long been in use in other disciplines, particularly in art in design where it generally means a 'portfolio of work'.

Advantages

Portfolios give learners the opportunity to present a 'big picture' of themselves and their achievements and to show their development over a period of learning. They can be used both formatively and summatively, particularly in conjunction with learning journals and diaries. As indicated in the section on competence-based learning, portfolios allow the collection of a range of assessment evidence, including written, visual, audio and artefacts. Increasingly learners are presenting this range of evidence as e-portfolios.

Disadvantages

The most obvious disadvantage of portfolios is that they can be difficult to assess, if only because of their bulk. There can also be problems with authenticity concerning the originality of the work submitted. As the word 'portfolio' has become widespread it seems to have lost its clarity – what exactly do we mean by a portfolio? Do our learners know what it means and why they are asked to produce them?

Presentations

Presentations are frequently used, even stipulated, in assessment. The most common form involves research into a subject accompanied by a presentation to peers supported by printed and projected resources, followed by questions and discussion.

Advantages

Presentations are invaluable for many reasons. Learners are very likely to present in some form in their working lives, if only at a job interview. Presentations are excellent for developing Key Skills and confidence.

Disadvantages

Teachers are generally very confident presenters and, consequently, we tend to forget some learners dread presentations and worry about them for weeks in advance. Another downside of presentations, particularly in large groups, is that they are time-consuming. Some teachers, particularly those delivering A-levels, who have extensive content to cover in a limited time, find the time spent on presentations outweighs their value.

Displays and exhibitions

These can range from simple poster displays to the full-blown art and design exhibition with VIPs and free wine on the opening night.

Advantages

Displays and exhibitions can be good motivators for learners because it gives them a chance to demonstrate their learning and skills to a wider public. This form of assessment can also develop team-working and time management skills as well as publicity and marketing skills. For adult learners who may not have enjoyed success in education before, displays and exhibitions are good opportunities to share and celebrate success. In some cases, particularly art and design, the work shown at the exhibition is assessed by external verifiers and examiners. At the less sophisticated end, simple poster displays give alternative ways of presenting and assessing work, particularly for learners with a visual preference.

Disadvantages

The main disadvantage of mounting exhibitions is the time and cost of preparing them (including the wine and nibbles on opening night!).

Learning journals, diaries and logs

These are not simply methods of assessment; they are also strategies for learning and development.

Advantages

Journals should be used to help learners reflect on their learning and to identify areas for improvement. This makes them invaluable in the development of independent learning, especially when used in conjunction with ILPs and as part of the Improving Own Learning Key Skill. Diaries and logs may also be used for assessment; one of their main benefits is that they provide continuity and structure for learners, making them look back on what they have just done but also look forward and plan for the next sessions.

Disadvantages

Journals, diaries and logs can be less valuable if learners don't understand why and how they should do them. There is a danger that they will perceive them as merely something to be done for the teachers but of little value to themselves.

Informal methods of assessment

Teachers should make it apparent to learners that assessment is not always a formal and/or summative activity. Formative assessment, as previously discussed can utilise a wide range of informal ways of assessing, checking and adjusting learning. These include:

- discussion;
- question and answer;
- group work and activities;
- quizzes;
- gapped handouts;
- observation;
- reflection.

Convergent and divergent assessment

When designing and delivering assessment techniques you should consider to what extent you wish to develop *convergent* or *divergent* responses in your learners. Convergent and divergent are not mutually exclusive; your assessments may be either or both, or a range in between the two.

Convergent assessment is relatively 'closed' or focused; that is, one particular answer or solution to the problem. Multiple-choice, computerised objective tests or short answer tests tend to be convergent. Convergent assessments are easier to mark, especially in computer-aided form but can end up just as 'quiz' type tests which only measure learners' recall.

Divergent assessment tends to be more open and is aimed at generating a range of response or alternative solutions to problems. Divergent activities are good for problem-solving, creativity and generating ideas. Assessments and activities such as case studies and brainstorming sessions are divergent. Essays can involve divergent thinking and encourage learners to explore a range of ideas and theories.

Giving feedback

Anecdotes of school are full of references to teacher feedback. 'Could do better', 'must try harder', even just 'good' or 'fair'. Here's an example from my own school report for 1963 (see Figure 7.1). One of my greatest achievements was to come top in composition and bottom in literature! My purpose in reproducing this is to demonstrate that limited feedback such as this is at best uninformative; at worst, demotivating. Nothing in this indicates how improvements can be made, what 'fair' means or what 'good' means. Clearly this is a worst-case scenario but you will probably have seen a few examples from post-compulsory education which 'could do better'.

What is feedback and what is it for?

Feedback is an essential element in effective communication between teachers and learners. This interpretation of feedback is used in the same

Subjects	Marks		Position	Remarks	Initials
	Max.	Actual			
English Studies:					
Composition ...	100	78	1	Some good work done.	
Comprehension ...	100	44	35		
Language ...	75	38	28		
Literature ...	25	9	44		
Mathematics ...	200	132	31	Has made progress.	D.T.
Geography ...	100	48	29	Only fair.	
History ...	100	47	22	Fairly good	
Science ...	100	82	4	Very good progress made.	
Biology ...					
Handicraft (Wood) ...		c		Fair	
Handicraft (Metal) ...		c+		Fair	
Tech. Drawing ...	50	19	19	Not enough Hand work done.	
Homecraft ...					
Needlecraft ...					
Art and Craft ...		c		Tries - but finds the subject difficult	D.P.S.
Music ...	100	43	29	Fair	
Divinity ...					
Physical Education ...		B-		His enthusiasm has brought about good result. Keep it up.	

Figure 7.1 School report.

way when we look at assessment *for* learning; the willingness of learners and teachers to give and receive feedback is at the heart of formative assessment. Moorse and Clough (2002) state that assessment should involve learners; it is a two-way process. Feedback makes communication, teaching, learning and assessment into a two-way process. Feedback is one of the most powerful methods for improving learning. In this section I want to concentrate on the more specific meaning of feedback: the giving of information, advice and guidance to help learners improve using written and/or oral methods.

Guidelines for giving feedback to learners

- Feedback should be positive. In both written and oral feedback teachers should indicate learners' achievements and areas of strength. The 'positive sandwich' is made up two slices of positive, encouraging feedback, with a filling of specific reference to areas for improvement. In oral feedback, the positive element is reinforced by body language and tone of voice.
- Feedback should be targeted and identify specific areas for development in knowledge and skills.
- Feedback should be positive. In any area of life we feel better when people tell us that we have done something well; this is especially true of education and learning. However, students can soon become habituated to constant praise without any points for improvement.
- Feedback should be motivating and should encourage learners to want to do more. Limited or excessively critical feedback is demotivating.
- Feedback should be clear and unambiguous and, wherever possible, clearly related to learning outcomes.
- Feedback should take time. When learners have spent a lot of time on their work, cursory feedback or just a brief written comment is very dispiriting. Plan time to give whole-group feedback on general points, but also allow time for individual tutorials; you might think it's costly in time, but remember the power of feedback.
- If a student's work is a fail or a referral you must indicate precisely what they need to do in order to achieve a pass.
- Use feedback as 'scaffolding' to help them get to the next stage of their learning.
- Feedback should be part of a culture of high expectations. All learners can improve and we should expect them to. There is no point in 'labelling' learners as 'successes' or 'failures'; 'academic' or 'not academic'. Think back to humanism in Chapter 3, 'Learning theories' – effective learning requires low threat (negative feedback can feel like

a threat) with high challenge.

- When marking written work, don't return scripts covered in wounds inflicted by red pen, and avoid crosses and crossing out. When writing feedback remember that students can't hear you; be careful about the 'tone' of your comments.
- When giving grades in marked work, make sure that students know how to interpret their grades; share the criteria with them.
- In tutorial sessions or ILP reviews, feedback from individual pieces of work can contribute to an overall picture of the learner's progress and identify any general trends or areas for development.

The emotional impact of assessment

One of the basic tenets of this book is that there is both an intellectual and an emotional component in learning; I would suggest that the emotional element has the greatest impact on learners' achievements. Nowhere is this emotional impact more pervasive than in the area of assessment. Assessment experiences have lifelong effects on people's lives and their life chances. Assessments of our performance are intimately bound up with our feelings about ourselves, our confidence and self-esteem. For many adults, their perceptions of themselves as 'successes' or 'failures' or as intelligent or not, stem in no small part from their experiences of assessment and the judgements made about them. In the lifelong learning sector we have to help learners, and potential learners, to change their self-concept even before they cross the threshold.

Anxiety about tests, it appears, begins quite early in life. Recent research suggests that the happiness and well-being of children begins to decline from Year 6, in part, it is suggested, because of the introduction of formal testing. With formal testing there is always the danger that the tests will become the end rather than the means and that children – and teachers, managers, parents and politicians – will judge them solely on test results. Excessive formal, summative testing can reinforce young people's and adults' views of their abilities and the factors to which they attribute success or failure. This is particularly true of learners who are less able and who can't achieve success within the fairly narrow range of teaching and assessment they encounter.

Much of the above discussion underlines our beliefs about ability and intelligence and the extent to which we believe these are innate and fixed or acquired and, therefore, susceptible to improvement. Claxton (1999) contrasts Chinese and Asian cultural attitudes towards learning in which, with effort and persistence, anyone can learn and achieve, with Western cultures which hold 'ability' to be the major determinant of success in learning. Such beliefs in innate ability match the belief in the importance and the measurability of something called IQ. Intelligence quotient continues to be perceived, both in educational reality and public perception, as an innate and fixed quality which means that some people are 'bright', 'academic' or 'gifted' whilst others are not. You can read criticisms of IQ elsewhere but, suffice to say, many educationalists have criticised IQ tests as being a measure of a limited set of skills and abilities – particularly mathematical and logical – if, indeed they are a measure of anything at all.

Such is the pervasiveness of these notions of fixed ability that they disproportionately influence learners' self-esteem and confidence. As Claxton (1999: 27) says, 'On this Western view, it is one's own personal identity that is a stake. To be lacking in ability is to be wanting as a person.'

Attribution, performance goals and learning goals

Key to understanding learners' self-esteem is the idea of attribution – do they attribute their success or a failure to something they have control over and can change and improve or, conversely, do they believe that some people are just naturally bright and intelligent whilst others aren't? Carol Dweck (2000) suggests that learners have two different goal orientations. These are:

- *learning goals* – in which individuals strive to increase their competence, to understand and master something new; and
- *performance goals* – in which individuals strive either to document, or gain favourable judgements of, their competence or to avoid negative judgements of their competence.

To use a footballing analogy, a young person who dazzles with his ball skills will often be applauded by his peers and teachers as someone with an innate ability. Others, no matter how hard they try, might make marginal improvements but can never achieve such heights of skill. The presence or absence of the skill is regarded just as a matter of good fortune. When applied to football, this seems a relatively harmless doctrine, but when applied to learning and general ability it can be devastating.

Dweck suggests that those with learning goals have a belief in themselves and their ability to learn; they view challenges positively, tend to be less put off by failure, persist in efforts to improve and tend to have an incremental rather than a fixed theory of intelligence. Conversely, those with performance goals tend to see ability as a fixed entity and attribute failure to low ability. They tend to give up, or become upset, in the face of difficulty. They tend to concentrate their efforts on getting favourable results and praise.

Teachers should reject ideas of fixed ability and commit ourselves to the notion that everyone can learn and develop. Whilst we recognise that some will learn and develop more rapidly than others, it is our job to support all learners and to help them to believe that they can succeed and to have some control over their own learning and development. These principles should be uppermost in our minds when designing and implementing learning and assessment schemes.

For your journal

If you haven't already done so for your ILP, carry out an audit of the assessment methods you use. Ask yourself why you use them. Is it habit, because someone else suggested it or because that's the way it's always been done?

What assessment methods have you not used? Could they be incorporated into your teaching?

In what ways have you given feedback to learners? How have they reacted to it and have there been signs of development?

Carry out some research with your learners; ask them what forms of assessment they find most helpful for learning.

Journal extract: Philip

Last week I set an essay on the sociology of the family. I was really rushed to get them marked and returned on time – I didn't want to keep them waiting. When I gave them back they didn't seem very interested and just stuck them in their files. I tried to go over some of the main points applicable to them all but there wasn't much discussion. My mentor said that my comments were too brief and that I hadn't really said how they could improve. She suggested that I should try individual tutorials to discuss their work. This is very time-consuming. They need practice writing essays because they have to do them in the exam, but I'm not sure essays are always the best way.

Further reading and useful websites

Ecclestone, K. (2005) *Understanding Assessment and Qualifications in Post-compulsory Education and Training: Principles, Policies and Practice*, 2nd edn. Leicester: NIACE.

Tummons, J. (2005) *Assessing Learning in Further Education*. Exeter: Learning Matters Ltd.

www.qca.org.uk Qualifications and Curriculum Authority. Download copies of *Characteristics of Assessment for Learning* and *The 10 Principles of AfL*.

8 Resources for teaching and learning

What this chapter is about

- Critically examining a range of resources, including: printed, projected, non-projected, digital
- Selecting appropriate resources
- Designing, making or adapting resources as appropriate
- Design principles for printed and projected resources
- Advantages and disadvantages of different resources
- Evaluating and improving teaching and learning resources

LLUK standards

This chapter covers:

BK 1.3; BK 2.1; BP 2.1; BK 2.2; BP 2.2; BK 2.3; BP 2.3; BK 3.1; BP 3.1
BK 5.1; BP 5.1 BK 5.2; BP 5.2
CK 3.5; CP 3.5
DK 1.2; DP 1.2

What is a resource?

The precise definitions of and differences between methods, strategies, techniques and resources occupy considerable space in some texts; I don't intend to add much to that debate here. Methods and strategies are generally concerned with the selection, combination and use of various teaching and learning activities, such as discussion, role play or demonstration. Resources are the things which teachers, and learners, use to support that learning. They are sometimes referred to as 'learning aids'. Thus a demonstration of using a microphone in music technology might be supported by real microphones and/or a PowerPoint presentation.

Why use resources?

This is probably a more important question than what a resource is because if we consider *why* we use resources, we are on the way to using them appropriately to suit the learners and the learning outcomes. It will help us to become more reflective in the selection, use and evaluation of a range of resources.

These are some of the reasons why we use a range of resources:

- *They add variety.* Effective learning requires a range of inputs and stimuli to engage and maintain the interest of learners.
- *They appeal to different senses.* Spoken input from a teacher loses its effect quite quickly. The introduction of a visual or moving image, sound, objects or a combination of these will arouse other senses and can help to re-engage your learners.
- *They appeal to different learning styles.* Well planned and imaginative use of resources will meet the preferences of all learners – visual, auditory and kinaesthetic.
- *They reinforce learning.* Multisensory inputs such as a spoken description of photosynthesis accompanied by an animated projected diagram, can help to reinforce learning.
- *They help understanding.* The use of visual images, particularly, can help learners to see 'the big picture' and to connect ideas more effectively.
- *They aid retention.* If learning resources help learners to visualise and connect learning they will also aid retention of learning.
- *They develop thinking skills.* Using a range of resources can help learners to retain information but also to use it more effectively for analysis, synthesis and evaluation.
- *They support explanations and demonstrations.* Effective use of resources make it easier for teachers to explain concepts and facilitate demonstrations.

Being visual

Very young children look at pictures and then start to associate words with them. Thus, a picture of an apple is accompanied by the word 'apple'. As the child becomes older the picture is removed and only the word (spoken or written) remains. Hearing or seeing the word 'apple' will produce a mental referent or image in the child's mind. This transition from recognising pictures to recognising words is the transition from *iconic* to *symbolic representation*. Icons are representations – photographs, pictures or drawings – which actually look like the real thing, as in the picture of the apple. Words are symbols which don't physically resemble the real thing; they've just become associated with it. Pictures of apples are the same in English or French; the words 'apple' and 'pomme' are not the same.

There is a temptation to assume that maturity means we should be able to understand most things by words rather than by visual images. The question, 'Do you want me to draw you a picture?' is generally intended as an insult to people unable to understand something represented in written or spoken words. However, when we encounter a new concept or idea it can be difficult to visualise it and to connect it to previous learning; a visual image often helps understanding. Obviously, a physics teacher will show a visual image of various atoms when explaining them, or art students will need pictures by Van Gogh before they can discuss his work, but perhaps we can consider using visuals in less obvious cases. As a social sciences student, initially I struggled to grasp Marxist theory but it became clearer when I drew a big box labelled 'Proletariat' with a much smaller box, labelled 'Bourgeoisie', above it. Having started with a simple, static framework I could add an increasing number of complicating factors. It's easier to start simple and add complexity. The level of simplicity you start at is negotiated with your learners.

Choosing, using and evaluating resources

The ASSURE model

Heinich et al. (1999) recommend a six stage model for the use of resources. The model fits in with reflective practice and can also be used as a method of reviewing and evaluating resources in your PDJ and session evaluations. The stages are:

Analyse learners
State objectives
Select resources
Use resources
Require learner participation
Evaluate and revise

Analyse learners

Knowing your learners is the key to planning and preparing effective teaching and learning, especially the selection and use of resources. Factors which will influence your choice of resources include:

Level. Resource choices will vary according to the level of your learners. Those working at entry level will require different content and style of resources on punctuation and grammar from students on an AS English language course. The style is also important; many pre-prepared worksheets for Skills for Life have rather childish drawings and presentation which is inappropriate for adults with reading and writing difficulties.

Age. Materials designed for 16–19-year-old learners may prove unsuitable for adults. Design features and references in the text to popular culture probably won't work for adult learners. It's also important to bear in mind that younger learners will increasingly have become habituated to fast-moving, short attention span activities such as they might experience through digital technology at home.

Motivation. It's often assumed that those in further and adult education are there because they have chosen to be. Unfortunately, this isn't always true. Less willing learners will appreciate resources and teaching methods which involve and interest them in the topic.

Previous learning and experience. You will need to choose and plan your resources with consideration of prior learning and experience. Learners encountering difficult concepts for the first time need to have them clearly introduced and explained.

Learning styles. In any group of learners there will be a range of learning styles and preferences which you need to cater for. You won't be able to please all of the people all of the time, but a variety of resources – video, printed resources, ILT – will help to engage all of them for most of the time.

State objectives

When choosing teaching and learning resources you need to be clear about why you are using them and what it is that you want your learners to know or be able to do – what is the learning outcome? The objectives could be those, or one of those, you have written for your lesson plan. In a numeracy session for example, the objective 'learners will add and subtract numbers' could involve physical resources (counters, sweets, blocks) rather than paper-based sums.

Using objectives based on Bloom's taxonomy (knowledge, comprehension, application, analysis, synthesis and evaluation) will help you to define the learning experiences and appropriate resources.

Select resources

Having analysed your learners and identified the objectives, you will need to select resources which are most appropriate for learners and purpose. The bulk of this chapter is concerned with the discussion of a range of resources for teaching and learning. One of your first tasks as a beginning teacher is to familiarise yourself with the range of resources available to you where you work but also from other sources. In larger organisations there are likely to be media technicians and IT technicians who can advise you on resource provision.

The most frequently used resources, which we will examine in more detail later, include:

- whiteboards;
- overhead projectors (OHP);
- flipcharts;
- DVD/video;
- printed resources (handouts, worksheets, readings, gapped handouts);
- models and 'realia';
- libraries and learning centres;
- visits and trips;
- IT/Internet/digital technology;
- interactive whiteboards;
- PowerPoint presentations.

In many cases, you will be producing your own resources. These might vary from the relatively straightforward design and production of printed resources, PowerPoints, or card sort activities to more complex pieces of equipment. I have seen trainee teachers produce quite sophisticated resources, for example, a 'light box' to demonstrate the colour spectrum or a PowerPoint projection including film clips for textual analysis.

Use resources

This step is the whole point of the exercise – actually using the resources. However, be wary of diving straight in and using your resources without adequate trial and preparation. There is a series of five simple steps, recommended by Heinich et al. which will guide you through preparation and use of resources. These are the '5 Ps'.

1 Preview the materials. Don't use any thing you haven't previewed first to check for suitability and appropriateness for learners. The first time

you see a DVD shouldn't be when you use it in the session. It might be too long, contain inappropriate content, or simply just not work. You might find that you need to edit a DVD or just show part of it.

2   Prepare the materials. The resources need to built into the structure of your session plan and the order of their use determined. It's a good idea to have a column on your session plan for resources and to summarise them on the front sheet. If the resources include equipment for learners to use, be sure you have enough of them readily available and try to anticipate any other equipment they might need.

3   Prepare the environment. Check equipment is available and working. Some projected resources require a darkened room so you need to check that blinds are working and effective and also adjust seating arrangements so learners can see and hear properly.

4   Prepare the learners. The content and objectives of all learning sessions should be made clear to learners from the start. You must prepare your learners for the resource you are about to use. If it's a video or DVD, explain why you are showing it and what you want the group to get from it. A video might be supported by a question sheet or prompt sheet of things to look for.

5   Provide the learning experience. In other words, use the resource. If you have gone through the previous steps carefully, you will lessen the chances of thing going wrong.

Require learner participation

Learners should not just be passive viewers or consumers of resources. This book is based on the belief that learning should be active and based on constructivist principles of learning. A video should stimulate discussion, analysis and evaluation of its content and its application to the topic. PowerPoint presentations shouldn't merely present; they should leave spaces where learners can offer responses and ideas. Printed resources become more meaningful to learners if they can personalise them and interact with them in some way.

Evaluate and revise

All resources can and should be refined and improved with subsequent use. In some cases they might be rejected as unsuitable for purpose. Evaluation and revision is part of being a reflective teacher committed to continuing improvement. Part of your resource evaluation might be done by 'reflection in action': by watching your learners and their reactions to the resource. You can easily detect 'Death by PowerPoint' by observing your learners' body language. You can also seek specific feedback on it and ask learners if it helped their understanding of the topic. Course or module evaluation questionnaires usually include feedback on resource provision and use.

Obviously, the ultimate test of a resource is whether it achieved the required purpose. One test of this is learner performance: can they do what you wanted them to do or do they know what you wanted? You should also ask yourself, and your learners, if the resource can be used differently or adapted in some way; whether it represented an effective use of time. Did the resource arouse learners' interest and attention; did it stimulate discussion or encourage learners to engage with the task?

All of these questions should stimulate analysis and evaluation of the resource and any necessary modifications and improvements for future use.

Resources for teaching and learning

This section is an introductory survey of a range of resources; it is not an exhaustive list. You will find others or observe colleagues using others. You will also start to develop your own which will be hybrids of these, or something completely new.

Whiteboards

Whiteboards have almost completely replaced chalkboards in educational establishments. Rather than discuss the merits and demerits of whiteboards, I offer some guidance to their use.

Guidelines for using whiteboards

- Avoid 'absent-minded professor' style rambling, scrawling coverage of the board. Keep the content well organised and to a minimum.
- Use the right pens. Ensure that the pen you are using says 'dry wipe' or 'whiteboard marker'. Permanent markers are not suitable and require special solvents to remove them. Never keep permanent and dry wipe markers in the same place.
- An interactive board is *not* a whiteboard. You cannot write on an interactive whiteboard with any can kind of marker other than the stylus provided with it. If you're planning to use an interactive board, it's best not to bring any markers into the room.
- Keep the writing legible, clear and a size that can be read by all. If in doubt walk to the back of the room and see if you can read it.
- Use capitals and lower case printed letters. Don't use capitals only; they are more difficult to read.

- Organise your board use with headings, subheadings, boxes and bullet points.
- Use diagrams and concept maps.
- Keep board writing to a minimum. As far as possible use it to provide advance organisers and to summarise key points. You might find it useful to write your objectives on the board before the start of the session. If you have extensive written input, plan it in to your session and prepare an overhead transparency (OHT) or PowerPoint.
- Try to avoid lengthy periods with your back to the audience as you write and don't speak to the board.

Overhead projector

Data projectors and PowerPoint have not taken over completely. It's probably still true to say that the most widely used method of displaying information to groups, especially large groups, is by using overhead projection. Lifelong learning takes place in a variety of situations many of which will not have enough funds to install expensive data projectors and interactive boards.

First, let's get the terminology right. An OHT is an overhead transparency; the acetate on which you write or print what you want to project. An OHP, an overhead projector, is the device you put the OHT on to project it. The chief advantage of an OHP is that you don't have to have your back to the audience as you do when using a whiteboard. The key to using an OHP effectively is to practise and experiment. If you're a trainee teacher you should get the opportunity to use one – if not, ask for it.

Guidelines for using overhead projectors

- Experiment and practise so that you can be confident in classes. Practise placing and moving the OHP, adjusting the focus and moving the projector nearer or further away to alter the size of the image. Practise pointing things out by pointing at the transparency, not the screen.
- Design – the best OHTs are used as frameworks for learning. Keep the number of words to minimum. Try to limit the number of lines to 8–10, double-spaced, and use bullet points to increase emphasis and focus.
- Design – use twenty point minimum font size to ensure that the OHT is visible by all. Go to the back of the room and check visibility; you shouldn't have to ask people if they can see.
- Use capitals and lower case letters, not all capitals. Use landscape rather than portrait layout.
- OHT pens come in a variety of colours in both permanent and non-

permanent forms. However, it's probably best to design your OHT on a computer and then use inkjet or laser printer transparencies to print directly on to. Alternatively, you can photocopy directly on to transparencies but be sure to use ones which are specifically designed for this purpose. Using write-on acetates in a photocopier will cause serious damage – not to mention embarrassment!

- You can amend and annotate your OHTs in use with non-permanent marker pens.
- Do not copy a page from a book directly on to a transparency. People will not be able to read it and you will rarely need everything that's on the page. Isolate key points or quotes and prepare them using the guidelines above.
- Don't have a series of transparencies of things for learners to copy down. There's little point in copying things. If you have designed your OHTs well, you can give learners copies which they can amend and personalise.
- Don't leave the projector running longer than necessary; the noise is annoying and the continued projection will be distracting if you've moved on to the next point.

Flipcharts

Flipcharts are large pads of paper, usually supported on a stand, which can be used in a similar way to a whiteboard when there isn't one available. Flipcharts can be used in more informal, student-centred sessions where you want to record, and refer back to, the narrative of the session and identify the key points. Individual sheets can be torn off and given to learners to use in group activities, which are then stuck on the walls for student presentations and reference purposes. Some teachers use prepared flipchart sequences which they can take to learning sessions at a variety of venues. However, the production of these is time-consuming and increasingly is not necessary where OHPs or data projectors are available.

DVD, video and audio

I have to admit that in my early days of teaching liberal studies to day-release, vocational students in a further education college, I frequently found myself with little time to prepare and only a vague idea of what to teach. Like many of my colleagues, I found the answer in an extensive collection of videos kept in a cupboard. 'Show 'em a video,' was the maxim of the hard-pressed liberal studies lecturer. This is very bad advice and, under no circumstances, should it be followed. Being a reflective teacher, however, I learned a lot from this experience; mainly, not to use too much video. Audio recordings are still used but generally in specific subjects or topic areas. Studying poetry is enhanced by hearing the poems recited and it's easy to locate recordings, often by the poet, from various websites. Music, obviously, needs to be heard. Audio allows learners to concentrate on the sound and structure of musical pieces, without the competing stimulus of the visual element. Digital technology is making it much easier to find and select music; you can even incorporate sound clips into PowerPoint presentations. Video recordings, and increasingly DVD, provide valuable learning experiences provided that their use is properly planned and prepared.

Guidelines for using video and DVD

- In the session planning and resource selection stages, it is important to be sure if and why you need to use video recordings. In some instances it is the only alternative; if hairdressing students want to observe a particular technique by a famous stylist, a video or DVD might be the only way. Video and DVD offer the possibility for learners to see experts operating in a particular field. Your reason for using video could be to provide variety in teaching techniques; there's nothing wrong with this provided the piece is relevant and brief.
- You can use video to provide an introduction or an overview to a topic; to provide 'the big picture'. A video can be used to stimulate discussion and explore issues, particularly in science, social science or humanities. Some training videos, in sport for example, can be used to demonstrate and exemplify good practice or technique.
- Having prepared the session you need to prepare the learners. State clearly what the video extract is, why you are using it and how it relates to the topic. It can be useful to point out what learners should look for or particular questions they might consider. A question sheet or key points sheet can be distributed prior to viewing, although there is a danger that learners will concentrate on the printed sheet and only look for those suggested.
- If you are using a video recording, have it set at the right starting point to avoid embarrassing searching while the group grows restless. Be sure that you know the controls of that particular machine and that the conditions – lighting, seating, visibility – are appropriate. Ensure the quality of sound and vision.
- Break up the viewing of a long extract to allow for checking of learning and discussion. Remember that people watching TV and videos at home have made a choice; in teaching you have imposed your choice. Learners will have varying attention spans and you should monitor the learners for signs of boredom or distraction.

- DVD and digital technology is more manipulable and this makes selection and editing easier. You can record your own DVD of particular extracts so that you don't have to sit, or fast forward, through irrelevant material. Video clips can be inserted into Power-Point presentations and, thus, be more integrated in to the session.
- Video sites, such as YouTube, carry a bewildering variety of short films. It might be more convenient for you to use this than go to the trouble of setting up the equipment.
- There must be a proper follow-up to the use of video; this is more likely to happen if you have prepared learners beforehand. Remember, a video is not an end in itself; it has a purpose. That purpose may be to stimulate discussion, to identify key points, for analysis, for recognition of good practice or for criticism and evaluation.
- Whatever happens, don't let the end of the video coincide with the end of the session. If it does, there will be no time for discussion or feedback and learners will not easily recall in the next session.

Printed resources

Handbooks

Course handbooks are vital if learners are to have 'the big picture', even if it's a short course. Learners feel ill at ease when they can't see the framework of what, why, when and how they are doing things; a course handbook provides this information and forms an intrinsic part of the course induction. It's worth spending time on the original version of the course handbook; subsequent versions will only need additions and improvements. Make it look professional and well presented by taking time and seeking advice on the design and content; it's one of the first things learners will see and helps to form an impression of the organisation and its staff. Remember, the more informed and supported learners feel, the more likely they are to achieve.

The exact contents of a course handbook will vary from course to course, but the following provides some suggestions:

- details of course, title, level, relevant extracts from the specifications;
- details of staff, locations, where resources can be found;
- course map, showing the sequence and timings of the units or modules. Try to provide a visual map of the course structure;
- schedule or scheme of work. You don't need to give learners the same scheme of work document as you use but a schedule of dates with key topic areas shown is useful for them;

- key dates, for example a calendar showing dates of assessments, visits, tutorials and support sessions;
- resources – give your learners a reading list and details of relevant websites and journals;
- assessments – indicate the range, frequency and type of assessment during the course.

Design the handbook so learners can add to it and personalise it and make sure it's a working document that is regularly referred to by learners and teachers. You can make them available electronically via an intranet for students who prefer to work this way and access things from home.

Module handbooks provide specific details of each element of the course and serve as an introduction to new modules or units. Module handbooks provide specific details of the assessments and can also include overviews of any relevant theories or key ideas. A good module handbook will serve as an advance organiser for a module and will aid learners in making sense of and organising their work.

Handouts

What is a handout? The easy answer is that it is a paper-based resource that you hand out to learners. But do we think enough about why and how we use them? Do our learners know clearly what they are for and what to do with them? Student feedback often criticises the use of too many handouts. Conversely, handouts can encourage laziness and poor attendance; if students think that the handouts equal the lesson, all they need to do is collect them at a later date.

Let's identify the range of handouts and why they are used:

Information sheets. A handout giving background, facts, information, statistics, can be a useful accompaniment to input from the teacher. The content should be kept to a minimum and not contain information irrelevant to the topic. The handout should support the input not distract from it. You should, wherever possible, make it interactive in some way so that learners can add to it and personalise it. This helps to make the learning meaningful.

Worksheets. These give learners something to do: they have to answer questions, add information or complete it in some way. An obvious example would be an English grammar worksheet on using apostrophes. You can obtain or produce a range of worksheets at different levels so that you can differentiate the learning within a group. They can also be used independently by learners in their own time.

Activity sheets: These are similar to worksheets, but are generally used to support a student (often group) activity. Examples would be a problem that learners have to solve, a mini-case study or a discussion point. Instructions for a particular exercise can be provided on an activity sheet.

Notes. These might be more appropriate for a lecture where you provide copies of your notes, or PowerPoint presentation, to your learners. Again, the question is, why? You might feel it's wasted effort for learners to write as much as they can of what you say or to copy every slide you project so you provide them with copies of the notes. It's important to ensure that learners do something with them to make them personal and to incorporate the learning.

Readings. It's sometimes appropriate to give learners a reading – perhaps an extract from a book, journal, newspaper or magazine article. Be prepared to edit and keep it to the minimum required. Avoid photocopying a page from a book because it can look scruffy and unprofessional; scanners are easy to use and a scanned copy can be stored electronically, retrieved and modified as required. Newspaper articles can generally be downloaded from the site and adapted to purpose. You might want to provide some questions and activities at the end of the article.

Gapped handouts. These are a useful learning and assessment device. The text of the handout leaves gaps for learners to fill or to answer questions. A particular form is the cloze exercise in which learners have to supply specific words to fit in the gaps, either from a list provided or from learners' memories.

An example of a cloze exercise in literacy on the use of 'their', 'there' and 'they're', could include the following examples:

'_ _ _ _ _ _ _ coming for dinner'

'I left my bike over _ _ _ _ _ '

'Have you seen _ _ _ _ _ photographs?'

A house style for printed resources

This is not just a case of style over content. Using a document template for your printed resources looks professional but also can help your learners to organise their files and resources more easily (see Figure 8.1). Use the organisation logo and perhaps a course logo you have designed. Include the course and unit or module title and a space for the learners to write the date. Dating printed resources is one of the most useful things you can do to help students organise their work in their files. If the budget will run to it you could print different modules on different coloured paper, but check with your learners to see if it suits them – some dyslexic learners prefer everything on yellow paper.

**FAB
College**
*Further and
Better*

AS Media Studies

Module 2:   Analysing Media Texts

Date_____

Figure 8.1 Example of handout template.

Design guidelines for printed resources

It's worth spending some time considering the design and presentation of your printed resources to make them more attractive and easier to use. The Basic Skills Agency provides an excellent guide to readability which can be downloaded from their website (*www.basic-skills.co.uk/resources/resources searchresults/detail.php?ResourceID=1603834202332*). This guide provides valuable design advice for materials for all learners, not just those with reading problems.

- *White space*. Avoid handouts which are too crowded. Leave space between paragraphs and wide margins to allow for easier reading and to give room for learners' annotations. Acres of densely packed text are off-putting for anyone. Avoid using newspaper-style columns.
- *Line spacing*. Lines too close together can be difficult to read. Consider using 1.5 line spacing; in some cases double line spacing might be necessary.
- *Font choice and size*. Modern computers provide a huge variety of fonts, many of which just look silly. You can use a fancy font or WordArt design for a logo or heading, but for text the best choices are those given in Figure 8.2.
- *Headings*. Use headings to organise the text. The heading can be in a larger or emboldened typeface to provide emphasis. Don't use capital letters for headings. In general, it's best to avoid overuse of capitals.
- *Illustrations and clipart*. These can help to break up text and make it more interesting and readable. You should choose the number and style of illustrations to suit your learners; some might feel patronised by excessive and or irrelevant clipart.

Learning centres and libraries

If you teach in college, school or university you will almost certainly have access to a learning centre – most people working in information services

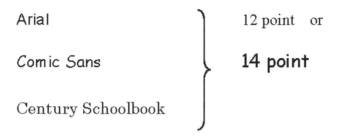

Figure 8.2 Recommended fonts and sizes for printed resources.

prefer the term 'learning centre' because they don't just provide books. A well-equipped learning centre is likely provide, at least, the following:

- books;
- academic journals;
- newspapers and magazines;
- video/DVD and audio recordings;
- CD–Rom;
- Internet access;
- inter-library loans and electronic access to materials in other places;
- study skills materials;
- photocopying/laminating/binding facilities.

In addition, your learning centre should provide access to vast stores of research and knowledge through information systems such as ERIC (Educational Resource Information Centre) which is the world's largest educational database. Similar services are provided by EBSCO, who specialise in electronic journals; InfoTrac for online newspaper archives, and several publishers who provide e-books. There are many reference services, such as the Oxford Reference Online, which provides dictionaries, thesauruses and a wide range of specialist dictionaries.

Get to know your learning centre colleagues

People who work in learning centres are proud of what they do and want to use their skills and knowledge to help you. In many organisations they are encouraged to provide sessions for learners on, for example, finding books or finding electronic resources. Learning centre staff can advise you on finding information, with developing the stock of books and materials for you and your learners, and can even help you devise assignments.

Digital technology is bringing a convergence of the activities of learning and teaching, learning and information services and ILT. To provide the best for your learners you should develop good working relationships with these colleagues. Your induction into the organisation should include these elements; if it doesn't you should seek it out.

If you don't work for a large organisation or work at an outreach centre you may not have such easy access to facilities. If you have computers and Internet access you will be able to access almost as much information as anyone else, although some subscriber services will be beyond the reach of your budget. If you have space you can start your own mini-library of books and other printed materials relevant to your teaching area. Your learners can be co-opted into this enterprise by locating and providing resources which the whole group can share.

Models and 'realia'

'Realia' is a horrible word; it simply means real things. In junior school we had a nature table to which I, being a country kid, contributed armfuls of sticky buds. Sometimes we need not only to see things but also to touch, move and manipulate them; this is especially true for learners with a kinaesthetic preference. In the first FE college I worked at the motor vehicle department had an excellent cutaway engine which could be turned by means of a handle to show the movement of pistons, valves and other elements. Such sophisticated working models are rare now because of expense, but it's worth approaching manufacturers and employers for help or for old things you can modify or adapt.

Models can be used to support demonstrations. I recently observed a trainer in the ambulance service explaining anatomy using a full-scale, accurate skeleton which could be disassembled and assembled. It was particularly useful in asking the learners to identify bones, groups of bones and the relationships between them.

In the skeleton example, scale and accuracy are important, but models don't always have to be so accurate. In science teaching models of atoms enlarge the structure and allow learners to disassemble and manipulate the electrons and protons. Many objects can be pressed into service to demonstrate and explain; I recall my brother using a football, marbles, apples and oranges to explain the solar system to me. The exact proportions and distances could not be accurately scaled down but the demonstration really captured my imagination.

Visits and trips

Sometimes you just have to go and see things. Anyone studying the Industrial Revolution in England will find the learning significantly enhanced by a visit to Ironbridge and Coalbrookdale to see where it all began. Museums and art galleries are the obvious choices for visits and the educational facilities are becoming increasingly sophisticated and interactive. Most museums and art galleries have websites which show some of their major exhibits; a virtual visit is not as good as the real thing but it can help you to plan and prepare for the actual visit and decide what you most need to see and do.

Visits can be arranged to give learners insights into particular areas of work, for example, business and retail, childcare, health care, construction and engineering. Before taking learners on visits you must check the policy and guidelines relating to visits and seek permission from parents if necessary. You must also ensure that appropriate insurance, health and safety regulations and risk assessments are arranged.

ILT

It isn't compulsory to use ILT but it's increasingly difficult not to and you and your learners will be missing a great many opportunities if you don't integrate it into your work. Furthermore, because of regular use in schools and elsewhere, your future learners will arrive with the expectation that ILT is central to the process of learning not just a resource. Using ILT won't make a bad teacher good; an ineffective teacher with a data projector and PowerPoint will probably remain ineffective but in new and surprising ways. An effective and reflective teacher will use ILT to enhance and develop her *teaching*, not just her use of ILT.

It's useful to speculate on the future by considering the concept of 'digital immigrants' and 'digital natives' put forward by Marc Prensky (2001). 'Digital immigrants' includes anybody above the age of about 20 who, though they try to learn and catch up with the latest digital technology, have not grown up with it. 'Digital natives' have never known life without digital technology and its concomitant devices. Prensky suggests, somewhat controversially, that their brains have developed differently. The following is a description of a 'digital native' from a *Sunday Times* article by Richard Woods:

> Emily Feld is a native of a new planet. While the 20-year-old university student may appear to live in London, she actually spends much of her time in another galaxy – out there, in the digital universe of websites, e-mails, text messages and mobile phone calls. The behaviour of Feld and her generation, say experts, is being shaped by digital technology as never before, taking her boldly where no generation has gone before. It may even be the next step in evolution, transforming brains and the way we think.

> 'First thing every morning I wake up, check my mobile for messages, have a cup of tea and then check my e-mails,' says Feld. 'I may have a look at

Facebook.com, a website connecting university students, to see if someone has written anything on my "wall". I'm connected to about 80 people on that. It's really addictive. I'll then browse around the internet, and if a news article on Yahoo catches my eye, I'll read it. And I may upload my iTunes page to see if any of my subscribed podcasts have come in.

'The other day, I went to meet a friend in town, and was about two minutes away when I realised I'd left my mobile phone at home. I travelled the five miles back to collect it. I felt so completely lost without it, I panicked. I need to have it on me at all times. I sound really sad, but everyone I know is the same. Everyone talks to each other through the internet or with mobiles. Technology is an essential part of my everyday social and academic life. I don't know where I'd be without it. In fact, I've never really been without it.'

(Woods 2006)

This person might represent an extreme version of the 'digital native' and Marc Prensky's dichotomy between 'native' and 'immigrant' is too rigid for some educationalists, but it does underline the rapid and continuing change which the lifelong learning sector will have to fit in with. The key point is the convergence of a range of devices and practice round one technology – digital.

An extensive investigation and evaluation of ILT is beyond the scope of an introductory text such as this, but we need a brief survey of the field and the ways in which it can enhance learning and teaching.

Terminology

Powell et al. (2003) developed the diagram shown in Figure 8.3, based on the original by Markos Tikris of the Learning and Skills Development Agency to explain the relationship between the key terms.

Information technology (IT) simply refers to the equipment such as, computers, printers and scanners. The computer is the hub around which all the various technologies converge and interact.

Information and communication technology (ICT) is what you get when you connect computers within an institution via a local area network (LAN) or an intranet, or beyond it via the Internet.

E-learning is the use of IT/ICT to support teaching and learning specifically not including the management of the business. e-learning ranges from the provision of, for example, computers and CD-Roms in a teaching room, through to the provision of wholly on-line learning which can be accessed

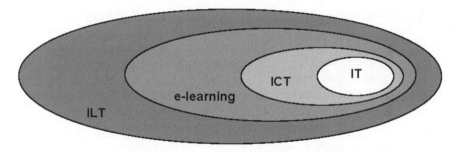

Figure 8.3 The relationship between the key elements of ILT.

at any place and time. The mixing of traditional teaching and learning with e-learning in various proportions is often referred to as *blended learning*.

Information and learning technology (ILT) refers to the application of IT/ICT to the main business of the organisation, learning and teaching, but also the management and business systems.

Using ILT to enhance and develop teaching and learning

You might not consider yourself a champion of e-learning but it's almost certain that you will have been involved in some way, even if only limited. If you have used word-processing and clipart to produce handouts, accessed the Internet or used PowerPoint then you're already on the way. This introductory survey will include the following:

- data projectors
- interactive whiteboards
- PowerPoint
- digital cameras (still and video)
- the Internet
- blogs and e-portfolios.

Data projectors

These are the starting point for projecting anything from an electronic source to whole groups of learners. The most common uses are projecting Power-Point presentations, projecting the teacher's computer display so that it can be seen from a distance and showing video film or clips.

At present it's probably still true that most rooms used across the lifelong learning sector – FE colleges, work-based learning, adult and community learning – will not have data projectors. Some rooms will have fixed projectors, in other cases you will need a portable one. If they are available to you make sure that you get the proper training in their use and know where you can find technical support in case of problems. Unless you're an expert, it's not a good idea to stand on a table and start fiddling hopefully with the equipment. You will also need to know how to connect your laptop to the system and connect to a network, if available. Learn and practise the use of the technology before you meet the learners.

Interactive whiteboards

The interactive whiteboard looks like an ordinary whiteboard but with a computer image projected on to it. The teacher, or learners, can touch the board to control the computer or write on the board electronically. The interactive whiteboard has many uses; here are a few:

- You can display any file from your computer or display Internet pages.
- You can project PowerPoint displays. Just tapping, or double tapping, the board progresses the slides or brings in animated sections.
- Using the stylus markers provided, you can use it like a conventional whiteboard, with the added facility of turning your writing into text and save it. Never have a conventional whiteboard marker anywhere near an interactive board.
- You, or the learners, can annotate PowerPoint slides using the stylus pens.
- You can save your 'board work' and convert it to handouts for your learners or store it on an intranet.
- You can use drag and drop and reveal techniques, particularly in PowerPoint and invite learners up to the board to operate these facilities.
- Drawing packages in Microsoft Word, Visio or other programs can be used to add visual elements.
- Interactive boards usually have object galleries of clip art and shapes. I've used these successfully with trainee teachers who have dragged and dropped tables and chairs around on the board to explore different room layouts.
- A whole range of programs can be used with interactive boards. Concept-mapping programs are excellent; they can be prepared beforehand and expanded and collapsed to explore connections.
- Learners and teachers can control the board and edit displays using a wireless keyboard and mouse or a tablet PC.

PowerPoint

This was designed for presenting information at conferences and meetings; it was not designed as a teaching resource. Used well PowerPoint is a useful tool which can enhance and enliven teaching presentations; used badly it can make learners passive and teachers lazy. Your session planning shouldn't start with the design of a PowerPoint presentation.

When we prepare our PowerPoint presentation for the learning session, we forget that it might easily be the second, third or even fourth time that day that learners have been exposed to this resource. 'Death by PowerPoint', is a result of this program being used in dull, didactic sessions where teachers bring up a succession of slides and talk learners through them. Trainee teachers are warned of the dangers of 'chalk and talk'; the new hazard is 'click and talk'. Whilst there are no recorded cases of 'Death by PowerPoint' there are certainly instances in which learners have been bored into a state resembling death quite closely. PowerPoint used in this way is nothing more than a 'posh' use of OHTs, especially if learners are required to copy the content of each slide. Excessive reliance on this program, like excessive use of OHTs, can have a 'distancing' effect in that it separates teachers from learners and comes between them. In the worst instances, teachers stop being teachers and just operators of technology.

Another downside of PowerPoint is that it can encourage the over-use of flashy, animated graphics; inappropriate clipart and animations flying in from all angles accompanied by the sound of applause, screeching tyres or ricocheting bullets. We know that a variety of stimuli – visual, colourful, moving, auditory – can help to engage learners with different learning styles, but excessive use of these things can result merely in style over content. Just because the program can do it doesn't mean you've got to use it.

Having apparently demolished the potential of this resource, we can now consider how it can be used effectively in teaching and learning. The best use of PowerPoint involves using it in a way which provides a framework for the session. If there are things that you would regularly write on a whiteboard in more or less the same way, you could put them on to PowerPoint slide; the slides then become a backdrop to the session rather than the main focus of it. Using bullet points can be a useful device for summarising the key points of a topic or of a learning session and it's a good technique to use custom animation to introduce them one by one. You should remember to include learners' summary points otherwise it just gives the appearance that the teacher knows all the answers. PowerPoint can be used successfully with an interactive whiteboard to add learners' points and convert them to text.

Design hints for PowerPoint slides:

- Font size should be 24pt minimum. Design templates are often set with 40pt for titles and 28pt for body text; this can be too much, so feel free to adjust it.

- Line spacing should ideally be 1.5 or even double. As with OHTs, avoid too many lines per slide, perhaps 6 maximum.
- Avoid too much content. Slides which are crowded with text and/or graphics can be too 'noisy' and make it difficult for learners to see the main points. Remember – less is more!
- PowerPoint provides some nice design packages which automatically adjust and coordinate design, colour and font. However, you should consider designing your own, especially if you want a 'corporate image'.
- White backgrounds can be too dazzling; use a gentler, pastel shade. Some font colours, particularly bright and light ones, are difficult to read. It's generally best to stick to dark colours for fonts. If you have learners with dyslexia or sight difficulties ask them what they prefer so that you can design slides to suit them.

Be creative with PowerPoint. It can do a lot of things which many teachers don't even know about, let alone use. Features include: action buttons, animation, incorporation of video and sound, hyperlinks to other presentations, programs and websites. Try designing a PowerPoint package which is non-sequential and in which you can go to different places using action buttons. I've designed a package on using thinking skills where I can choose a topic area from the introductory page and go to it by action buttons. You can develop packages which use 'drag and drop' as matching exercises and invite people up to the board to use them. You can also use reveal techniques to uncover answers to a quiz or an assessment or to uncover concealed information. Using action buttons you can devise assessments or quizzes where people select an answer to a question and the button reveals the right or wrong answer with explanations and further information. You can download quiz timers and question ladders (see further reading, p. 225) to make them more fun. There are many gaming packages which you can download, sometimes for free.

Finally, PowerPoint can also be used by learners. Increasingly they use it give presentations of their work and in assessments (some obvious Key Skill opportunities here). They can also use it to design individual or group revision packages. You should encourage this but remind them of design principles and the danger of PowerPoint-induced boredom.

Digital cameras (still and video)

Using photography with students used to be so difficult that teachers rarely bothered. With digital cameras, some of which are very cheap, it's no longer a problem. Think of ways in which you can motivate and involve your learners by letting them use digital cameras to include images in their work and presentations, to include in blogs or on websites. Just experiment. If an image is no good, just delete it; all you are using is battery power. For example, a Key Skills Communication session on body language and facial expression could be enhanced by learners taking pictures of different expressions and using them to assess others' understanding of NVC. Clearly, the possibilities can be further extended by using video clips.

The Internet

This is so commonly used that I don't need to explain what it is. Its use is widespread in colleges and schools, not to mention controversial. Let me express my bias immediately. I feel uncomfortable when a learner's first action in any research or problem-solving is to look on the Internet. However, whether or not I feel uncomfortable is largely irrelevant because it's what young learners do. My problem is the tendency to regard everything found on the Internet to be of equal value. A search for information on Mozart will bring thousands of hits, many of which will be reliable, trustworthy and accurate; others, however, will be the products of Mozart-obsessives who have a less than impartial interpretation of him and his works. Quality control is a problem with the Internet. On the other hand, it is a very democratic medium which allows people with no previous opportunities for publishing to share ideas. It can break down the notion of experts and amateurs. Wikipedia is a very good example of a shared community of knowledge which is updated and modified by its users.

Having offered some words of caution we must accept that the Internet is a central part of life for 'digital natives' and many 'digital immigrants' and that, therefore, we need to embrace it as part of our work as teachers. It offers quick and easy access to a vast amount of information which can be accessed at any time in any place. Specialist websites exist for all areas of learning. Teachers in the lifelong learning sector are increasingly well catered for: check out the Gold Dust resources which have been developed by the Standards Unit of the DfES.

Blogs

This is shorthand for 'weblogs'. These are online personal logs or diaries which groups or individuals develop to share ideas and points of view. Many of your learners will write their own weblogs and will want to use this format to record their learning journals and submit them for assessment. Some colleges actively encourage this and have developed systems to accommodate them. Personalised learning is likely to become electronic with the development of e-portfolios. Futurelab's report 'Personalisation and Digital Technologies', states that 'many learners today are already creating personalised environments for themselves outside school using digital resources' (Green et al. 2005).

For your journal

Use the ASSURE model to develop use and evaluate a learning resource.

Consider your use of PowerPoint. Do you use it sparingly or does every lesson include a PowerPoint presentation? Why do you use it? In what ways does it enhance the learning experience?

For your ILP, as well as your journal, you should consider your ILT skills and knowledge and identify areas you need to develop or improve.

Review your printed resources and your use of them. Have any learners complained of an excess of handouts? Always ask yourself why you are using handouts and what learners do with them. Do they just file them or do they personalise and integrate them into their own notes and resources?

Journal extract: Martyn, training to teach popular music

I've been developing the idea of a 'MySpace' website for the students. They'll be able to showcase their music, have a forum for discussion/moans and (most importantly) have a less formal outlet for written work which can provide assessment criteria without the stress. I launched this project and EVERYONE is up for it.

Further reading and useful websites

Hill, C. (2003) *Teaching Using Information and Learning Technology in Further Education*. Exeter: Learning Matters Ltd.

Whalley, J., Welch, T. and Williamson, L. (2006) *E-learning in FE*. London: Continuum.

www.becta.org.uk British Educational Communications and Technology Agency

http://ferl.qia.org.uk Further Education Resources for Learning. See, especially, the section on teaching and learning.

www.goldust.org.uk Learning and teaching resources developed by the Standards Unit at the DfES.

www.jisc.ac.uk Joint Information Systems Committee for leadership in the innovative use of ICT in education and research.

www.A6training.co.uk This site offers a range of timers for activities which can simply be downloaded and incorporated into PowerPoint presentations.

9 Motivation and behaviour

What this chapter is about

- The differences between extrinsic and intrinsic motivation
- The connections between motivation and behaviour
- The factors which influence learner motivation and behaviour
- The links between motivation and self-esteem
- Strategies to improve behaviour and motivate learners
- The importance of structure in planning teaching and learning to enhance motivation and behaviour

LLUK standards

This chapter covers the following standards:

AS 1; AS 1.1; AP 1.1; AK 4.1; AP 4.1
BS 1; BK 1.1; BP 1.1; BK 1.2; BP 1.2; BK 1.3; BP 1.3
BS 2; BK 2.1; BP 2.1; BK 2.2; BP 2.2; BK 2.3; BP 2.3; BK 2.5; BP 2.5
BS 3; BK 3.1; BP 3.1
CS 2; CK 2.1; CP 2.1
DK 1.2; DP 1.2

Motivation

What is motivation?

Motivation is what compels us to do things. The key point, as we shall see, is where the motivation comes from. Everyone is motivated to learn; it's part of what it means to be human. People have always learned, in fact if human beings couldn't learn we wouldn't have survived. Right from birth you learned language; nobody taught it to you, all you had to do was be surrounded by it. In school you would have been taught about grammar, spelling, punctuation and all the formal elements of language which, if they were taught well, enhanced your use and understanding of language. If they were taught badly and you didn't see the point of doing it or get any enjoyment from it, then you would have gained little – you wouldn't have been motivated to learn.

Learning is natural; education, unfortunately, isn't. This is why we need to emphasise learning more than teaching. Compared to the span of human life on Earth, formal education and its methods and purposes are relatively new. As Ian Gilbert says, 'The culmination of six million years' worth of neurological evolution is not the GCSE' (Gilbert 2002: 5). Everyone wants to learn; unfortunately they might not want to learn what *you* want them to learn, at the time and place you want them to learn or in the ways that you want them to do it. This chapter is about ways of resolving this fundamental conflict.

Activity

One way to understand motivation is to empathise with your students. Think about what does and doesn't motivate you, and then apply this to your learners; they're just the same as you.

- If you are currently on a teacher training course, what is your motivation for doing it?

- To what extent are you doing it because you want to and to what extent because you've got to?

- Which parts of the course have you most enjoyed, and which parts have you done because 'you just had to'? How and why are they different?

- Are there parts of a course that you teach which learners enjoy and are motivated by and those they 'just have to do'? Do they have to be this way?

What do we know from previous chapters?

Making links is what learning is all about and you should be making links between the various parts of this book in order to get a big picture of how learning works best. In Chapter 2, 'Communication and the teacher', we saw that learning is most effective when the *climate* is right, that is when our learners feel safe and not threatened but they also feel challenged. Nonverbal communication, including body language and voice qualities, are essential elements in creating a positive climate and motivating learners. We also discovered that the emotions affect learning more than any other factor; if learners are frightened, bored, frustrated or anxious then learning isn't possible. Daniel Goleman, says that

> Motive and emotion share the same Latin root, motere, 'to move.' Emotions are, literally, what move us to pursue our goals; they fuel our motivations, and our motives in turn drive our perceptions and shape our actions. Great work starts with great feeling.
>
> (Goleman 1998: 106)

Similarly, in the chapter on learning theories, we examined the humanist view of learning. Carl Rogers's humanist principles stress the importance of personal development and positive self-esteem. One of the main demotivators is low self-esteem and the accompanying lack of self-belief; this often arises from negative feedback from teachers and significant others earlier in life. Humanist theory also emphasises student-centred learning in which learners have some choice in what they learn and how they learn it; this helps to build positive motivation.

In Chapter 4 on planning we saw how structure and variety are essential elements of planning for motivation and learning. In addition, assessment *for* learning, in which constructive feedback is a vital element in helping learners to plan and develop, is another ingredient in creating motivated learners.

Intrinsic and extrinsic motivation

Where does motivation come from? Is it from within the individual learner or from outside factors? In considering this question we are dealing with the concepts of intrinsic and extrinsic motivation.

Intrinsic motivation

Do you have a personal interest or hobby? Perhaps stamp collecting, family history, Renaissance sculpture, the films of Alfred Hitchcock or ecclesiastical architecture. You might care to reflect on the genesis of this interest; did anyone tell you to do it? I mention ecclesiastical architecture, because many years ago I wandered in to Lincoln Cathedral and pondered the construction of such a vast edifice. The purchase of a little book on church architecture from the cathedral shop fired a lasting interest. Something similar will probably have happened to you. Intrinsic motivation comes from within the individual. It is generally driven by curiosity and the desire to learn and find out; it is learning for its own sake.

Young people, like most adults, come to education with a variety of motivations. In post-compulsory education there will be a significant number of learners who have actively chosen to study a particular course because of a genuine interest in the subject. Those studying several subjects may well have chosen, for example, physics, biology and English with real enthusiasm; their fourth choice, however, media studies, was just to fill the timetable.

For many adult learners, enjoyment and pleasure come from the social element of being with other people and learning and having fun together. Adult education, in its fullest non-vocational and general interest form, has been neglected in recent years, but still survives. Most people who attend pottery, painting, poetry, or Polish do it because they have a genuine desire to learn something or master a new skill. This skill might have a use beyond personal interest – improving job prospects or making communication easier on a foreign holiday – but the main drivers are interest and desire. The incorporation of colleges and changes in funding in the 1990s ushered in the development of accreditation of areas of adult learning which previously had none. Some curriculum planners felt that this accreditation would be a motivating force for adult learners. In reality this wasn't always the case; many adult learners didn't want a qualification and often resented the extra charge the assessment incurred. A qualification or a certificate was not what motivated them.

Extrinsic motivation

Some of the motivating factors in the list above are not, specifically, intrinsic or driven from within the learners. Gaining a qualification can be the key to improved career prospects or to promotion and pay increases. This kind of motivation is extrinsic, that is it comes from outside of the learner. Many young people are extrinsically motivated by the promise of bikes or computers if they are successful in exams or SATs. Examples of extrinsic motivation include:

- to achieve an end or goal;
- a means to an end, for example, taking a course or qualification which is a requirement of your work. Learners who have been told to do something provide considerable motivational problems for teachers;
- externally offered rewards including promotion or status-related rewards;
- avoiding negative sanctions or unpleasant consequences; avoiding 'failure'. Many people studied extremely hard and practised IQ tests in the 1950s and 1960s in order to pass the 11 plus examination because their life chances could be significantly affected by success or failure.

Adult learners' motivation

It is frequently assumed that adults return to learning because they choose to and because they are intrinsically motivated. The picture is much more complicated, however, and adult motivation comes from many different sources – educational, social and economic. Some will return to learning for something new and different to do, to develop an interest or learn a new skill. Others will return because they want to make real changes to their lives. People whose circumstances have changed, perhaps through redundancy or bereavement, may have a much more fundamental need to return to learning.

The National Institute for Adult and Continuing Education's briefing paper, *Learning in Later Life* (2000: 3), lists a number of reasons why adults return to learning. As we look at these, however, we might conclude that they are not very different from the factors that motivate learners of all ages. Even if a 16-year-old doesn't consciously decide to attend college to improve his social interaction, this could be a latent benefit.

- intellectual stimulation;
- to gain qualifications;
- to help find/change a job or to gain promotion;
- for fun;
- interest in a particular subject;
- personal development;
- better social interaction;
- to help other family members;
- ability to make demands more effectively;
- to help with voluntary or community work;
- to improve health – recent research by NIACE confirmed that concentration on study took the mind off many physical, mental and emotional problems.

Some adults will return to learning brimming with confidence, even to the point of arrogance; others are likely to have real problems with confidence and self-esteem. This variety provides challenges and opportunities for teachers in adult education which require skilful handling and sensitivity. Unfortunately, there are instances I am aware of where adult learners have complained of teachers who treat them like children or lack respect for their age and experience. There are those who will be returning to learning very tentatively because of previous negative experiences of learning in school and, as a result will have self-esteem problems and lack self-belief. This can be particularly true of those coming to improve their literacy and numeracy skills. As Lawrence (2000: xvii–xviii) points out:

what began a long time ago in school as an educational problem gradually becomes a social and emotional problem. With regular failure in a skill that society values, people eventually lose confidence in themselves generally. It should come as no surprise to discover there is an association between literacy skills and self-esteem. People who have low attainments in literacy have lower self-esteem than the rest of us.

Motivation and 14–19-year-olds

The old stage boundaries of education are changing. The 14–19 agenda was developed, in the main, to combat the very low staying-on rates in education post-16. The Increased Flexibility Programme has provided opportunities for young people to spend time in FE colleges studying vocational courses. Recent government plans to make attendance at school, college or workplace training compulsory until 18 offers a whole new range of challenges for those working in the lifelong learning sector.

The opportunities for vocational education and skill development are undoubtedly a motivating factor for some young people who find the school curriculum doesn't suit all their needs and abilities. Courses, for example, in construction, engineering, hairdressing and business administration are increasingly popular and there is evidence to suggest that those who undertake such courses during the last two years of compulsory schooling are more likely to stay in education and training post-16. Others, however, may feel that they have been 'dumped' by their schools because their behaviour is perceived to be too difficult to manage. More serious is the suggestion that those likely to 'under-perform' on the more academic courses will adversely affect the school's position in the league tables and, therefore, are best served by vocational courses elsewhere.

There is research evidence to support the view that many 14–16-year-olds prefer their college experience to school and from this we can draw some conclusions about motivation for this age group. A key factor in the college provision was the attitude of the teaching staff, who were reported by many learners to be more patient with them and respectful to them. Harkin's research (2006: 328) observes that:

> The characteristics of 'best' teachers, according to 14–16-year-old pupils attending college, are that they:
> • are friendly, can share a joke, and show respect for students;
> • know their subject and can make it interesting; and
> • can keep order but without undue authoritarianism.

In addition:

This sense of a more 'adult' environment in college is also, more importantly, about the way the students perceive that they are treated and spoken to by teachers:

> *School teachers tell you off for nothing and just tell you to do something ... they should be more like college teachers: let you do things in your own way; give you choice of what you want to do.'*

(Harkin 2006: 325)

The research also points to the value young learners place on being in a live working environment and their learning being relevant to this environment. Several young people referred to working in garage or hair salon environments where they had opportunities to make independent choices about how things were done, for example in dealing with customers and booking appointments. (See *situated learning* in Chapter 3, 'Learning theories').

How to motivate your learners

Reflective teachers can discover a lot by recalling the motivating and demotivating factors in their own education and applying them to their teaching. In addition, you should consider the following points as keys to motivation for learners of all ages.

Planning

Learner motivation is a vital element in planning teaching and learning. You should ensure that your planning covers a wide range of teaching and learning methods and different forms of assessment, particularly emphasising assessment *for* learning.

As we have discussed before, learners feel confused and frustrated if they don't have a clear picture of the what, why and how of their learning and how they can be successful. From the outset you should give learners a 'big picture' through the use of handbooks, information and induction sessions. This is the starting point of the learning journey; people will feel reassured if they know the destination and points along the way.

Your planning must aim to pitch the learning and tasks at the right level for the learners. This means you need to find out as much as you can about them as soon as possible: about their level, their previous experience, and their learning styles and preferences. Remember, you will be meeting a group of *individuals* and you need to find ways of differentiating (see Chapter 4, 'Planning for teaching and learning') to meet, as far as possible, the needs of each individual. Fear and boredom are the most significant demotivating factors for learners. If the learning and tasks are too easy they will become bored and frustrated – learners need a challenge. If tasks are too hard they will become fearful of failure and stigma. Learners need to feel stretched, but not stretched to breaking point. To help the development of all learners you will need, perhaps, to spend extra time guiding and supporting some of them, whilst ensuring that those who are ahead have some form of extension activities. Using ILPs will help you and the learner to set goals, agree targets and to tailor the learning to their particular needs and abilities.

Kyriacou (1998) emphasises that learners need to have an 'expectation of success', that they will be able to be successful at particular tasks or activities. Once again, level is important; tasks which are not challenging are unlikely to produce real feelings of success. Tasks which elicit the best learner motivation are those which are seen to be difficult but reachable. Learners' expectation of success should be matched by teachers' expectations of them; we should hold high but realistic expectations of all our learners. Many a learning journey has been disrupted by teachers who make remarks such, 'You won't pass', or 'You're not as clever as your sister'. Why any teacher would ever say such things to any of their students is a mystery.

It may possible with some groups to negotiate some of the content and methods. This is more likely to be true with adult learners, particularly if they are on non-vocational general interest type of courses. A photography teacher could spend some time initially discussing the group's particular interests and previous experience and to build the information into subsequent planning. Even with 14–19-year-olds, however, some element of negotiation is empowering and motivating.

Teaching and learning methods

In Chapter 3 on learning theories I described the 'empty buckets' theory of teaching in which learners are 'filled up' with knowledge from the teacher and then tested to assess to what extent they were 'leaky' buckets. Many learners will put up with this kind of passive and surface learning; very few will be motivated by it. Wherever possible you should plan to use techniques which maximise learner involvement and motivation. Active learning methods emphasise learner involvement; learning by doing; thinking and connecting – learners are actively involved in constructing their own learning. When choosing learning methods and activities, favour those which develop active learning, for example discussion, case studies, presentations. You should also plan to use a range of different teaching and learning activities within each session. Questioning is a good way of involving and motivating learners, particularly the use of higher-order questions which stimulate thinking and connecting ideas.

Assessment

For many of your learners assessment means testing, and testing often meant failure. Previous negative experiences of education have left many with a lack of belief that they can learn and succeed. We need to give people different experiences of assessment; in short, to use assessment *for* learning (see Chapter 7, 'Assessment for learning'). Remember the old adage 'success breeds success'. For those returning to learning or young people who have had negative experiences at school, a quick feeling of success is vital to re-engage and motivate them. Devise tasks which allow step by step learning so that learners can make steady progress and start to develop their self-esteem. Feedback on learners' progress should be positive, early and frequent.

When you need to use more formative methods of assessment which require learners to produce work which will be marked and graded, make sure the assessment is part of a planned programme of development for which they are adequately prepared and don't surprise learners by assessing without prior notice. Feedback should emphasise the positive but also include areas for development. Learners love good grades, but feel demotivated by poor ones. As far as possible try to de-emphasise grades, especially with learners who lack self-esteem; it's the feedback and support that's important.

Celebrate success. Achievement feels good in its own right but a certificate or some evidence of achievement is very important for learners, particularly if they haven't had many in the past. Organise events at which learners can receive their qualifications and congratulate each other on their success. Include displays and exhibitions of learners' work so that they can showcase their achievements to visitors, friends and relatives. Involve the management and if you can invite a few local dignitaries and the media, so much the better.

Teacher qualities

Learners don't always come ready motivated; even if they do it's part of our job to maintain and increase that motivation. Research into teacher effectiveness emphasises the importance of enthusiasm, subject knowledge, professionalism and being organised. Effective communication is also identified as an important quality of good teachers. We will consider this separately.

Enthusiastic teachers are likely to develop enthusiastic learners. If you don't feel and demonstrate enthusiasm for your subject area you cannot inspire and enthuse others. It can be difficult to maintain your passion for your subject and for teaching it in the face of long class contact hours and, sometimes, difficult learners. Enthusiasm comes from involving your learners. Using questions and discussion brings people in and means you not having to do all the input while they do all the listening. Learners are people too; they're full of ideas and opinions, some of which you won't agree with, which will challenge you and force you to think on your feet. One way to maintain your enthusiasm is to keep up to date with the latest subject developments, not only in the content and skills and knowledge, but also in the latest ideas in subject pedagogy and resources. It's exciting to try new ideas with your learners and have the feeling that you're working 'at the edge' and developing theory in practice. Personally, I have found my most stimulating teaching sessions are the ones in which I learned the most myself.

Being professional and being organised are linked points to do with how teachers look, talk, behave, treat their learners and plan and prepare thoroughly. Thorough planning and preparation show that you care about your learners and that you are prepared spend time and effort on them. Conversely ill-prepared teachers give the impression that this group of learners is not important to them; this does not produce motivated learners. Adult learners, in particular those who are very goal-oriented in terms of needing specific training or a qualification, expect a professional approach to teaching and learning. Many of these people are in business and want the same kind of professionalism and commitment as they would show their own customers. Teachers who arrive late, don't have all the materials they need, don't appear to know their subject or even be enthusiastic about it are a motivational turn-off.

Communication and motivation

Developing effective communication skills is one of the key themes of this book. Here we will briefly consider a few points specifically in relation to communication.

As discussed in Chapter 2 ('Communication and the teacher) effective learning and motivation are more likely when there is a positive climate for learning. Teachers can do much to create this climate. Nonverbally by posture, movement, eye contact and facial expression you can do a great deal to reassure your learners that you are business-like but supportive and fair. Remember that many will come to your sessions with self-esteem and confidence problems and will tend to notice those things which confirm their negative self-image more readily than those which challenge it. You need to be particularly careful about facial expressions and vocal qualities which can be seen as frustration, annoyance or criticism. Learners like to know they are being listened to and you will often have to consciously use NVC to demonstrate you are listening – looking at people when they speak, adopting an appropriate posture and reflecting back things they have said all help to reassure them that you are listening to and valuing what they are saying.

One of the simplest methods to find out what motivates learners is to ask them. The simple act of seeking learners' opinions is beneficial in itself but if you really listen to what they have to say about their learning preferences and interests then you will increase their feelings of involvement and empowerment, leading to, hopefully, increased motivation.

Motivation and emotional intelligence

This section draws mainly on Daniel Goleman's work (1995, 1998) on emotional intelligence and in particular on two concepts relating to motivation – optimism and flow.

Optimism

Why some people tend to be optimistic and others pessimistic is a complex issue, drawing on arguments relating to nature and nurture and questions of human nature. I think we can safely assume that no one is born either an optimist or a pessimist; it is learned behaviour and, as such, can to some extent be unlearned. Pessimism is often the result of repeated negative messages to an individual from significant others, leading to a general belief that things tend to go badly. Optimism, on the other hand, is likely to have a similar origin in messages received but this time positive and resulting in a general feeling that things will go well, even if there are setbacks. If as teachers we can start to change the messages people receive, we can, even if only to a small extent, help learners to develop a more optimistic view of life and, consequently, their ability to succeed and do well.

Optimism is related to success in learning and, it is claimed, is more likely to lead to achievement than skills and knowledge alone. Goleman refers to the work of the psychologist Martin Seligman. Goleman (1995: 88) writes:

> Seligman defines optimism in terms of how people explain to themselves their successes and failures. People who are optimistic see failure as due to something that can be changed so that they can succeed next time around, while pessimists take the blame for failure, ascribing it to some lasting characteristics they are helpless to change.

There are clear links here to learners' previous negative experiences and particularly their experience of assessment. Those who have been repeatedly tested and have failed can easily conclude that there is something fundamentally wrong with their ability to learn and, consequently, conclude that any future efforts will be equally fruitless. Psychologists use the term *self-efficacy* to describe the belief individuals have that they can take control over their lives and change them. Teachers are not psychotherapists or social workers but it should be abundantly clear that part of our role is to help learners feel good about themselves and to believe that they can achieve. Optimism breeds hope.

Flow

Have you ever been so involved in a task that time seems to fly by and you feel completely absorbed in your work? If so, you've experienced 'flow' and it's almost certain that everyone living human being can experience flow given the right task and the right environment. If we ask ourselves what the 'right' tasks are and what the 'right' environment is, we already know the answers. The right tasks are those which learners not only perceive to be interesting and relevant but also are at a level which is challenging but they feel they can reach with application and effort. The right environment is one in which they feel such challenges but feel supported and emotionally safe; that is safe from negative feeling like disapproval, humiliation or failure. Goleman (1998: 106) asserts that: 'Flow is the ultimate motivator. Activities we love draw us in because we get into flow as we pursue them. ... When we work in flow the motivation is built in – work is a delight in itself.' This might sound too idealistic a notion for learners in the lifelong learning sector but you will have seen learners experiencing flow and how motivated they become. The challenge, therefore, is to find tasks and methods which are most likely to bring this about. A word of warning – once a person has experienced flow other things can seem drab by comparison, so we have to bring people down from the experience by helping them to reflect on what they have learned and how they learned it.

Motivating learners is clearly one of the keys to unlocking good behaviour. This is the subject of the next section.

Behaviour

Understanding learner motivation is an essential prerequisite to understanding and improving the behaviour of learners. Well-motivated learners are likely to have fewer challenging behaviour problems. 'Bad' behaviour is one of the issues which most concern new teachers, in lifelong learning and in schools. The media and popular opinion tends to suggest that schools are populated by frightening and violent young thugs who terrorise their fellow learners and their teachers; for many people, further education colleges' reputation is not much better. Having worked with 16–19-year-olds, as well as adults, for more than twenty years, I have to say that the instances of extreme bad behaviour are very few and that for most of the time, most young people are pleasant, decent and want to learn.

The lifelong learning sector covers a wide variety of learners from 14–16-

year-olds to senior citizens, with many different reasons and motivations for being there. Behaviour problems are generally associated with young learners, increasingly with 14–16-year-olds in colleges, but adult education tutors would, undoubtedly, support the view that some adults can be difficult and demanding, indeed might exhibit 'bad' behaviour. In this section there will be some discussion of the 14–16 and 16–19 age groups specifically, but to a great extent the guidelines and advice on behaviour will be appropriate to learners of all ages.

What is 'bad' behaviour?

Activity

- List the kinds of behaviour that you consider to be 'bad'.

- What is about these behaviours that makes them 'bad'?

- What are the consequences of these kinds of behaviour a) for you, and b) for the other learners?

- If you have done this activity as a group, do you all agree about what 'bad' behaviour is? In what ways are your views different?

- What words other than 'bad' might describe this behaviour and its consequences more accurately?

This activity will almost certainly have revealed that we have different perceptions of learner behaviour and different thresholds of acceptability. One teacher might feel that groups should be run with military precision and with strict discipline and behaviour imposed on the learners. Another might prefer a noisy, physically active session in which learners have considerable freedom about how they behave and personal choice regarding how, what or even whether they learn. These two teachers – who I have lazily typified as 'the sergeant-major' and 'the hippy' – represent extreme views of attitudes towards behaviour and would probably regard each other's methods as anathema. As reflective teachers, we would argue that the most appropriate methods are the ones which are the most effective and that these will vary from teacher to teacher based on their understanding of individual learners and groups. Those who work for large learning organisations, however, should consider the policies relating to behaviour and discipline and try, as far as possible, to have the same expectations of acceptable and appropriate behaviour.

Describing behaviour as 'bad' is imprecise and not very helpful in promoting positive behaviour. As we have seen, one teacher's 'bad' behaviour might be another teacher's free expression for students. Both of these would, almost certainly, agree that there are behaviours which are 'challenging' or 'disruptive', even, to use a term from schools, describing some learners as having emotional and behavioural difficulties (EBD). In essence, they would agree that, for them, some kinds of individual or group behaviour cause concern and are not conducive to learning and achievement. Given that there are differing perceptions of behaviour and thresholds of acceptability, we have to consider carefully just how 'bad' is the bad behaviour? Incessant talking, inappropriate comments or rudeness are extremely irritating but not life-threatening, and often happen just because there is a room full of lively young people excited by each others' company. Teachers who respond disproportionately are in danger of escalating minor issues into major confrontations. The skill in teaching, as in personal relationships, is to recognise potential trouble spots and de-escalate them.

Structure and planning

Prevention is better than cure. There are many things you can do to create a learning climate which will encourage positive behaviour, particularly at the session planning stage. Television childcare experts emphasise the importance of structure and routine in children's lives and, I would suggest this desire for structure extends to learners of all ages. There is considerable evidence to support the view that youngsters in schools do not like lessons which are badly planned and if they don't feel sure about what they are doing or don't have enough to do.

You might find it useful to reread the section on session structure in 'Planning for teaching and learning', Chapter 4 (pp. 96–112). When planning think of these stages of the session:

Arrival. Wherever possible, arrive before your learners. This is important for several reasons. First, because it demonstrates that you are a professional who starts the session promptly and that you are prepared. Second, difficult groups will know from the outset that you are running 'a tight ship' and monitoring their behaviour. Wherever possible greet the learners at the door as they arrive, using their names. Most importantly, early arrival gives you time to set up your resources and materials for the session and ensure that everything is working. If you have to spend five or ten minutes of the lesson sorting things out, learners will feel cheated that they've made the effort to arrive on time but you're not ready for them. In addition, you can prepare the environment by adjusting the light and temperature if necessary, arranging the furniture in a way that best suits this group and making the place look tidy and business-like. The room should be safe; check there are no trailing wires, dangerous equipment or electrical hazards.

The establishment, or opening, phase of the lesson. This sets the tone of the whole session. Establish your authority from the outset and don't begin until you have silence and attention. Once you have silence and full attention, get straight into the lesson and don't wait for latecomers. Begin with a bang – set a question or pose a problem – and try to get people interested and engaged straight away.

In Chapter 4, 'Planning for teaching and learning', we considered the idea of the rhythm and a flow of a session. There should be smooth transitions between the different sections and the transitions should not leave any gaps which learners can exploit and use to pursue their own agenda. Above all, keep them busy with appropriately challenging tasks. If you consider your own attendance at staff development sessions, I'm sure you will have 'messed about' if there wasn't enough to do or tasks were allotted too much time for completion; there's no reason why the same shouldn't apply to your learners.

Ending. Plan so that you finish on time. Finishing too early sets a bad precedent and your learners will come to expect it every time. Don't over-run a session, even if it's been a great one; learners need their breaks. Having summarised the session, thank the learners for their attention and their activity and remind them of when and where the next session is.

Strategies to encourage positive behaviour

The remainder of this section provides some brief guidelines for developing positive behaviour. These cannot be applied to all learners at all times and as a reflective teacher you will need to develop a repertoire of techniques to draw on according to who you are working with. In the lifelong learning sector we are encouraging independent and active learning so it is important that our learners take responsibility for their actions and behaviour. We should aim to develop behaviour *for* learning; this emphasises the positive relationships we make with learners, rather than controlling and reprimanding them. Much of the following will apply to 14–19-year-olds; some will be useful when working with adult learners, but there will be some specific consideration of adult behaviour.

Rules and routines

As stated earlier, people like structure. Establishing and implementing appropriate rules and routines is part of providing structure. When establishing these we should remember that both learners and teachers have rights and responsibilities which have to be balanced.

- If you work for a college or a large learning organisation there will be policies and procedures relating to student behaviour. It is part of your job to know and apply these consistently; it makes life easier for teaching colleagues if these procedures are applied equally.
- You will want to develop your own rules and routines with your own learners. As far as possible, these should be discussed and agreed with them; be age-appropriate and apply them consistently. You could even draw up a contract which is printed and displayed.
- Your rules and routines will include behaviours which are unacceptable, for example: mobiles switched off; no inappropriate language, particularly racist or sexist; no lateness, unless explained and agreed.
- Remember that learners have expectations of you; meeting these will go some way to developing positive behaviour. They expect: well planned and stimulating sessions; respect, politeness and fairness; professional, well-organised teachers; fair assessment; feedback on their progress and support in their development.

Nonverbal communication

Chapter 2, 'Communication and the teacher', stressed the importance of NVC; it may be helpful to revisit that section. Here are some specific examples related to behaviour:

- Eye contact can be used positively to show that you are listening and interested in your learners. It can also be used to control learners who are behaving inappropriately; a prolonged look will generally change behaviour, if only briefly. Too much eye contact can, however, be confrontational.
- Posture – adopt a confident and assertive posture. You have legitimate authority within the classroom and you should not be frightened to appear in control.
- Movement – move around the classroom. 'Patrol' the classroom and be vigilant if you have lively, challenging learners. Movement is not just about control, however, it is also about being there to offer support, especially during individual and group activities.
- Proximity – use personal space appropriately. In some cases it will be effective to move into an individual's space in order deliver or reinforce sanctions. Regular invasions of a learner's space can be threatening and confrontational.

- If there are confrontations, don't 'square up' to people or invade their space face-to-face. It's better to stand back a bit and at right angles to the person.

Voice and voice qualities

- Shouting is rarely appropriate, even if a learner has raised their voice to you. You should aim to keep calm, speak slowly and clearly and to avoid escalating the tension.
- Speak clearly and at an appropriate pace and give clear instructions. Learners get frustrated and when they can't hear or understand you.

Politeness and respect

- Teachers should model good behaviour; this includes basic politeness such as saying 'please' and 'thank you'.
- Learners deserve respect. We demonstrate this by fairness and politeness and by listening to them and showing that we value them as individuals.
- Use learners' names. It shows respect and affirms relationships. 'No-naming' is impersonal and implies that you can't be bothered getting to know people.

Relationships

- Criticise the behaviour, not the person. Making personal comments, such as, 'You're an extremely rude person', attack the whole person. Be clear that you disapprove of what they've done or said, not of them.
- Use praise and reward regularly to recognise and encourage positive behaviour and achievements. You know how bad it feels when a manager consistently criticises you but rarely congratulates you on a job well done; it's the same for learners.
- Try using unconditional positive regard. This means that whatever the behaviour you maintain standards of respect and politeness with the individual and recognise their value as a person even if you disagree with their behaviour. I once had a tutee at college who had major attendance and punctuality problems and was an attention-seeker in class. During our tutorial sessions I was consistently calm and polite, used his name, listened to him and was calm and reasonable. It was hard work but we avoided confrontations and eventually it paid off, partly because he felt I was treating him as an adult.

Some thoughts on adult learners' behaviour

Activity

In what ways can adults show difficult or challenging behaviour?

To what extent do you think adult behaviour problems are the same in cause and effect as younger learners?

Discuss any examples of 'bad' adult behaviour you have experienced in classes you have taught or been a learner in.

Jenny Rogers (2001) discusses some ways in which adult learners can be challenging in their behaviour. These are:

- anxiety;
- memories of school;
- challenge to beliefs;
- differing expectations.

To a great extent, we have already discussed adult anxieties and memories of school at various points and concluded that we need to make positive attempts to understand their previous experiences and make learning a more positive experience for them.

Adult learners have had more experience of the world and more time to develop views and opinions; some of these are very firmly held and any challenges to them can be unsettling for the learners. Putting forward ideas and concepts backed by research and evidence will not necessarily cause a sudden change in learners' viewpoints. Adults are no less immune than youngsters from the belief that their experience of the world is a reliable guide to the way the world actually is. The important thing is not to mock or dismiss learners' views and ideas out of hand; patience is required to get people to challenge their own perceptions. Critical thinking inputs can help here by encouraging learners to look at issues dispassionately and objectively.

Adult learners might arrive with preconceived notions of how teaching and learning should happen; this usually results from their previous experience of education and training. For many adults, active and student-centred learning is a novelty and many complain that they have come to 'be taught'. Graduates with experience of lecture-dominated teaching may find it difficult to imagine that other kinds of teaching and learning are possible. I can recall at least one trainee teacher who insisted that her subject (engineering) could only be taught by lecturing and teacher input.

Fortunately she became more reflective and began to employ a much wider range of methods to suit her learners in FE colleges.

Activity

Discuss and explain how:

● planning and preparation;

● teaching and learning methods;

● communication;

● resources; and

● assessment

affect learner motivation and behaviour. You might find it useful to concept-map these points so that you can explore the connections more easily.

For your journal

Describe and analyse any critical incidents relating to motivation and behaviour you have experienced in your sessions.

What did you do to deal with the situation? How effective were your actions?

Have you developed your own principles and strategies for motivating learners and encouraging positive behaviour?

You should also consider ways in which you have created positive behaviour *for* learning and encouraged learners to take responsibility.

Journal extract: Russell, trained to teach construction

My plastering session with _ _ _ _ _ on Wednesday was not quite what I had imagined. The students were quite rowdy to begin with. I had planned to get them to plaster some columns but their behaviour was likely to get out of hand. I asked them to elect mixers and fixers to nail wooden battens to the wall and then put them behind an enclosed low wall. In my health and safety briefing I warned them that any carelessness with their steel floats could cause injury to their colleagues and that they would have to take turns sharing the limited space available. Due to the setting time of the undercoat plaster the mixers would have to watch the plasterers and the plasterers would have to watch each other.

It was gratifying to see formerly boisterous standoffish youths suddenly develop a sense of spatial awareness and the confidence and trust to move in close proximity to each other. The team spirit began to show and by the end they were moving gracefully like dancers, exhausted but content with their work.

Journal extract: Martyn, training to teach popular music

Sometimes I'm frustrated by the lack of attention paid by the students in the classes I'm observing. I have already 'put my foot down' over swearing and eating during the lesson and am frustrated when colleagues seem, to me, to let things go. I think that we need to establish some ground rules.

Further reading and useful websites

Vizard, D. (2007) *How to Manage Behaviour in Further Education*. London: Paul Chapman Educational Publishing.
Wallace, S. (2007) *Getting the Buggers Motivated in FE*. London: Continuum.
www.behavioursolutions.com Dave Vizard's website provides support and training for schools and FE colleges in behaviour management and the development of teaching and learning.
www.lifelonglearning.org/currentactivity/14-16_modules.html Working with Younger Learners. Support modules for post-16 staff from LLUK.

10 Skills for Life, Key Skills and thinking skills

What this chapter is about

- Defining and distinguishing Skills for Life; Key Skills; Functional Skills; personal, learning and thinking skills (PLTS)
- Planning teaching and learning to include and develop Skills for Life and Key Skills
- Defining 'embedded' skills and ways in which to embed Key Skills and Skills for Life
- Future developments, especially Functional Skills and PLTS
- What are thinking skills?
- Ways in which we can plan teaching and learning to encourage development of thinking skills
- The minimum core of language, literacy and numeracy for teachers in the lifelong learning sector

LLUK standards

This chapter covers the following standards:

AS 2; AK 2.1; AP 2.1; AK 2.2; AP 2.2
BK 1.3; BP 1.3; BK 2.2; BP 2.2; BK 3.2; BP 3.2
CK 3,1; CP 3.1; CK 3.3; CP 3.3; CK 3.4; CP 3.4

Introduction

'Skills' is one of the most widely used words in the lifelong learning sector: Basic Skills; Key Skills; Skills for Life; essential skills; Functional Skills, and, more recently, personal, learning and thinking skills (PLTS). What 'skills' actually means is not always clear. There are specific skills relating to particular areas of work, for example surgeons, architects, hairdressers, plumbers. Students have programmes of study skills to help them manage their learning and study. Social psychologists, and others, argue convincingly the importance of social, interpersonal and emotional skills and, more recently, there have been many interesting developments in thinking skills, particularly in schools.

Any discussion of skills will eventually include the controversy about the differences between education and skills. This mirrors the debate about vocational and academic education and, unfortunately, skills are still equated by many with manual skills and having sufficient literacy, numeracy and ICT skills to function in employment. Regardless of our definitions of skills and their value, for our current purpose of learning and teaching in the lifelong learning sector 'skills' refers to language, literacy, numeracy, ICT and the 'wider' Key Skills.

The importance of the continuing development and improvement of skills was further underlined in *Prosperity for all in the Global Economy: World Class Skills* (Leitch 2006), otherwise known as the 'Leitch Review'. Lord Leitch set new targets for the achievement of skills and, whilst recognising progress made so far, suggested that if the targets are not met we would have 'been running just to stand still'.

Our first task is to get some clarity about these different skills, how they relate to each other and what developments there will be in the future. To get some clarity a brief history lesson is necessary.

A brief overview of the development of 'skills'

Basic Skills are defined by the Basic Skills Agency as: 'The ability to read, write and speak in English/Welsh and to use mathematics at a level necessary to function and progress at work and in society in general.' By the mid-1990s there was no doubt in educational, economic and government circles that Britain had an unacceptably high number of people with poor or very poor literacy and numeracy. Not only was this recognised as a personal problem for each of these people but it also had significant consequences for the economy. The government commissioned Sir Claus Moser to investigate the scale of the problem and make recommendations on how it could be tackled. His report, *A Fresh Start* (DfEE 1999), generally known as the Moser Report, was published in 1999 and painted a bleak picture of the national situation on literacy and numeracy. Moser's research suggested that 7 million adults had literacy skills at or below those expected of 11-year-olds; the situation regarding numeracy was at least as bad. Moser demanded a national strategy to reduce the numbers of adults with low levels of Basic Skills.

In 2001 the government launched its Skills for Life strategy aimed at tackling the literacy and numeracy skills needs of adult learners. To support this strategy the Adult Core Curriculum documents set out the content of what should be taught in literacy and numeracy programmes for adult learners in the lifelong learning sector. The core curriculum documents cover literacy, language (ESOL), numeracy and, from 2007, ICT.

The term 'skills for life', whilst not formally adopted by the Basic Skills Unit, has tended to replace the term Basic Skills. 'Skills for life' is considered by most practitioners as a preferable term because it removes the overtones of deficiency and 'remedial education' which many learners felt labelled by in their early education.

The Skills for Life levels are, from the top down:

- Level 2 (Intermediate level)
- Level 1 (Foundation level)
- Entry level 3
- Entry level 2
- Entry level 1

So far, so skilled. The next area of possible confusion comes when we consider Key Skills. Prior to the Dearing Review of post-16 education (1996) there was a variety of different kinds of skills, including Common Skills and Core Skills. Dearing recommended the adoption of the single term Key Skills, and that these should be available across academic and work-based routes. Key Skills are defined by the QCA as: 'the skills that are commonly needed for success in a range of activities in education and training, work and life in general'.

Confusion frequently results from the overlap of Key Skills and Skills for Life at levels 1 and 2. Because of this anomaly, and for many other reasons, the DfES announced in 2004 that they intended to explore ways to merge Key Skills and Skills for Life into one coherent framework. As now seems clear the new name will be 'Functional Skills'. The development of Functional Skills fits in with a number of policy and curriculum initiatives, mainly the 14–19 agenda and the development of specialised diplomas, which will be considered further later.

In summary, the present situation is:

- Skills for Life remain offering language (ESOL), literacy, numeracy and ICT from entry level 1 to level 2.
- Key Skills remain and are offered from levels 1–4.

The likely future situation will be:

- Functional Skills offered in one framework from entry level 3 to level 3. 14–19-year-olds will be expected to achieve Functional Skills alongside their GCSEs and other qualifications.

- Young people taking the new specialised diplomas will also develop personal, learning and thinking skills.
- The main Key Skills (Communication, Application of number and ICT) will remain in place until at least 2010.
- The 'wider' key skills will remain for the foreseeable future.

We will now consider each area – Skills for Life, Key Skills and Functional Skills – in more detail. This will be followed by an introduction to, and discussion of, thinking skills.

Skills for Life

The term 'Skills for Life' simplifies a previously confusing curriculum area and replaces such terms as Adult Basic Skills; Adult Literacy, Numeracy and ESOL; and Language, Literacy and Numeracy (LLN).

Following the publication of the Moser Report in 1999, the government launched the Skills for Life national strategy in 2001 which aimed to significantly improve the literacy, numeracy, ICT and language skills of adults in England. The key documents you will need to understand and plan delivery of Skills for Life are:

- *Skills for Life: The National Strategy for Improving Adult Literacy and Numeracy Skills* (DfES 2001)
- *Skills for Life: The National Strategy for Improving Adult Literacy and Numeracy Skills: Focus on Delivery to 2007 (DfES, 2007)*
- *Adult Literacy Core Curriculum*
- *Adult Numeracy Core Curriculum*
- *Adult ESOL Core Curriculum*
- *Adult ICT Core Curriculum*
- *Adult Pre-entry Core Curriculum*
- *Access for All*

These documents can be obtained through the Read Write Plus website, (*www.dfes.gov.uk/readwriteplus*).

The *Access for All* strategy document is aimed at making the core curricula accessible to all, including those with disabilities and/or learning difficulties. It is essentially about inclusive learning strategies and ways of removing barriers to learning.

The 'learning journey'

The 'learning journey' is a useful framework to understand and organise not only Skills for Life but also any programme of learning. It provides a structure for both learners and teachers. For Skills for Life the points on the journey could be as follows:

- initial advice and guidance to help learners choose a learning programme;
- initial assessment to discover the learner's skill levels;
- diagnostic testing to provide detailed assessment of the learner's skill needs;
- an ILP – agreed between learner and teacher and regularly reviewed together;
- teaching and learning based around vocational or other learning contexts, using as far as possible embedded methods;
- assessment for learning to help learners develop through structured, positive feedback;
- summative assessment leading to the next stage in the learner's progression.

An important element in the successful delivery of Skills for Life is 'embedded' learning in which the skills and the learning context are holistic and integrated.

'Embedded' Skills for Life

One of the key issues in both Skills for Life and Key Skills is how they are taught. Should they be taught as an integral part of the learning programme or by separate provision? Increasingly, the consensus is that Skills for Life should be 'embedded'. The Skills for Life Strategy Unit defines embedding as follows:

> Embedded teaching and learning combines the development of literacy, language (ESOL), and numeracy with vocational and other skills. The skills acquired provide learners with the confidence, competence and motivation necessary for them to succeed in qualifications, in life and at work.
>
> (DfES 2001)

Research by the National Research Development Centre for Adult Literacy and Numeracy (NRDC) (Roberts et al. 2005; Casey et al. 2006) suggests that embedding is preferable to stand alone delivery not only because it is more motivating and relevant for learners, particularly those on vocational courses, but because it also leads to increased retention and achievement. The NRDC's research indicates that:

- on courses where skills were embedded retention was 16 per cent higher than non-embedded;
- on fully-embedded courses, 93 per cent of those with an identified literacy need achieved literacy/ESOL qualification, compared to only 50 per cent on non-embedded courses;
- for learners on fully-embedded courses 93 per cent of those with an identified numeracy need achieved a numeracy/maths qualification, compared to 70 per cent on non-embedded courses.

(Casey et al. 2006: 5)

Research suggests that on programmes where the skills are embedded learners feel more motivated because they can see their skills being developed in a specific context in which they are interested. At a deeper level embedding helps learners to discover what it means to be a professional and with

> learning what is worth knowing, how far they can draw on their existing expertise and what are the risks and challenges in taking on this new identity. This new professional identity is what motivates such learners and for young people this identity is often in contrast to their former experience as 'school pupils'. Teachers are both teachers and mentors. Learners are both 'doing things' and understanding the culture of their chosen jobs ...

(Roberts et al. 2005: 7)

Embedding Skills for Life might seem the natural and obvious thing to do, particularly given what we know about 'situated' learning, which is relevant to learners' interests and vocational areas. Quite simply, there are many courses in which numeracy is an everyday requirement, most notably in engineering or construction. Similar arguments also apply to literacy, language and ICT in vocational and other contexts. In reality, because of funding and staffing issues, not all learning providers embed the skills provision.

Providing embedded learning is a challenge for providers in terms of organisation and funding. The range of 'embeddedness' is a continuum but there are four main points along it:

- *non-embedded*: skills and vocational learning/context are almost entirely separate;
- *partly embedded*: skills and vocational learning/context are embedded to some degree;
- *mostly embedded*: skills are mainly acquired and developed in context but some elements are separately taught;

- *fully embedded*: learners experience their skills development and vocational learning as an integrated whole.

It should not be assumed that all learning must be integrated at all times. It may be appropriate on occasions, for example, to offer literacy support to business and administration students as separate provision so that they can develop the skills in writing letters and reports in a vocational context. It is vital that vocational teachers and Skills for Life teachers work together to plan and prepare schemes of work and learning activities and resources; vocational area staff should include Skills for Life staff in team and planning meetings. Vocational staff do not have to become literacy and numeracy teachers but they can learn about the barriers to skills development their learners experience. Equally, Skills for Life teachers do not have to become plasterers or hairdressers but an understanding of the vocational contexts will better equip them to support learners and vocational staff and to develop learning and assessment materials which are set in a vocational context.

The Minimum Core

Everybody teaching in the lifelong learning sector has a responsibility for the development and improvement of Skills for Life and Key Skills; not just Skills for Life and Key Skills specialists. Every teacher should have a working knowledge of the skills requirements and a prescribed level of skills and knowledge themselves. Teachers will usually be expected to have a minimum of Level 2 in literacy and numeracy. Lifelong Learning UK publish the Minimum Core document which describes the minimum skills and knowledge teachers should have. More importantly, however, the document is about teachers recognising and understanding barriers to skills learning and developing inclusive learning practices which are designed to include all learners. At the time of writing a new Minimum Core document is being drafted by LLUK.

> ### Journal extract: Darren, training to teach Skills for Life (literacy)
>
> I've been working with the Hairdressing students on my placement for two weeks now and haven't felt particularly welcome. They're all at level 1 and I've got to get them up to Level 2 but they're not really interested in writing. Talking – fine. Writing – NO!
>
> Up to now they've been working on standard worksheets on spelling, punctuation and grammar. Even I think these are boring. I visited the hairdressing team and discussed some ideas about

connecting their written work to their vocational stuff more. They didn't seem particularly keen and didn't really think literacy was their business. But, we started to work out a few ideas for the students to do some relevant written work. So far, we've come up with writing some publicity materials and adverts, plus an idea for a short magazine piece about hairstyles and colours. At present the last idea seems to have grabbed the interest of most of them. Still a lot of spelling, punctuation and grammar problems but at least they're more interested and I've got some of their work I can talk to them about.

To make a bridge between the section on Skills for Life and Key Skills, Table 10.1 provides an overview of the differences between the two.

Key Skills

What are Key Skills?

Key Skills are essential, generic skills which are the basis of all successful lifelong learning and personal development. By 'generic' we mean that key skills are not applicable to any one programme, age, ability range or context. They are appropriate for all learners, teachers, employers and employees in all settings. In reality teachers have always wanted learners to acquire and develop key skills, particularly in literacy and numeracy, it's just that they weren't referred to as Key Skills.

Key Skills should be practical and applied and are best learned in realistic and meaningful contexts, either vocational settings such as apprenticeships, or subject-specific courses. Many learners complain that, for example, they already have English or maths GCSE and, therefore, do not have to take Key Skills. This misses the point and suggests that teachers have not explained these skills properly to their learners. Key Skills are there to be used and developed; getting a qualification doesn't mean you don't have to think about the skill again. Like Skills for Life, learners are less likely to be successful if the Key Skills are delivered through separate provision.

Table 10.1 Skills for Life and Key Skills: similarities and differences

What's the same?

Skills for Life	Key Skills
The national tests for literacy and numeracy are the same as the Key Skills tests for communication and application of number respectively.	
At Levels 1 and 2 the skills, knowledge and understanding are similar for both Skills for Life and Key Skills.	

What's different?

Skills for Life	Key Skills
Skills for Life in: • Literacy • Numeracy • Language (ESOL) • ICT	Six Key Skills: • Application of number • Communication • ICT • Improving own learning and performance (IOLP) • Working with others • Problem solving
Skills for Life are broken down into: • Entry 1 • Entry 2 • Entry 3 • Level 1 • Level 2 Entry level is subdivided into three stages to recognise the smaller steps of learning at lower levels.	Each skill has four levels: • Level 1 • Level 2 • Level 3 • Level 4
To achieve a Skills for Life qualification in literacy and numeracy, a learner must pass a national test.	To achieve a Key Skills qualification for communication or application of number, a learner must pass the test and also complete a portfolio.
Literacy, ESOL, numeracy and ICT have a core curriculum based on the national standards.	There are no curriculum documents for Key Skills

Source: Adapted from LSC Skills for Life Quality Initiative 2005–6.

What are the Key Skills and how are they assessed?

DfES (2005: 6) states that:

> In July 2001, the then Secretary of State confirmed a wish to see key skill programmes offered to all post-16 learners. Where learners have not already achieved A*–C grades in GCSE English, maths, or ICT, their programmes should lead to the formal acquisition of the relevant key skills qualifications at level 2. Where young people are starting on advanced level programmes with the aim of pursuing a professional or higher qualification post-19, then institutions should support them in gaining at least one relevant key skill qualification at level 3. These expectations apply equally to apprentices and trainees on Government funded work-based programmes as well as to pupils and students in schools and colleges.

There are six Key Skills:

- Communication
- Application of Number
- Information Technology
- Improving Own Learning and Performance
- Working with Others
- Problem-Solving

The first three Key Skills are, essentially, the same as Skills for Life literacy, numeracy and ICT at levels and 1 and 2. The last three are sometimes known as the 'wider' Key Skills. Research suggests that employers have always placed high value on these 'wider' skills and want employees who are good at team-working, self-management, communication, problem-solving and using initiative.

The six Key Skills are now all included in the National Qualifications Framework (NQF) (see Appendix 1). For learners taking Communication' Application of Number or ICT, the assessment is by external test and the production of a portfolio. Some previous qualifications which learners have gained can be considered as suitable proxy qualifications. For the wider Key Skills, assessment is by portfolio alone.

How are Key Skills most effectively learned?

The answer is quite simple – they are best acquired and developed when they are integrated, or, to use the most recent terminology, embedded. There are so many instances in which embedding is natural and easy. In retail, for example, learners can regularly demonstrate development of skills in working with others. When planning projects in vocational or subject-specific settings learners should be able to evidence the development of the wider Key Skills without creating a lot of extra work for themselves.

The essence of Key Skills is that they are designed around the following principles set out in the QCA guidance documents (2004) in which learners are encouraged:

- to think about their intentions and purposes;
- to plan a course of action;
- to implement the plan;
- to reflect on their progress towards the plan;
- to review the plan to suit changing circumstances or to overcome problems;
- to devise a new plan when the original one has been fulfilled.

This process is the guiding principle for all the Key Skills but is most apparent in Improving Own Learning and Performance, which could be regarded as the 'key' Key Skill. You will also have noted the similarity of the Plan; Do; Reflect: Review cycle (see Figure 10.1) to Kolb's learning Cycle (see Chapter 3, 'Learning theories'). If Key Skills are to be delivered and assessed effectively, they should be seen as a framework that underpins the planning and delivery of learning, rather than treating them as an 'add on'. They must be planned into schemes of work from the outset and Key Skills/Skills for Life specialists should work closely with vocational and subject teams during the planning stages. Most importantly, Key Skills opportunities can only meaningfully

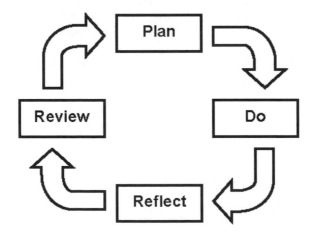

Figure 10.1 Learning cycle.

occur in programmes where this is learner-centred, active learning. If Key Skills don't make us consider the appropriateness of our learning and teaching methods, then we are doing something wrong.

What follows is an overview example of an integrated activity and the Key Skill opportunities it provides.

Learning activity for retail

Students have been asked to design and evaluate a display strategy for a new product in store. The Key Skills opportunities could include:

Communication

- meetings to plan and discuss initial ideas;
- writing notes of meetings; writing letters;
- keeping a learning log;
- designing questionnaires for the public to evaluate the display;
- interviewing members of the public;
- giving a presentation at the end of the project;
- discussion of working practices and skills developed.

Application of number

- design, sizing and positioning of displays;
- interpreting feedback from questionnaires and presenting statistics.

ICT

- keeping learning logs;
- using digital cameras to record visual images of display;
- using video to record interviews with public (useful for portfolio evidence);
- designing and producing display materials;
- using design packages to design displays;
- preparing PowerPoint and handouts for the presentation.

Working with others

- working in a team with fellow learners;
- working with work placement colleagues;
- talking to members of the public.

Problem-solving

- making decisions about most effective display ideas;
- overcoming difficulties in developing the display;
- piloting the questionnaires.

Improving Own Learning and Performance

- setting goals, targets and milestones for the completion of the project;
- reviewing and monitoring plans and targets;
- reviewing and evaluating the displays;
- reviewing and evaluating working methods;
- identifying skills developed and concluding lessons for future activity.

Journal extract – Martyn

One of the students asked me the difference between a manager and an agent and I was able to introduce a key skills element by way of a Venn diagram … If I can bring maths into a chat about the music business then I can do it anywhere. I've come home feeling good.

The future: Functional Skills

Functional Skills are being developed, partly, in response to the realisation that it was possible for young people to achieve grade C in GCSE English and maths but not have a satisfactory standard of literacy or numeracy. The QCA is currently developing these skills in three main areas: maths, English and ICT.

The QCA defines Functional Skills as: 'those core elements of English, mathematics and ICT that provide an individual with essential knowledge, skills and understanding that will enable them to operate confidently, effectively and independently in life and at work' (quoted in Owen-Evans and McNeill 2006). It is envisaged that Functional Skills will be offered to learners as stand-alone qualifications, integrated within GCSEs and included in specialised diplomas and in apprenticeships. At the time of writing, qualifications are being piloted. The final qualifications in English and ICT will be introduced for first teaching in 2009 and in mathematics in 2010. See *www.qca.org.uk/functionalskills* for further information and developments.

Thinking skills

Activity

Let's begin this section with some activities to make you think. Consider the following questions and, if possible, discuss them with colleagues or fellow trainees.

1 What are the differences between:
   - information;
   - knowledge; and
   - thinking?
2 What does 'thinking' mean? What are you doing when you think about something?

3 Can you describe the way you think? How similar or different is your way of thinking from other people's?

4 What are the differences between thinking about what you did on your holidays and thinking to solve a problem?

In considering these questions you've been involved in 'metacognition', that is thinking about thinking, particularly your own thinking. Metacognition is one of the most powerful methods of improvement for learners and teachers.

What are thinking skills?

We all think, more or less all of the time. Much of our thinking involves random, unstructured thoughts, daydreams, reminiscences and just general ideas popping into our heads. This kind of thinking is effortless and frequently serves no particular purpose – sometimes it is a source of pleasure; sometimes anxiety.

Thinking skills are centred on more deliberate, purposeful, structured thinking processes which are learned and developed through application and practice. When we talk about thinking skills we are usually referring to a range of higher-order thinking processes. Fisher (2006: 25) suggests that 'Such processes include remembering; questioning; forming concepts; planning; reasoning; imagining; solving problems; making decisions and judgements; translating thoughts into words and so on.'

McGuiness (1999: 3) says that thinking skills include:

- collecting information;

- sorting and analysing information;
- drawing conclusions from information;
- 'brainstorming' new ideas;
- problem-solving;
- determining cause and effect;
- evaluating options;
- planning and setting goals;
- monitoring progress;
- decision-making;
- reflecting on one's own progress.

Clearly, the thinking skills outlined by Fisher and McGuiness coincide with a number of teaching and learning methods and processes discussed elsewhere in this book. For example, these kinds of thinking skills can be applied to learners devising and monitoring their own projects; using their ILPs to identify their strengths and ways to improve, and working out the ways in which they learn most effectively.

Why are thinking skills important?

Thinking skills are important for two main reasons: first, for their benefits to the economy and society and, second, their impact on learners and teachers.

The importance of developing skills for the needs of the economy in an increasingly competitive world is beyond question. We have always needed the skills of literacy and numeracy, that's basically why the 1870 Education Act made schooling compulsory. Without a fully skilled workforce we can't compete. We, rightly, recognise the skills of literacy, numeracy and ICT for individual and economic success, but we live in a rapidly changing world in which these 'basics', on their own, will be insufficient. They need to be matched by the development of the kinds of higher-order, transferable skills outlined above because individuals, in an 'information society', will be unable to 'store' sufficient knowledge in their memories for the future and the rapid rate of information increase will require individuals to develop higher-order skills which are transferable to other contexts.

Guy Claxton writes persuasively about 'information' and argues against the simplistic view of learning as the 'application and manipulation of information'. You will be familiar with learners whose first instinct on being given a task to complete or being asked to find information is to use a search engine to trawl the Internet for them. Whilst this method will yield much useful, reliable and accurate information it will, most likely, bring forth a greater amount of material of doubtful and unreliable origin. Thinking skills approaches would require learners to justify their use of the Internet as well as to demonstrate judgement in selecting and evaluating information sources. As Claxton points out:

> Info-evangelists ... seem to talk as if the endless accumulation of up-to-the-minute information were the answer to all the world's ills ... Access to avalanches of information, loosely connected by threads or casual associations, does not of itself bring about the transformation of that information into knowledge or wise judgement, nor the development of the requisite skills and dispositions for doing so. It is the business of education to foster the development of the ability to select, integrate and evaluate theories and opinions, not to drown in information ...
>
> (Claxton 1999: 224)

From the learners' and the teachers' point of view the development of thinking skills has many benefits. The most obvious is that it improves achievement. The CASE (Cognitive Acceleration through Science Education) programme developed at Kings College, London, develops thinking skills in schools through science education. The most recent evidence suggests that students in schools using this at Key Stage 3 achieve 19 per cent more A–C grades in GCSE science than those using traditional methods. Significantly, the CASE science students achieve 16 per cent more A–Cs in English and 15 per cent more in maths, suggesting that students have transferred their thinking skills to other subjects.

The importance of the thinking skills approach is underlined by Geoff Petty (2006: 283) with his idea of the 'content trap'. He suggests that 'Weak teachers spend almost all their time teaching content; thinking skills are relatively ignored. They teach the easy stuff and ignore the hard. Teaching both skills *and* content gets much better results.' One can possibly understand that busy teachers in colleges, training providers and schools feel that they only have time to teach to the exam or test and that wider skills and higher-order thinking are luxuries they cannot afford, but thinking skills programmes integrated across the curriculum seem to improve results and, most likely, will make the experience more active and enjoyable for learners and teachers.

How can thinking skills be developed in the lifelong learning sector?

Learning is lifelong; not just an activity which happens at specific times in our lives and in certain places such as school, college, workplace or training courses. It is a natural human activity which we do all the time, particularly at times of change such as when we start a new job or a new relationship or, on a simpler level, when we buy a new piece of technology. Learning is, on a simple level, about working things out; it requires the conscious application of thinking, adaptation and development. Formal learning in formal situations has traditionally been based on the acquisition of knowledge and, to a great extent, our examination system reinforces this view of learning; that is, learning as a body of knowledge which you own rather than as a set of skills which you use and refine. Thinking skills go beyond the acquisition of knowledge. In formal learning situations we need to recognise and develop our higher-order skills through learning which makes us think and construct, test and justify our learning. Some of the best practice in FE colleges and adult learning (for example, reflection and evaluation, discussion, collaborative group working) has been based on these principles for a long time and is, in many ways, ahead of schools in the development of thinking skills.

Thinking skills can and should be taught; the main question is how? There are two main approaches: either by specifically designed thinking skills courses or by embedding thinking skills activities across the curriculum by using teaching and learning techniques chosen to encourage higher-order skills. As with key skills the best practice, I feel, is via the embedded route. This approach is sometimes referred to by thinking skills experts as 'infusion', but this is the first and last time I will use the term; I'll stick with 'embedding'.

This section will consider a range of techniques and ideas for developing thinking skills for learners, and teachers. Many of these ideas are underpinned by the active and constructivist learning principles discussed throughout this book and some, especially questioning and problem-based learning, have already been considered in detail in their own right. However, developing a thinking skills approach to learning and teaching is not just a matter of acquiring some new techniques; it's more an attitude of mind based on enquiry, curiosity and, to some extent, risk-taking.

Using Bloom's taxonomy

Bloom's taxonomy (see Chapter 4, 'Planning for teaching and learning', p. 104) is a framework which can be used to develop thinking skills, especially the higher-order elements – analysis, synthesis and evaluation. Using the taxonomy in your session planning will encourage you to include higher order activities and develop thinking skills. Share the taxonomy with your learners; get them to identify when they are using particular elements of it and, especially, get them to evaluate their learning either through written evaluations or discussions and presentations. This can happen in each session through a debriefing at the end.

Debriefing

A debriefing at the end of each session, or at the end of an extended task over several sessions, is one of the most valuable ways to get learners to reflect on and evaluate their learning. It also provides an excellent method of linking forward to the next session. Here are some tips for debriefing:

- Get learners to restate the 'big picture'; what was the task or what was the problem they set out to solve?
- Ask them to explain their methods and activities. Ask them to explain and justify choices of method and ways of working.
- Ask them to describe methods they rejected and explain their reasons.
- Use higher-order questions to help learners connect and extend their thinking.
- Ask them to identify methods they have used and skills and knowledge which can be transferred to other learning.
- If it's a debriefing at the end of a major project make it a more intensive activity. Learners could give presentations and take part in discussions.

Discussion

We have seen the benefits of using discussion in the chapter on learning methods. A thinking skills approach can help to improve the quality of discussion. A particularly useful method is Edward de Bono's *Six Thinking Hats* (1985) which is designed to get learners to discuss and analyse ideas and problems from different perspectives. If, for example, a learner proposes an idea which is really 'off the wall' and derided by fellow learners it can be evaluated using this method with individual learners 'wearing' a particular hat and using the approach that goes with it. The six thinking hats are:

White hat is neutral and objective and encourages the wearer to consider the facts;
Red hat is emotional and involves the expression of subjective points of view and feelings;
Black hat urges a careful and cautious approach and looks for the weakness in an idea;
Yellow hat is positive and optimistic and recognises the benefits of the idea. It's the 'let's go for it' hat;
Green hat is the creativity hat. It encourages new ways of thinking and alternative approaches;
Blue hat encourages metacognition, thinking about the thinking involved and the use and control of the other hats.

A similar approach, frequently used in business, is the SWOT analysis in which learners consider the strengths, weaknesses, opportunities and threats of a particular proposal.

Reflection and evaluation

Encourage learners to reflect on and evaluate their work. Learning logs can be a useful way to record and reflect on learning. You can apply the same principles as outlined in Chapter 1, 'The reflective teacher', particularly 'reflection in action' and 'reflection on action'.

Thinking circles and 'café philosphique'

In a thinking circle, groups of learners, and teacher/s, are given a written or visual stimulus as a starting point for discussion. The idea of the 'café philosophique' conjures visions of French philosophers in black polo-neck jumpers vigorously debating and exchanging ideas through a thick fog of cigarette smoke; this is a great idea, but you should omit the cigarettes. This is much more informal than a debating society or a seminar, so don't do it in a classroom; find somewhere more relaxed where people can lounge around and get drinks and food. Doing it using a blog is far less effective because it lacks the immediacy of response, the passion and the social contact. It's a great format for discussing 'big issues'; *The Philosopher's Magazine* has examples on their website (see Further Reading, p. 272). Scientists can develop a 'café scientifique'. We are all affected by science but very few of us will become scientists; the 'café scientifique' is where scientists can explain and justify their views to non-scientists.

What if?

This is sometimes referred to by historians as 'counterfactual' history; what would things be like now if history had been different? The clichéd example is what the world would be like if the Nazis had won the Second World War. This method is not just for history; English literature students could explore what would have happened if Bathsheba Everdene hadn't sent Farmer Boldwood the Valentine card in *Far from the Madding Crowd*; travel and tourism students could consider what the world would be like if planes hadn't been invented; engineers could speculate about engineering if there was no such thing as steel. These activities might begin with instant, unsupported speculation but learners must research and justify their speculations and make imaginative connections.

Reading images

This is a technique which I, and many other media teachers, have employed successfully. A photograph or an image is a frozen moment in time; it's a good thinking skills exercise to imagine and explain what happened immediately before and after that moment; where it is and who the people are. You can use the concepts of 'denotation' and 'connotation' here. Denotation requires learners to describe what they see, for example, a man with a gun and a child crying. Connotation is about interpretation and how the image makes you feel: the man with the gun could either represent a threat or protection; the child may be crying because it is frightened or relieved to be protected. Learners' interpretations of the image will be affected by where and when they think the image is set.

The methods outlined here are intended as a kind of 'starter pack' for thinking skills activities. I urge you to try some of these techniques and to follow up further methods and ideas, not only because they are more effective but also because they are more fun.

PLTS in the new specialised diplomas

Specialised diplomas are a new qualification for 14–19-year-olds which will be introduced from September 2008. They combine theoretical and applied learning together with Functional Skills and personal, learning and thinking skills. They will be available at Levels 1, 2 and 3 in 14 employment areas. The first diplomas starting in 2008 will be:

- construction and the built environment;
- creative and media;
- engineering;
- health and social care;
- IT.

By September 2010 this will be extended to include:

- land-based and environmental studies;
- manufacturing;
- hair and beauty;
- business administration and finance;
- hospitality and catering;
- public services;
- sport and leisure;
- retail;
- travel and tourism.

The main elements of the diplomas are:

principal learning: which develops knowledge, understanding and skills within the context of a particular sector;

generic learning: functional skills in English, maths and ICT, and personal, learning and thinking skills;

additional/specialist learning: which offers the opportunity to study a particular topic in more depth or broaden through complementary learning;

a project: in which learners plan and organise their own learning;

work experience.

The framework for PLTS is set out by the QCA (2007). These skills are integrated into the assessment criteria for the principal learning component. The framework makes specific reference to the development of young people's skills; however this can also serve as a comprehensive framework for learners of all ages so I have reproduced it here in full:

Independent enquirers

Young people process and evaluate information in their investigations, planning what to do and how to go about it. They take informed and well reasoned decisions, recognising that others have different beliefs and attitudes.

- identify questions to answer and problems to resolve;
- plan and carry out research, appreciating the consequences of decisions;
- explore issues, events or problems from different perspectives;
- analyse and evaluate information, judging its relevance and value;
- consider the influence of circumstances, beliefs and feelings on decisions and events;
- support conclusions, using reasoned arguments and evidence.

Creative thinkers

Young people think creatively by generating and exploring ideas, making original connections. They try different ways to tackle a problem, working with others to find imaginative solutions and outcomes that are of value.

- generate ideas and explore possibilities
- ask questions to extend their thinking
- connect their own and others' ideas and experiences in inventive ways
- question their own and others' assumptions
- try out alternatives or new solutions and follow ideas through
- adapt ideas as circumstances change.

Reflective learners

Young people evaluate their strengths and limitations, setting themselves realistic goals with criteria for success. They monitor their own performance and progress, inviting feedback from others and making changes to further their learning.

- assess themselves and others, identifying opportunities and achievements
- set goals with success criteria for their development and work
- review progress, acting on the outcomes
- invite feedback and deal positively with praise, setbacks and criticism
- evaluate experiences and learning to inform future progress
- communicate their learning in relevant ways for different audiences.

Team workers
Young people work confidently with others, adapting to different contexts and taking responsibility for their own part. They listen to and take account of different views. They form collaborative relationships, resolving issues to reach agreed outcomes.
- collaborate with others to work towards common goals
- reach agreements, managing discussions to achieve results
- adapt behaviour to suit different roles and situations
- show fairness and consideration to others
- take responsibility, showing confidence in themselves and their contribution
- provide constructive support and feedback to others.

Self-managers
Young people organise themselves, showing personal responsibility, initiative, creativity and enterprise with a commitment to learning and self-improvement. They actively embrace change, responding positively to new priorities, coping with challenges and looking for opportunities.
- seek out challenges or new responsibilities and show flexibility when priorities change
- work towards goals, showing initiative, commitment and perseverance
- organise time and resources, prioritising actions
- anticipate, take and manage risks
- deal with competing pressures, including personal and work-related demands
- respond positively to change, seeking advice and support when needed.

Effective participators
Young people actively engage with issues that affect them and those around them. They play a full part in the life of their school, college, workplace or wider community by taking responsible action to bring improvements for others as well as themselves.
- discuss issues of concern, seeking resolution where needed
- present a persuasive case for action

- propose practical ways forward, breaking these down into manageable steps
- identify improvements that would benefit others as well as themselves
- try to influence others, negotiating and balancing diverse views to reach workable solutions
- act as an advocate for views and beliefs that may differ from their own.

Some ideas for integrating PLTS into the specialised diplomas

The guidelines for the delivery of specialised diplomas make clear that the personal, learning and thinking skills are integrated into the assessment criteria for the principal learning and can be developed and also included as part of the project and work experience. Like Key Skills, PLTS will not be effective if they are treated as a 'bolt-on' extra; they need to be planned in right from the start and this means using learning and teaching methods which necessitate the application and development of these skills: teacher-dominated, transmission teaching will not do. The specialised diplomas could provide an ideal opportunity for developing problem-based learning (see Chapter 5, 'Teaching and learning methods). Time taken over planning will show that it may also be possible to meet the criteria for Functional Skills and ECM, as well as PLTS, within the same activities.

Here are a few starter ideas for embedding personal, learning and thinking skills into some of the new specialised diplomas:

Health and social care

Organising a 'Healthy Life' exhibition would offer a wide variety of evidence for PTLS (or Key Skills), Functional Skills and Every Child Matters. The spider diagram in Figure 10.2 suggests just a few; you will be able to think of many more.

Engineering

Engineering offers many opportunities for problem-based learning and the development of PLTS. Learners could be encouraged to identify and analyse an engineering problem and plan, research, produce, analyse and evaluate their solutions. Such a project would involve all elements of the PLTS framework.

Creative and media

Media planning and production projects – for example, the development of an advertising campaign – can be structured around PLTS and functional

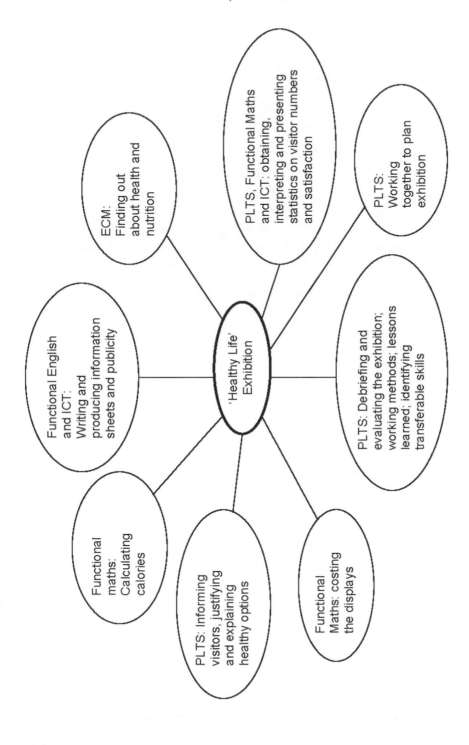

Figure 10.2 Healthy Life exhibition: combining Functional Skills and PLTS

skills. In media projects it is particularly important for learners to match the campaign to the needs and lifestyles of the target audience and to create products in the appropriate style, tone and presentation to suit that audience. It's pretty much what teachers have to do for learners!

Journal extract: Jo, doing a Cert Ed while teaching biology in an FE college

I've been thinking about some of the things staff have been discussing to do with the new science curriculum. Some of them think it's dumbed down and the students won't develop scientific skills. But most of them won't be scientists. We'd also been looking at thinking skills in Cert Ed. I'm doing genetics with one group and it was all getting a bit dull, so I thought we should have a discussion about transgenic animals and cloning and such-like. Some people had very strong opinions and just about everyone had something to say. I used some connected to questions to try to get them to develop their ideas. We didn't do much specific content but they seemed a bit more enthused and had more of an idea about why we're studying it.

Skills for Life: further reading and useful websites

www.basic-skills.co.uk This site provides a wide range of publications and support, including a series of leaflets which give accessible information about the reading, writing, speaking, listening and mathematical demands of a range of occupations.

www.dfes.gov.uk/readwriteplus Adult Basic Skills Strategy Unit (ABSSU): this site is intended to be the main source for information and advice on all aspects of implementing Skills for Life. The Embedded Learning Portal is at: *www.dfes.gov.uk/readwriteplusembeddedlearning/*

www.sflqi.org.uk Skills for Life Quality Initiative (SfLQI) provides a downloadable pack *Practical Guidance for Embedding Skills for Life*.

The National Institute for Adult and Continuing Education (NIACE) provides some excellent case studies in embedded learning, particularly learners with disabilities and/or learning difficulties: *Learning from Experience www.niace.org.uk/Projects/learningfromexperience*

The National Research and Development Centre for Adult Literacy and Numeracy (NRDC) carries out significant research into learning and teaching in this area.

Two reports referred to above on embedding are:

Embedded Teaching and Learning of Adult Literacy, Numeracy and ESOL: Seven Case Studies (August 2005).
'You wouldn't expect a maths teacher to teach plastering ...' Embedding Literacy, Language and Numeracy in Post-16 Vocational Programmes – The Impact on Learning and Achievement (August 2006).

The NRDC also publishes specific case studies on embedding Skills for Life in vocational areas such as childcare, construction and horticulture.
These can be downloaded from *www.nrdc.org.uk/projects*

www.bbc.co.uk/skillswise BBC Skillswise provides a wide range of materials to support Skills for Life, including embedded materials.
www.skillsforlifenetwork.com See this site for news, resources, jobs and information. You will need to register.
www.hm-treasury.gov.uk/leitch See this site for full and summary versions of the Leitch Review.

Key Skills: useful websites

www.qca.org.uk The QCA Key Skills qualifications standards and guidance Levels 1–4 for:
- Communication: Application of Number: ICT
- Working with Others; Improving Own Learning and Performance; Problem Solving

www.keyskillssupport.net Key Skills Support Programme publishes a wide range of publications including, *Supporting Centres to Innovate and Develop Effective Key Skills and SfL practice* (2007).
www.dfes.gov.uk/keyskills
www.keyskills4u.com This site is useful for explaining Key Skills to young learners.
www.ksspforwork.org.uk See this site for the Key Skills Support Programme for work-based learning.
www.totallyskilled.co.uk This site is useful for embedding Key Skills and Skills for Life in vocational qualifications.

Thinking skills: further reading and useful websites

Bowkett, S. (2006) *100 Ideas for Teaching Thinking Skills*. London: Continuum.
Claxton, G. (1999) *Wise Up. Learning to Live the Learning Life*. Stafford: Network Educational Press Ltd.

de Bono, E. (1985) *Six Thinking Hats*. London: Penguin Books.

DfES (2005) *Leading in Learning: Developing Thinking Skills at Key Stage 3. Handbook for Teachers*. London: DfES.

(These materials are intended for schools but there are a lot of good ideas you can use or adapt.)

Fisher, R. (2003) *Teaching Thinking*. London: Continuum.

McGregor, D. (2007) *Developing Thinking: Developing Learning* Maidenhead: McGraw-Hill/Open University Press.

www.case-network.org See this site for further information on CASE.

www.cheshire-learning.co.uk Follow the link to *Mind Friendly Learning*.

www.teachthinking.com This is the site of the *Teaching Thinking and Creativity Magazine*.

www.philosophersnet.com The *Philosopher's Magazine* has a section on 'café philosophique' and some interesting and amusing debates, a recent example, 'Shakespeare vs. Britney', considers questions of what art is.

For your journal

Skills for Life are a concern of all teachers in the lifelong learning sector. To what extent does the delivery of skills affect your planning, preparation, delivery and assessment? Do you consciously plan for skills development?

To what extent and in what ways have you embedded Skills for Life and Key Skills into your planning and delivery? How successful has this been and what have been the learners' reactions to the inclusion of these skills?

Do you plan for the development of thinking skills in teaching and learning activities and methods? What methods and activities have you tried? To what extent do you think that learning has improved and learners have responded positively?

11 Equality, diversity and inclusion

What this chapter is about

- Defining and explaining equality, diversity and inclusion
- Inclusive learning
- Widening participation
- Disability legislation
- Specific Learning Difficulties (SpLD), e.g. dyslexia
- Every Child Matters (ECM)

LLUK standards

This chapter covers the following standards:

AS 1; AK 1.1; AP 1.1; AS 3; AK 3.1; AP 3.1; AK 6.1; AP 6.1
BS 1; BK 1.1; BP 1.1; BK 1.2; BP 1.2
CK 3.2; CP 3.2
DS 1; DK 1.1; DP 1.1

Introduction

Diversity and inclusion are, in essence, quite simple ideas to understand. Everyone is a potential learner and there is an enormous diversity of learners out there with all sorts of needs, abilities and experiences. Unfortunately, many of them have experienced difficulty in finding out about and accessing learning opportunities. People may have experienced difficulties in accessing learning for many reasons, for example, disability or health problems, prejudice or economic problems. However, as professionals in the lifelong learning sector it is our job to be inclusive and offer learning to all.

Some definitions

Equality or equal opportunities, refers to the whole organisation in which you work, its general ethos and its attitudes towards providing equal opportunities for learners and staff.

Diversity means the whole range of different individuals and groups in your community – and possibly beyond it – who are your potential learners. There are six recognised strands of diversity:

- gender
- disability
- ethnicity
- age
- sexual orientation
- religion and/or belief.

Widening participation describes the positive attempts made by learning organisations to bring people from across the diversity of the community into learning, particularly those who have experienced difficulty, disadvantage, discrimination and disappointment in their earlier learning.

Inclusion embraces the whole learning institution. As Wright et al. (2006) point out it is different from integration which refers to the process of putting people with learning difficulties and disabilities into mainstream provision with the implicit expectation that it is *they* who need to change.

> Inclusion is very different. Inclusion requires the institution to change and not the learner. In inclusive settings, the learner is intrinsically valued and accepted and it is the institution that must change its policies, structures and curricula if these restrict access or present any barrier to full participation by the learner.

(Wright et al. 2006: 3)

Inclusive learning is learning which meets the needs, learning styles, abilities and experiences of all who come into our institutions. We can't just say, 'This is how we teach' and expect everyone to fit in with it. We need to find out how people learn and to develop provision, methods and resources to suit them. This takes us on to a consideration of the Tomlinson Report.

The Tomlinson Report *Inclusive Learning* (1996)

Professor John Tomlinson was asked to research and report on educational provision for learners with learning difficulties and disabilities. The final document, however, had implications for all learners and was a keystone in the development of inclusive education. The Tomlinson Committee moved the focus from those with learning difficulties and disabilities to a more a learner-centred approach for all and, in essence, makes clear that all learners are unique individuals with their own particular needs and experience. The report moves away from labelling and asserts that difficulties are not located within the learner; rather it is the duty of educational providers to understand individual learners and to find ways to meet their requirements. There is a clear link here to more recent trends with the development of ILPs and the move towards 'personalised learning'.

The key message of Tomlinson is summed up by his statement that:

> The aim is not for students to simply take part in further education but to be actively included and fully engaged in their learning. At the heart of our thinking lies the idea of match or fit between how the learner learns best, what they need and want to learn and what is required from the FE sector, the college and teachers for successful learning to take place.
>
> By inclusive learning therefore we mean the greatest degree of match or fit between the individual learners' requirements and the provision that is made for them.
>
> (Tomlinson 1996: 10)

In a later article, Tomlinson (2003) reviews and reaffirms the centrality of inclusive learning and puts it into a contemporary context and makes clear that it applies right across the lifelong learning sector in work-based learning, adult and community learning, colleges and sixth forms. He reminds us that inclusive learning is not just for those with learning difficulties and disabilities; 'Inclusive learning also applies to all learners, teachers and providers'.

Tomlinson recommends an individually designed learning environment as the best way to ensure that provision meets learners' needs. This environment would have, and develop for all, these components:

- an individual learning programme;
- a curriculum which promotes progress in learning;
- effective teaching;
- counselling, guidance and initial assessment;
- opportunities for students to discuss and manage their own learning;
- support for learning;
- support for learners, such as crèche facilities;
- procedures for assessing, recording and accrediting achievement;
- learning materials and resources;
- technical aids and equipment;
- learning technology;
- trained staff.

Activity

To what extent do you think that your institution meets the criteria for an individually designed learning environment as set out by Tomlinson?

Widening participation

The key document here is *Learning Works: Widening Participation in Further Education* (Kennedy 1997), commonly referred to as the Kennedy Report, which stated the 'irresistible case' for widening participation in education. Recently we have heard a great deal, rightly, about the importance of learning and skills for economic success. Kennedy recognised this but added, perhaps more importantly, the case for learning as a way to develop social unity and lessen social exclusion. Kennedy understands that many people who have failed in their early learning have suffered economic and social disadvantages from which they may not easily recover. Far too many people have come out of school believing that education is over and they never return to it; as Kennedy wryly says, 'If at first you don't succeed ... you don't succeed.' For the health of society and the economy these people need to be given opportunities to return to, and succeed in, learning.

Kennedy (1997: 15) stated that:

> We must widen participation not simply increase it. Widening participation means increasing access to learning and providing opportunities for success and progression to a much wider cross-section of the population than now. All those who are not fulfilling their potential or who have underachieved in the past must be drawn in to successful learning. Widening participation in post-16 learning will create a self-perpetuating learning society.

In May 2003, following a consultation process, the Learning and Skills Council launched its *Successful Participation for All: Widening Adult Participation* strategy. This built on the Tomlinson and Kennedy reports and reflected the LSC's concern that a significant number of adults do not continue in education or training beyond school and the implications of this for individuals and the economy as well as wider social issues including crime, health and community cohesion. The important implication for our practice as teachers is that the strategy brings together two key ideas. It states that:

> We cannot separate widening participation from inclusive learning. Widening participation is about seeking to reach under-represented groups and retaining these groups in learning. Inclusive education addresses the learning programmes needed for individuals and groups to succeed in learning.
>
> (LSC 2003, para. 49)

Further, the strategy provides important messages for the ways in which we plan, prepare, deliver and assess learning. It highlights some of the ways in which many people were turned off learning by early negative experiences, including:

- too much teaching and too little learning;
- content which had little interest to them or relevance to their lives;
- frequent experiences of failure and humiliation.

In considering ways in which learners can be encouraged to return to, and remain in, learning the report asserts that: 'Nothing is more likely to demotivate learners than to feel they are being criticised as failures. Nor are they likely to be willing participants in a process that is "being done to them"' (LSC 2003, para. 50).

Activity

Consider the above points.

In what ways can you link these to the theory and practice discussed elsewhere in this book, particularly learning theories, teaching and learning methods, assessment and motivation?

Learners with learning difficulties and/or disabilities

The Disability Discrimination Act (1995) defines a *disability* as: 'a physical or mental impairment which has a substantial and long-term adverse effect on your ability to carry out normal day-to-day activities'.

This can include:

- sensory impairments, e.g. people with visual impairments or who are hard of hearing;
- learning difficulties, including specific learning difficulties such as dyslexia;

- mental health conditions ('clinically well recognised');
- severe disfigurements;
- progressive conditions, such as multiple sclerosis, cancer and HIV;
- conditions which are characterised by a number of cumulative effects such as pain or fatigue;
- a past history of disability.

The Learning and Skills Act (2000) states that a disability 'prevents or hinders [a person] from making use of facilities of a kind generally provided by institutions providing post-16 education or training'.

A *learning difficulty* is when someone has greater difficulty in learning than the majority of persons of their own age. A person who has a learning difficulty may also have a disability, for example a person who has Down's syndrome may have some degree of learning difficulty.

A brief review of the legislation

The Disability Discrimination Act (DDA) (1995) made it unlawful to discriminate against a disabled person in the provision of a job, services or property. The Special Educational Needs and Disability Act (2001) amended the DDA (1995) to make it unlawful for educational providers to discriminate against learners with disabilities. Education providers must make 'reasonable adjustments' to ensure that disabled learners do not suffer a substantial disadvantage in comparison to people who are not disabled. Such adjustments might include:

- changes to admissions, administrative or examinations procedures;
- changes to course content;
- changes to physical features and the learning environment;
- providing information in alternative formats;
- additional teaching;
- providing auxiliary aids, communication or support services.

Institutions should also anticipate the likely needs of disabled learners as well as respond to individual needs as they arise. For example, an institution might not previously have had learners who are wheelchair users but provision should still be made.

The Disability Discrimination Act (DDA) (2005) develops previous legislation by placing a 'disability equality duty' (DED) on all public sector institutions to become proactive agents of change. This duty means that all institutions, including educational, must have due regard to the need to:

- promote equality of opportunity between disabled people and other people;
- eliminate unlawful discrimination;
- eliminate disability-related harassment;
- promote positive attitudes towards disabled people;
- encourage participation by disabled people in public life;
- take account of disabled people's disabilities, even where that involves treating disabled people more favourably than others.

(see Rose and Faraday 2006: 9)

Rose and Faraday provide a rebuttal to staff in institutions who say that the disability equality duty is yet another example of 'political correctness gone mad'. They state that:

There are clear and irrefutable facts that disabled people experience discrimination. For example, disabled people are twice as likely to be unemployed, compared with non-disabled people, despite many having the satisfactory skills and qualifications, and wanting to work. Disabled people are twice as likely to have no qualifications, compared with non-disabled people.

(Rose and Faraday 2006: 39)

Perhaps we should all remember that disabled people aren't a race apart and that any one of us who is able-bodied could become disabled through illness or accident. I am certain that none of us would, if disabled, accept that we should have fewer rights or opportunities than we previously had.

The medical and social models of disability

To help us understand the background to the DDA (2005) and the disability equality duty the *medical* and *social* models of disability describe different attitudes towards disability and its consequences.

The medical model focuses on the person's disability and sees it in terms of what they can and cannot do. There is an implicit assumption in this model that the difficulties disabled people encounter are the direct result of their disability rather than the fact that society and institutions do not adequately provide for them. This model of disability leads to a labelling approach which takes a narrow view of disabled people and ties them into cultures of dependency.

The social model doesn't view disabled people as having something wrong with them and shifts the focus to society and its institutions and attitudes. The social model takes as its starting point the belief that all disabled people have a right to belong and not be discriminated against. The DED places an obligation on institutions to 'understand and dismantle barriers before they have an impact on individuals' (Rose and Faraday 2006).

Activity

The Learning and Skills Council requires all providers to have a disability statement.

Have you found and read the disability statement for your institution? Is it widely available to all learners in a variety of formats?

Specific learning difficulties (SpLD)

SpLD refers to a range of learning difficulties, including dyslexia, dyspraxia, dyscalculia, attention deficit hyperactivity disorder (ADHD) and autistic spectrum disorders. Individually and collectively these conditions have been widely researched and there is a great deal of information in specific texts and websites to support you and your learners. The following is a brief overview of specific learning difficulties, some words of advice and references to further reading and websites.

Dyslexia

About 4 per cent of the population is affected by dyslexia to a significant extent and a further 6 per cent to a lesser degree. We know that until recently dyslexia was not fully understood and many dyslexic children and adults were regarded as stupid or lazy. The percentage of the prison population who are dyslexic is higher, certainly above 10 per cent and it has been suggested that in some prisons more than 50 per cent of the population is dyslexic.

Wright et al. provide a comprehensive list of symptoms that a dyslexic person may have some or all of:

- Generally disorganized – the student's file is always in a mess with pieces of work missing or 'mislaid'.
- The student is often late or misses appointments because he or she has forgotten the time, place, and so forth.
- He or she may seem 'clumsy', always knocking things over or bumping into objects.
- The student avoids reading aloud in class and always takes a passive role in group discussion.

- The student has difficulty with pronunciation, particularly with multi–syllabic words.
- The student has difficulty with writing essays, although he or she appears to understand the subject during the lessons. Generally he or she is 'good' orally, but has not produced much written work and may even avoid it completely.
- The student consistently makes spelling errors, even though he or she has had those errors corrected several times.
- The student's handwriting may be messy and immature.
- The content of the student's work may be inspiring but there is a lack of appropriate punctuation and grammar.
- The student may be a very good artist, hairdresser, musician or mechanic, but struggles to meet deadlines with assignments.

(Wright et al. 2006: 71–2)

It could be argued that dyslexia is more properly referred to as a learning difference rather than a learning difficulty, since dyslexic people can often be innovative and creative thinkers with intuitive problem-solving skills.

There are several ways in which you can help dyslexic learners and, fortunately, most of these are good methods for all learners.

- Like most learners dyslexic students benefit from seeing the big picture. Use some form of advance, particularly graphic, organiser such as a concept map or diagram to introduce topics and highlight key points
- Make learning multi-sensory – looking, listening, saying and doing. Using different materials and objects for writing with. One teacher working with prisoners describes her learners' success when writing in sand or on to a bar of soap.
- Flow charts are good for explaining procedures.
- Spelling – dyslexic learners like to visualise, so look for words within words, e.g. *bus* in *business*.
- Keep your boardwork neat and use colour to highlight different elements. Keep essential points grouped together.
- Provide glossaries of abbreviations and jargon.
- Don't use light text on a dark background. Use coloured paper for handouts; off-white or cream is good. Matt paper reduces glare.
- Give clear instructions and avoid long, complicated explanations.
- Assess work positively and provide positive feedback.
- Encourage learners to word-process their work.

This last point is particularly important because research suggests that dyslexic people lack 'automaticity'. For most of us such things as word recognition and multiplication tables become automatic and the retrieved information can be accessed rapidly without the brain having to process individual units of information. For dyslexics these processes are not so automatic and they have to think about them as well as the content and style of what they are writing. Louise Green has carried out research using word-processing with dyslexic learners in schools. In her article 'Freed from the pen', she concludes:

> So dyslexic pupils find it helpful to write using a keyboard not because they cannot write by hand, are lazy, or want to rely on a computer program to help them spell. It is because the demands on their working memory are reduced when they are allowed to use a keyboard rather than having to retrieve from memory each time how to form a letter or spell a word. Typing provides far less distraction from expressing what they want to write. Quite simply most dyslexics report that they can 'think better' when they type.
>
> (Green, 2007)

Under the Disability Discrimination Act, education providers are obliged to make 'reasonable adjustments' to support learners with dyslexia. This support may take the form of assistive technology, such as voice recognition software; specialist support from a specialist dyslexia tutor to assess and support learners; mentoring; specialist assessment and any necessary changes to the presentation of documents.

Dyscalculia

Dyscalculia is similar to dyslexia; learners have difficulty with numbers rather than words. Professor Mahesh Sharma explains that dyscalculia is, 'dysfunction in the reception, comprehension, or production of quantitative and spatial information', which results in difficulty 'in conceptualizing numbers, number relationships outcomes of numerical operations and estimation' (Sharma 2003).

Teachers can help learners who have dyscalculia by:

- improving understanding and self-esteem by making number work relevant to everyday life, for example checking change or estimating quantities in specific vocational areas. Clearly, such 'situated learning' would have benefits for all learners;
- using Socratic questioning to structure and scaffold learning;
- encouraging visualisation;
- getting them to read problems out loud and discuss mathematical problems;

- using repetition and practice;
- using technology.

Dyspraxia

Dyspraxia is a complex neurological condition which can affect many areas of life. The Dyspraxia Foundation estimates that up to 10 per cent of the population are affected, 2 per cent severely. It is characterised by difficulty in planning and carrying out complex movements. Additional difficulties include:

- 'clumsiness' and dropping things;
- problems judging distance;
- problems distinguishing between left and right;
- inability to do two tasks at once;
- taking a long time to complete tasks;
- poor handwriting.

Ways in which the teacher can help learners with dyspraxia include the following:

- Be patient and stay calm. Dyspraxic learners can be emotionally fragile and a careless comment or a harsh word can produce a disproportionate response.
- Offer encouragement. Be positive and recognise achievement.
- Ensure that learners know where they are in the session. Provide structure.
- Break down tasks into smaller, more manageable components.
- Provide staged processes and logical sequences.
- Provide regular routine and firm guidelines.

For further advice and discussion see Brookes (2007).

Every Child Matters (ECM)

Following the death of Victoria Climbie it was recommended that all children's services should work together and share information to improve child welfare and to ensure a 'joined up' approach to the inspection of children's services. The Children's Act 2004 placed a requirement on inspectors to pay attention to the well-being of young people. Inspections of college's provision will be included in joint area reviews of all children's services in every local authority. These reviews will evaluate to what extent the following outcomes are being met:

- being healthy;
- staying safe;
- enjoying and achieving;
- making a positive contribution;
- achieving economic well-being.

Attention will be paid to all students aged 14–19, but particularly to vulnerable groups, including those over 19. These groups may include:

- students with learning difficulties and/or disabilities;
- looked-after children;
- those at risk of under-achieving;
- young carers;
- statemented children;
- 14–16-year-old learners.

Evidencing the five themes

A fuller guide and range of examples is provided in *Every Child Matters: What it Means for Colleges* by Rosemary Clark (2006).

Being healthy. Evidence that young people:

- are physically healthy;
- are mentally and emotionally healthy;
- are sexually healthy;
- have healthy lifestyles;
- are encouraged to choose not to take illegal drugs.

To evidence this, colleges may consider a range of health promotion and awareness activities and development days. Some subject areas will lend themselves to inclusion of these issues, for example biology and psychology.

Staying safe. Evidence that young people are safe from:

- maltreatment, neglect, violence and sexual exploitation;
- injury and death;
- bullying and discrimination;
- crime and anti-social behaviour.

Much evidence for this will come from the existence and promulgation of policies and procedures relating to welfare of learners, including CRB checks, child protection issues and security.

Enjoying and achieving. Evidence that young people are:

- attending and enjoying college;
- making good progress and achieving stretching national educational standards;
- achieving personal and social development and enjoying recreational activities.

Enjoyment and achievement are likely to be enhanced if teachers have planned learning activities to suit the needs, styles and interests of their learners. In addition, celebrations, award presentations and displays of work also contribute to enjoyment and achievement.

Making a positive contribution. Evidence that young people:

- engage in decision-making and support the community and environment;
- engage in law-abiding and positive behaviour;
- develop positive relationships and choose not to bully and discriminate;
- understand their rights.

This theme gives opportunities for a range of community-based, voluntary and fund-raising events. These kinds of events and activities will also generate many key skill opportunities. Student bodies and councils can be set up to represent student views and contribute the institution's planning.

Achieving economic well-being. Evidence that young people:

- are provided with good impartial information, advice and guidance on future choices of career, education and training;
- are provided with opportunities for work experience and other work-based learning opportunities;
- acquire skills needed for employment and which will assist them in taking a full part in society.

Again there are clear links to key skill development, here, especially application of number. Financial literacy programmes can be integrated into a variety of curriculum areas and tutorial programmes. Small business projects would meet a number of ECM and key skill outcomes.

For your journal

Are you aware of all your learners who have specific learning difficulties?

What methods and techniques are most valuable in supporting these learners? What specialist support, information, advice and guidance do you get as a teacher?

Have you had any training in the legislation relating to disability and learning difficulties? For your ILP you should consider what further knowledge and skills you need.

Consider any instances from your sessions in which you have been uncertain about how you should support or communicate with a learner who has disability or a learning difficulty. For example, has your first instinct with a wheelchair user been to help him/her? Is there anything wrong with this instinct?

Further reading and useful websites

Clark, R. (2006) *Every Child Matters: What it Means for Colleges*. Support for Success Quality Improvement Programme downloadable from *www.s4s.org.uk*

Rose, C. and Faraday, F. (2006) *The Journey Towards Disability Equality: Responding to the Duty to Promote Disability Equality in the Post-school Sector*. London: Learning and Skills Network. This core document is accompanied by six more detailed documents on specific aspects of implementing the disability equality duty (DED).

Wright, A-M., Sina, A-J., Colquhoun, S., Spear, J. and Partridge, T. (2006) *FE Lecturer's Guide to Diversity and Inclusion*: London: Continuum.

www.drc-gb.org This is the site of the Disability Rights Commission.

http://www.direct.gov.uk/en/DisabledPeople/index.htm has information and directories of services for disabled people.

www.skill.org.uk Skill: National Bureau for Students with Disabilities

www.signcommunity.org.uk British Deaf Association Sign Community

www.rnib.org.uk Royal National Institute for the Blind

www.bdadyslexia.org.uk British Dyslexia Association. This provides very useful information and advice packages, including 'The Dyslexia Style Guide' for producing printed materials and teaching and learning advice in 'How FE and HE tutors can help'.

www.dyslexiaacction.org.uk Dyslexia Action (formerly The Dyslexia Institute)

www.bbc.co.uk/skillswise/tutors/expertcolumn BBC Skillswise. The Expert Column has advice and information sheets on a range of learning difficulties and specific learning difficulties, including dyslexia, dyscalculia, Asperger's syndrome and working with deaf learners.

www.dfes.gov.uk/readwriteplus/understandingdyslexia A Framework for Understanding Dyslexia – a comprehensive overview of theories of dyslexia and ways to help dyslexic learners.

www.dyspraxia.org.uk Advice for learners and teachers about dyspraxia

www.dyscalculia.org.uk Advice for learners and teachers about dyscalculia

www.addiss.co.uk Attention Deficit Disorder Information Service

www.nas.org.uk National Autistic Society, for information about autism and Asperger's syndrome

www.aspergerfoundation.org.uk Asperger's Syndrome Foundation provides useful advice sheets for teachers working with adolescents and adults.

www.speakability.org.uk Aphasia and dysphasia

www.everychildmatters.gov.uk Every Child Matters

http://inclusion.ngfl.gov.uk Inclusion: Supporting Individual Learning Needs

12 Synthesis and evaluation

What this chapter is about
- Bringing together the various elements of teaching and learning
- Recognising the connections between these elements
- What is effective teaching and learning?
- The Hay McBer model of teacher effectiveness applied to lifelong learning
- Evaluating your teaching

LLUK standards

This chapter includes, at least, the following standards:

AS 1; AK 2.1; AP 2.2; AS 2; AK 2.1; AP 2.1; AS 3; AK 3.1; AP 3.1; AS 4; AK 4.2; AP 4.2; AK 4.2; AP 4.2; AK 4.3; AP 4.3; AS 5; AK 5.2; AP 5.2; AS 6; AK 6.2; AP 6.2; AS 7; AK 7.2; AP 7.2; AK 7.3; AP 7.3
BS 1; BK 1.1; BP 1.1; BK 1.2; BP 1.2; BK 1.3; BP 1.3; BS 2; BK 2.6; BP 2.6
DS 1; DK 1.1; DP 1.1; DS 3; DK 3.1; DP 3.1; DK 3.2; DP 3.2

Introduction

This brief, concluding chapter takes its title from the highest two levels of Bloom's taxonomy. *Synthesis* because effective teaching and learning is when the various elements – for example theory, planning, resources, assessment – are all working together in concert and the teaching matches the learning. *Evaluation* because effective teachers evaluate teaching and learning as part of the reflective process and the drive for continual improvement.

Synthesis

At various points throughout this book I have encouraged you to make connections between the different elements of teaching and learning and to consider the effects they have on each other. Competence-based systems of learning and assessment can, all too frequently, break things down into their constituent elements but forget to put them back together; they forget the 'big picture'. A great car is a more than just the sum of its parts: its gearbox, transmission, steering and aerodynamics are designed as individual parts but they are also designed to work together so that the whole of the car is greater than the sum of its parts. Great teaching is the same and good teachers ensure that all the elements are aligned to meet the needs of the learners. Good teaching and effective learning is creative – it is a synthesis of, at least, knowledge, skills, methods, theory, experience and reflection.

Activity: case study

Ron, our fictional teacher from the discussion case study, is meeting a group of young learners for their first (all day) session in a further education college. They have come from various local schools but none of them has enjoyed learning or had any significant achievements. Now that Ron is a wiser and more experienced teacher, he knows that he can make a difference to these people and, hopefully, re-engage them in learning. He knows that getting it right in this first session is vital to success.

This first session has two purposes. The stated, explicit purpose of the session is to induct them and carry out initial assessments – potentially a dull and anxiety-inducing experience. The implicit, but far more important purpose of this session, is to show the learners that they will have a different experience in college; that they will be respected and treated more like adults than in school; that teachers will have high expectations of them and provide challenging but achievable learning activities; that they will be listened to and their experiences valued; and that the learning environment will be emotionally safe. In short, to make them want to keep coming to college and learning.

Going back over all that you have read and learned so far, consider each of the following and discuss how they can contribute to making a better learning experience for them:

- communication;

- learning theories;

- planning;

- teaching and learning methods;
- motivation;
- assessment;
- resources;
- inclusive learning.

What is effective learning and teaching?

What do we mean by effective teaching and effective learning? Effective for whom or for what?

Effective teaching could be teaching that gets results. In an assessment-driven system, teachers who produce the best results are highly valued – rightly so. Good results mean a better reputation and more secure funding and future for the organisation and its teachers. Better results mean more people progressing to higher levels of learning. Conversely, effective teaching in an assessment-driven system can mean a narrowing of the curriculum and the content and an emphasis on transmission-based teaching; at its worst, teaching to the test. Good teaching which produces good results does not necessarily produce lifelong learners. Teaching which gets results is also, we are told, good for the economy and society. People need skills to get on in their lives and work and the lifelong learning sector can provide these skills, but does it also produce lifelong learners?

Another view is that good teachers create frameworks in which people can learn, rather than just be taught. Effective teaching encourages learning. This is why the best teachers are always a bit subversive; they acknowledge the importance of results for learners and institutions and strive to improve them, but they also know that creating excitement and enthusiasm for learning is the greater prize.

There are many analyses and models which attempt to describe effective teaching. One of the most useful is that provided by the Hay McBer (2000) *Research into Teacher Effectiveness*. The report was commissioned to provide a framework to describe effective teaching in schools, but with a few modifications and provisos, it is equally useful for teachers in the lifelong learning sector. Figure 12.1 shows the three main, interlinked, components of the model. Each element breaks down into categories and sub-categories which constitute a valuable toolkit for teachers to evaluate their effectiveness.

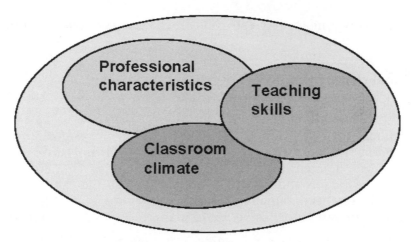

Figure 12.1 Hay McBer's three measures of teacher effectiveness.

Teaching skills

Teaching skills has six categories (I have omitted the 'homework' category).

1 *High expectations.* Effective teachers have high expectations of all their learners which they communicate to them and support them in achieving. These expectations will be differentiated to meet the needs of all learners.

2 *Planning.* Effective teachers set clear frameworks and objectives and share them with their learners.

3 *Methods and strategies.* Effective teachers use and develop a variety of teaching and learning methods to meet the needs of a wide range of learners. They use active learning methods to develop higher-order skills and encourage learning.

4 *Management and discipline.* Effective teachers establish a physically and emotionally safe and secure learning environment. They set boundaries, often in negotiation with learners, in which inappropriate behaviour is censured and appropriate behaviour is recognised and encouraged.

5 *Management of time and resources.* Effective teachers are skilled managers of time and resources to maximise learning. Learning sessions are clearly structured and make full use of time.

6 *Assessment.* Effective teachers use a wide range of methods to check understanding and assess learning. They consciously use teaching, learning and assessment methods which are based on assessment *for* learning.

All these elements combine to create well-structured sessions which flow and keep learners on task.

Professional characteristics

The Hay McBerReport (2000: 14) states that:

> Professional characteristics are deep-seated patterns of behaviour which outstanding teachers display more often, in more circumstances and to a greater degree of intensity than less effective colleagues. They are how the teacher does the job, and have to do with self-image and values; traits, or the way the teacher habitually approaches situations; and, at the deepest level, the motivation that drives performance.

This statement should be read in conjunction with the LLUK Standards Domain A: Professional Values and Practice which provide the underpinning values for those teaching in the lifelong learning sector.

The professionalism cluster has five elements:

1 *Professionalism*
   - *Respect for others*. This is the core value and is based on respect for all learners and colleagues (teaching and non-teaching). It is closely linked to valuing diversity and inclusive practice.
   - *Challenge and support* are related to high expectations of learners and to helping all learners develop their self-esteem as well as their learning.
   - *Confidence*. Effective teachers are confident in their role and their self-image as professionals. They are emotionally intelligent, positive and believe in success.
   - *Creating trust*. Effective teachers are consistent and fair. They keep their word and don't betray the trust of learners or colleagues.
2 *Planning and setting expectations*
   - *Drive for improvement*. Teachers in lifelong learning set targets and measure them against internal and external data and benchmarks.
   - *Information seeking*. As well as seeking information about standards and achievement, effective teachers constantly seek to find out about their learners in order to meet their needs and provide differentiated learning.
   - *Initiative*. Effective teachers use their initiative and take opportunities to deal with problems before they escalate. In addition, they seize opportunities to develop positive aspects of learning sessions in response to feedback from learners and unplanned events.

3 *Thinking*
   - *Analytical thinking.* This is related to reflection and evaluation. Effective teachers analyse their practice as a key to improvement.
   - *Conceptual thinking.* Effective teachers are able see patterns and links and to make connections. They provide the 'big picture' for themselves and their learners.
4 *Relating to others*
   - *Understanding others.* This relates to communication skills, emotional intelligence and recognising feedback. Effective teachers have insight into their learners and what motivates them and overcoming barriers to learning.
   - *Impact and influence.* Effective teachers recognise and use their ability to impress and influence others – colleagues and learners – to produce positive outcomes.
   - *Team-working.* Effective teaching in the lifelong learning sector requires teachers to cooperate and collaborate with a range of people – learners, colleagues, managers, external bodies.
5 *Leading*
   - *Managing learners.* Effective teachers are adept at keeping their learners on task and engaged in learning.
   - *Passion for learning.* This is self-evident, really. They are committed to their subject area but, above all, committed to learning.
   - *Flexibility.* Teachers in lifelong learning are flexible in their approach to learners and learning, as well as seeking opportunities to develop and extend their range of teaching and depth of learning.
   - *Holding people accountable.* Effective teachers hold people, learners and colleagues accountable. For learners this means taking some responsibility for their own learning and developing independent learning.

Classroom climate

It will be useful to read this section in conjunction with the 'Communication climate and emotional intelligence' section in Chapter 2, pp. 53–4.

In the lifelong learning sector there is a wide variety of learning situations, including classrooms, laboratories, workshops and workplaces. In addition, some learning will happen in situations other than a conventional class, NVQ assessment, for example.

Given the much wider range of learning situations than in schools, however, Hay McBer's guidelines for classroom climate are still useful. They are essentially about the ways in which 'effective teachers use their knowledge, skills and behaviours to create effective learning environments'. The key elements are:

1 *Clarity* about the purpose of the learning; the aims and objectives; activities and assessment. It refers to clarity, also, about the 'big picture' and how the current learning fits in with and connects to previous learning.
2 *Order.* This isn't just to do with maintaining discipline, it's also about having a structured and business-like attitude to learning sessions.
3 *Standards.* For many groups of learners it will be appropriate to have a set of standards relating to behaviour. These standards could be negotiated and contracted with learners.
4 *Fairness.* This means the degree to which there is an absence of favouritism. It also means avoiding bias, stereotypes and making assumptions about learners. It's about equality.
5 *Participation.* Effective teachers use methods to encourage and develop active learning. They provide opportunities for learners to participate by using discussion, higher-order questions and similar activities.
6 *Support.* This is part of providing an emotionally safe environment in which learners can seek guidance and support as well as take risks and learn from mistakes.
7 *Safety.* This is about the degree to which learners feel that the learning environment is an emotionally and physically safe place free, as far as possible, from fear-inducing factors.
8 *Interest.* Effective teachers strive to make the learning environment interesting, exciting and stimulating.

Evaluating your sessions

There are probably as many session observation and evaluation forms as there are learning providers. Many of these will provide useful advice and guidance to help teachers improve; some won't. You are probably working quite happily with a standard lesson evaluation format but if you're not and you need to create your own here are some suggestions.

First impressions

This an unscientific, 'gut feeling' approach to evaluating sessions which needs to be backed up by a more analytical approach but makes a useful starting point.

- How did you feel at the end of the session?
- How do you think your learners felt?
- Was there a buzz about the session?
- What was the learners' nonverbal communication like? Did they look as if they were enjoying themselves?

Some general questions to ask yourself

- What were you planning to do:
  - with whom?
  - how?
  - why?
- What happened?
- What went well?
- What was effective? How? Why?
- What went according to plan/what didn't?
- What were the causes of difficulties/changes etc.?
- What would you do again?
- What wouldn't you do again?
- What was unaccounted for/not planned for?
- How will your planning for the future change?

To the above you could add the kinds of questions inspectors ask:

- Do the learners know *what* they are learning and *why* they are learning it?
- Were they learning? Were *all* of them learning? How do you know?
- How did you assess the learning and check understanding?
- What did you do to help those who weren't learning?

A lesson observation and evaluation checklist

Checklists can assume mammoth proportions and, as a result, become just a box-ticking exercise. They should always be used as a basis for discussion with your mentor, tutor, colleague or with yourself. The checklist in Table 12.1 is intended simply as guide to the elements of an effective teaching and learning session.

Conclusion

Educationally, we live in an age in age of frequent changes in policy, quality systems, audit trails, checklists, tickboxes and accountability. Accountability should be welcomed because we are in receipt of public money which should be spent wisely and well. The preceding items in the checklist can contribute positively to accountability; used badly they reduce the art of teaching to merely a set of competences.

In her review of the research into teacher effectiveness, Alma Harris writes of the research tradition based on the notion of 'teacher artistry': 'Within this

Table 12.1 Evaluation and observation checklist

Planning

- Scheme of work ☐
- Session plan ☐
- Aims and objectives – precise and SMART ☐
- Structure and timings ☐
- Variety of teaching and learning methods ☐
- Differentiation planned in ☐
- Resources and equipment prepared and ready ☐
- Room layout appropriate ☐

Start

- Prompt start ☐
- Learning set in context ☐
- Refers to/links to previous session ☐
- Gets learners' attention before starting ☐
- Purpose and content of session explained ☐
- Structure provided ☐
- Objectives shared (as appropriate) ☐
- Registration ☐
- Lateness challenged or managed ☐
- ILPs reviewed (as appropriate) ☐

Communication

- Appropriate use of voice: pace, pause, volume, variation ☐
- Appropriate use nonverbal communication/body language ☐
- Relationship/rapport established ☐
- Appropriate level of language for learners ☐
- Technical terms explained ☐
- Avoidance of jargon ☐
- Listening skills ☐
- Learners' communication/feedback noticed and responded to ☐

Methods and strategies

- Variety of methods used to stimulate and motivate learners ☐
- Promotes inclusive learning ☐
- Methods selected to suit learners, levels and tasks ☐
- Whole group/small group/individual learning as appropriate ☐
- Questions used to check learning ☐
- Questions used to extend and develop learning ☐
- Clear explanations provided ☐
- Clear instructions provided ☐

Learning

- Learners on task
- Learners involved
- Learners interested
- Learners understand
- Learners motivated
- Appropriate level for these learners
- Learning extended

Resources

- Appropriate resources selected/created
- Resources used competently
- ILT incorporated as appropriate

Skills

- Skills for Life embedded
- Key Skills embedded
- Thinking skills planned in

Behaviour management

- Behaviour managed appropriately
- Positive behaviour recognised and rewarded
- Negative behaviour censured

Monitoring and assessment

- Range of methods used to check understanding
- Assessment *for* learning
- Assessments clearly explained
- Assessments relevant, fair and valid
- Developmental feedback provided

Ending

- Debriefing session (as appropriate)
- Main points summarised and recapped
- Learners given opportunity to apply and discuss learning
- Link forward to next session
- Crisp ending; on time

research tradition there is the central recognition that teaching involves creativity and is carried out in a highly personalised way' (Harris 1998: 178). Professional teachers must work within and meet the demands of the organisations and systems of their profession, but they also have a personal, professional responsibility to reflect, learn, develop and be creative.

Further reading

Harris, A. (1998) 'Effective teaching: practical outcomes from research', in F. Banks and A. Shelton Mayes (eds) (2001) *Early Professional Development for Teachers*. London: David Fulton.

Hay McBer (2000) *Research into Teacher Effectiveness*. London: Hay Group/ DfEE.

Appendix

NVQ	Skills for Life	Key Skills		HE Level
NVQ Level 5		Key Skills Level 5	Level 5	HE Level 8 – Doctorate 7 - Masters
NVQ Level 4		Key Skills Level 4	Level 4	HE Level 6 - Degree 5 - Diploma 4 - Certificate
NVQ Level 3		Key Skills Level 3	Level 3 Advanced A-level	
NVQ Level 2	Skills for Life Level 2	Key Skills Level 2	Level 2 Intermediate GCSE A*-C	
NVQ Level 1	Skills for Life Level 1	Key Skills Level 1	Level 1 Foundation GCSE D-G	
	Skills for Life Entry 3			
	Skills for Life Entry 2			
	Skills for Life Entry 1			

The National Qualifications Framework (NQF)

Bibliography

Adler, R., Rosenfeld, L. and Towne, N. (1998) *Interplay: The Process of Interpersonal Communication, 7th edn.* New York: CBS Publishing.

Argyle, M. (1994) *The Psychology of Interpersonal Behaviour*, 5th edn. London: Penguin.

Association of Colleges/FENTO (2001) *Mentoring Towards Excellence.* London: FENTO.

Atherton, J.S. (2005) *Teaching and Learning: Assessment* [On-line] UK: *http://www.learningandteaching.info/teaching/assessment.htm#Validity* (accessed 29 January 2007).

Berliner, D. (2001) Teacher expertise, in F. Banks and A. Shelton Mayes (eds) *Early Professional Development for Teachers.* London: David Fulton Publishers.

Berlo, D. (1960) *The Process of Communication: An Introduction to Theory and Practice.* New York: Holt, Rinehart and Winston.

Biggs, J. (2003) *Teaching for Quality Learning at University,* 2nd edn. Maidenhead: McGraw-Hill/Open University Press.

Black, P.J. and William, D. (1998) Assessment and classroom learning, *Assessment in Education: Principles, Policy and Practice*, 5(1): 7–73.

Blakemore, S-J. and Frith, U. (2005) *The Learning Brain: Lessons for Education.* Oxford: Blackwell.

Bourdillon, H. and Storey, A. (2002) *Aspects of Teaching and Learning in Secondary Schools: Perspectives on Practice.* London: Routledge Falmer.

Brookes, G. (2007) *Dyspraxia*, 2nd edn. London: Continuum.

Brookfield, S. (1995) *Becoming a Critically Reflective Teacher.* San Francisco, CA: Jossey-Bass.

Brown, G. (1978) *Lecturing and Explaining.* London: Methuen.

Brown, G. and Atkins, M. (1997) Explaining, in O. Hargie (ed.) *The Handbook of Communication Skills.* London: Routledge.

Bruner, J. (1966) *Towards a Theory of Instruction.* Cambridge, MA: Harvard University Press.

Burton, G. and Dimbleby, R. (1995) *Between Ourselves: An Introduction to Interpersonal Communication*, 2nd edn. London: Arnold.

Callaghan, J. (2004) Diversity, ILPs, and the art of the possible, in *Reflect: The Magazine of the NRDC*, Issue 1, October.

Capel, S., Leask, M. and Turner, T. (2001) *Learning to Teach in the Secondary School*, 3rd edn. London: Routledge Falmer.

Casey, H., Cara, O., Eldred, J. et al. (2006*) 'You Wouldn't Expect a Maths Teacher to Teach Plastering . . .' Embedding Literacy, Language and Numeracy in Post-16 Vocational Programmes – The Impact on Learning and Achievement.* London: NRDC.

Clark, R. (2006) *Every Child Matters: What it Means for Colleges.* Support for Success Quality Improvement Programme. *www.s4s.org.uk* (accessed 21 April 2007).

Clarke, A. (2006) *Teaching Adults ICT Skills.* Exeter: Learning Matters Ltd.

Claxton, G. (1990) *Teaching to Learn.* London: Cassell.

Claxton, G. (1999) *Wise Up. Learning to Live the Learning Life.* Stafford: Network Educational Press Ltd.

Clow, R. and Dawn, T. (2007) *The Ultimate FE Lecturer's Handbook.* London: Continuum.

Coffield, F., Moseley, D., Hall, E. and Ecclestone, K. (2004) *Should We be Using Learning Styles?* London: Learning and Skills Research Centre.

Curzon, L.B. (2004) *Teaching in Further Education*, 6th edn. London: Continuum.

de Bono, E. (1976) *The Greatest Thinkers.* New York: G.P. Putnam.

de Bono, E. (1985) *Six Thinking Hats.* London: Penguin Books.

Dewey, J. (1933) *How We Think.* New York: D.C. Heath.

DfEE (Department for Education and Skills) (1999) *A Fresh Start – Improving Literacy and Numeracy: The Report of the Working Group Chaired by Sir Claus Moser.* London: DfEE.

DfES (Department for Education and Skills) (2001) *Skills for Life. The National Strategy for Improving Literacy and Numeracy Skills.* London: DfES.

DfES (Department for Education and Skills) (2005) *Leading in Learning: Developing Thinking Skills at Key Stage 3. Handbook for Teachers.* London: DfES.

DfES (Department for Education and Skills) (2005) *Key Skills Policy and Practice: Your Questions Answered.* Sheffield: DfES.

DfES (Department for Education and Skills) (2004a) Key Stage 3 National Strategy *Pedagogy in Practice; Unit 7 Questioning.* London: DfES.

DfES (Department for Education and Skills) (2004b) Key Stage 3 National Strategy *Pedagogy in Practice; Unit 8 Explaining.* London: DfES.

DfES (Department for Education and Skills) (2006) *Personalising Further Education: Developing a Vision.* London: DfES.

DfES (Department for Education and Employment (2007) *Skills for Life. The National Strategy for Improving Literacy and Numeracy Skills: Focus on Delivery to 2007.* London: DfES.

Dillon, J.T. (1995) *Using Discussion in Classrooms.* Buckingham: Open University Press.

Driscoll, J. and Teh, B. (2001) The potential of reflective practice to develop individual orthopaedic nurse practitioners and their practice, *Journal of Orthopaedic Nursing*, 5: 95–103.

Dweck, C.S. (2000) *Self-theories: Their Role in Motivation, Personality and Development*. Philadelphia, CA: Psychology Press.

Ecclestone, K. (2005) *Understanding Assessment and Qualifications in Post-compulsory Education and Training; Principles, Policies and Practice*, 2nd edn. Leicester: NIACE.

Exley, K. and Denick, R. (2004) *Giving a Lecture: From Presenting to Teaching*. London: Routledge Falmer.

Fisher, R. (2003) *Teaching Thinking*. London: Continuum.

Fisher, R. (2006) Thinking skills, in J. Arthur, T. Grainger and D. Wray (eds) *Learning to Teach in the Primary School*. London: Routledge Falmer.

Flanagan, F. (2006) *The Greatest Educators ... Ever!* London: Continuum.

Gardner, H. (1993) *Multiple Intelligences: The Theory in Practice*. New York: Basic Books.

Gibbs, G. (1988) *Learning by Doing*. London: Further Education Unit.

Gilbert, I. (2002) *Essential Motivation in the Classroom*. London: Routledge Falmer.

Gill, D. and Adams, B. (1998) *ABC of Communication Studies*. Surrey: Nelson.

Ginnis, P. (2002) *The Teacher's Toolkit*. Camarthen: Crown House Publishing Ltd

Goleman, D. (1995) *Emotional Intelligence*. London: Bloomsbury.

Goleman, D. (1998) *Working with Emotional Intelligence*. London: Bloomsbury.

Gowers, E. (1986) *The Complete Plain Words*, 3rd edn. London: Penguin.

Green, H., Facer, K., Rudd, T., Dillon, P. and Humphreys, P. (2005) *Personalisation and Digital Technologies. www.futurelab.org.uk/research/personalisation.htm* (accessed 29 March 2006).

Green, L. (2007) Freed from the pen, *Times Educational Supplement*, 30 March.

Green, M. (2003) *Improving Initial Assessment in Work-Based Learning*. London: Learning and Skills Development Agency.

Hargie, O. (ed.) (1986) *A Handbook of Communication Skills*. Beckenham: Croom Helm.

Hargie, O. and Dickson, D. (2004) *Skilled Interpersonal Communication*, 4th edn. London: Routledge.

Harkin, J. (2006) Treated like adults: 14–16-year-olds in further education, *Research in Post-Compulsory Education*, 11(3): 319–39.

Harkin, J., Turner, D. and Dawn, T. (2001) *Teaching Young Adults*. London: RoutledgeFalmer.

Harris, A. (1998) Effective teaching: practical outcomes from research, in F. Banks and A. Shelton Mayes (eds) *Early Professional Development for Teachers*. London: David Fulton Publishers.

Harris, I. and Caviglioli, O. (2003) *Think It – Map It! How Schools Use Mapping to Transform Teaching and Learning*. Stafford: Network Educational Press Ltd.

Hartley, P. (1999) *Interpersonal Communication*, 2nd edn. London: Routledge.

Hay McBer (2000) *Research into Teacher Effectiveness*. London: Hay Group/DfEE.

Heath, H. (1998) Keeping a reflective practice diary: a practical guide, *Nurse Education Today*, 18: 592–5.

Heinich, R., Molenda, M., Russell, J.D. and Smaldino, S. (1999) *Instructional Media and Technologies for Learning*. New Jersey: Prentice-Hall.

Henry, J. (1994) *Teaching Through Projects*. London: Kogan Page.

Hill, C. (2003) *Teaching Using Information and Learning Technology in Further Education*. Exeter: Learning Matters Ltd.

Hillier, Y. (2005) *Reflective Teaching in Further and Adult Education*. London: Continuum.

Hillier, Y. (2006) *Everything you Need to Know about FE Policy*. London: Continuum.

Honey, P. and Mumford, A. (1986) *Manual of Learning Styles*, 2nd edn. London: P. Honey.

Hughes, M. (1997) *Closing the Learning Gap*. Stafford: Network Educational Press Ltd.

Jones, C.A. (2005) *Assessment for Learning*. London: Learning and Skills Development Agency.

Kennedy, H. (1997) *Learning Works. Widening Participation in Further Education*. Coventry: FEFC.

Kerry, T. (1982) *Effective Questioning*. London: Macmillan.

Kerry, T. (2002a) *Explaining and Questioning*. Cheltenham: Nelson Thornes.

Kerry, T. (2002b) *Learning Objectives, Task Setting and Differentiation*. Cheltenham: Nelson Thornes.

Knowles, M.S. (1978) *The Adult Learner: A Neglected Species*. Houston, TX: Gulf Publishing Co.

Kolb, D. (1976) *The Learning Style Inventory*. Boston, MA: McBer.

Kolb, D.A. (1984) *Experiential Learning– Experience as the Source of Learning and Development*. New Jersey: Prentice Hall.

Kyriacou, C. (1998) *Essential Teaching Skills*, 2nd edn. Cheltenham: Nelson Thornes.

Lasswell, H. (1948) The structure and function of communication in society, in L. Bryson (ed.) *The Communication of Ideas*. London: Harper and Row.

Lave, J. and Wenger, E. (1990) *Situated Learning: Legitimate Peripheral Participation*. Cambridge: Cambridge University Press.

Lawrence, D. (2000) *Building Self-esteem with Adult Learners*. London: Sage.

Le Versha, L. and Nicholls, G. (2003) *Teaching at Post-16: Effective Teaching in the A-Level, As and VCE Curriculum*. London: Kogan Page.

Learning and Skills Council (2003) *Successful Participation For All: Widening Adult Participation Strategy. For Consultation*. LSCA March 2003. *www.lsc.go.uk* (accessed 19 April 2007).

Lefrancois, G. (2000) *Psychology for Teaching*, 10th edn. Belmont, CA: Wadsworth Thomson Learning.

Legge, K. and Harari, P. (2000) *Psychology and Education*. Oxford: Heinemann.

Leitch, A. (2006) *Prosperity for all in the Global Economy: World Class Skills* London: HM Treasury.

Lifelong Learning UK (2006) *New Overarching Professional Standards for Teachers, Tutors and Trainers in the Lifelong Learning Sector*. London: Lifelong Learning Sector.

Lipman, M. (1982) *Philosophy for Children:* Thinking: The Journal for Philosophy for Children, quoted in Fisher, R. (2003) 'Teaching Thinking' London: Continuum.

Longworth, N. (2003) *Lifelong Learning in Action*. London: Kogan Page.

Lumby, J. and Foskett, N. (2005) *14–19 Education: Policy, Leadership and Learning*. London: Sage.

MacLennan, N. (1995) *Coaching and Mentoring*. Aldershot: Gower Publishing Limited.

Marland, M. (2002) *The Craft of the Classroom: A Survival Guide*. Oxford: Heinemann.

McCarthy, M. (2006) Message understood? *The Guardian*, 11 April.

McGregor, D. (2007) *Developing Thinking; Developing Learning*. Maidenhead: McGraw-Hill Open University Press.

McGuiness, c. (1999) *From Thinking Skills to Thinking Classrooms: A Review and Evaluation of Developing Pupils' Thinking*. Nottingham: DfEE Publications.

Marland, M. (2002) *The Craft of the Classroom: A Survival Guide*, 3rd edn. London: Heinemann.

Mehrabian, A. (1972) *Non-verbal Communication*. Chicago; Aldine Atherton.

Minton, D. (2005) *Teaching Skills in Further an Adult Education*, 3rd edn. London: Thomson.

Moon, J. (1999) *Reflection in Learning and Professional Development*. London: Kogan Page.

Moon, J. (2005) *Guide for Busy Academics No. 4: Learning Through Reflection*. York: Higher Education Academy.

Moorse, R. and Clough, L. (2002) *Recognition and Reward: Using Feedback for Learner Success*. London: Learning and Skills Development Agency.

Mortiboys, A. (2005) *Teaching with Emotional Intelligence*. London: Routledge.

National Association for Adult and Continuing Education (2000) *Learning in Later Life*. NIACE Briefing Paper (November 2000).

Nashashibi, P. (2002) *Learning in Progress: Recognising Achievement in Adult Learning* London: Learning and Skills Development Agency.

National Institute for Adult and Continuing Education (2000) *Learning in Later Life: NIACE Briefing Sheet No. 15*. Leicester: NIACE.

Neary, M. (2003) *Curriculum Studies in Post-compulsory and Adult Education: A Teacher's and Student Teacher's Study Guide*. Cheltenham: Nelson Thornes.

Ofsted (2006) *Handbook for Inspecting Colleges*. London: Ofsted.

Ofsted (2004a) *Why Colleges Fail*. London: Ofsted.

Ofsted (2004b) *Why Colleges Succeed*. London: Ofsted.

Owen-Evans, S. and McNeill, P. (2006) *Paving the Way: From Key Skills to Functional Skills*. London: DfES. (Available from *Pwww.Keyskillssupport.net).*

Petty, G. (2004) *Teaching Today*, 3rd edn. Cheltenham: Nelson Thornes.

Petty, G. (2006) *Evidence Based Teaching*. Cheltenham: Nelson Thornes.

Powell, B., Knight, S. and Smith, R. (2003) *Managing Inspection and ILT*. BECTA: *ferl.becta.org.uk*

Prensky, M. (2001) Digital natives, digital immigrants, *On the Horizon*, NCB University Press, (9:5).

Pritchard, A. (2005) *Ways of Learning: Learning Theories and Learning Styles in the Classroom*. London: David Fulton Publishers.

QCA (Qualifications and Curriculum Authority) (2004) *Key Skills Standards: Improving Own Learning and Performance. www.qca.org.uk/libraryAssets/ media/6349_iolp-level-3.pdf* (accessed January 2007).

QCA (Qualifications and Curriculum Authority) (2001) *Assessment for Learning. http://www.qca.org.uk/ca/5-14/afl/* (accessed January 2007).

QCA (Qualifications and Curriculum Authority) (2007) *The Secondary Curriculum Review. Curriculum Lenses: The Personal, Learning and Thinking Skills Framework. http://www.qca.org.uk/secondarycurriculumreview/lenses/ skills/personal-learning/definitions/* (accessed 15 May 2007).

QCA (Qualifications and Curriculum Authority) (n.d.) *NVQ Portfolios* at *www.qca.org.uk/printable.html?url=/610_1746.html&title=NVQportfolios* (accessed February 2007).

Race, P. (2001) *The Lecturer's Toolkit*, 2nd edn. Abingdon: Routledge Falmer.

Reece, I. and Walker, S. (2006) *Teaching, Training and Learning*, 6th edn. Sunderland: Business Education Publishers.

Reid, G. (2005) *Learning Styles and Inclusion*. London: Paul Chapman Publishing.

Reynolds, B. (1965) *Learning and Teaching in the Practice of Social Work*, 2nd edn. New York: Russell and Russell.

Roberts, C., Baynham, M., Shrubsall, P. et al. (2005) *Embedded Teaching and Learning of Adult Literacy, Numeracy and ESOL: Seven Case Studies*. London: NRDC.

Rogers, J. (2001) *Adults Learning*, 4th edn. Maidenhead: Open University Press.

Rollet, B.A. (2001) How do expert teachers view themselves? in F. Banks and A. Shelton Mayes (eds) *Early Professional Development for Teachers*. London: David Fulton Publishers.

Rose, C. and Faraday, F. (2006) *The Journey Towards Disability Equality: Responding to the Duty to Promote Disability Equality in the Post-school Sector*. London: Learning and Skills Network.

Rosenshine, B. (1971) *Teaching Behaviors and Student Achievement*. London: National Foundation for Educational Research.

Schön, D.A. (1983) *The Reflective Practitioner*. New York: Basic Books.

Schramm, W. (1973) *Men, Messages and Media*. New York: Harper and Row.

Sharma, M. (2003) *Dyscalculia*, Skillswise expert column. *http://www.bbc.co.uk/skillswise/tutors/expertcolumn/dyscalculia* (accessed 21 April 2007).

Shannon, C.E. and Weaver, W. (1949) *The Mathematical Theory of Communication*. Urbana, IL: University of Illinois Press.

Shaw, M. (2006) Death by ... PowerPoint, *Times Educational Supplement*, 1 September.

Skidmore, P. (2003) *Beyond Measure: Why Educational Assessment is Failing the Test*. London: Demos.

Stradling, B. and Saunders, L. (1993) Differentiation in practice: responding to the needs of all pupils, *Educational Research*, 35: 127–37.

Swan, M. (2006) Learning GCSE mathematics through discussion: what are the effects on students? *Journal of Further and Higher Education*, 30(3): 229–41.

Tanner, H. and Jones, S. (2003) *Marking and Assessment*. London: Continuum.

Thompson, N. (2002) *People Skills*, 2nd edn. Basingstoke: Palgrave Macmillan.

Toffler, A. (1970) *Future Shock*. London: The Bodley Head Ltd.

Tomlinson, J. (1996) *Inclusive Learning – Principles and Recommendations. A Summary of the Findings of the Learning Difficulties and Disabilities Committee*. Coventry: FEFC.

Tomlinson, J. (2003) Notes towards a definition of inclusive learning, *Learning and Skills Research*, Summer 6(5–7).

Torrance, H. and Pryor, J. (1998) *Investigating Formative Assessment: Teaching, Learning and Assessment in the Classroom*. Buckingham: Open University Press.

Torrance, H., Colley, C., Garratt, D. (2005) *The Impact of Different Modes of Assessment on Achievement in the Learning and Skills Sector*. London: Learning and Skills Development Agency.

Tummons, J. (2005) *Assessing Learning in Further Education*. Exeter: Learning Matters Limited.

Wallace, S. (2002) *Teaching and Supporting Learning in Further Education*, 2nd edn. Exeter: Learning Matters.

Wallace, S. (2007) *Getting the Buggers Motivated in FE*. London: Continuum.

Weeden, P., Winter, J. and Broadfoot, P. (2002) *Assessment: What's in it For Schools?* London: Routledge Falmer.

Whalley, J., Welch, T. and Williamson, L. (2006) *E-learning in FE*. London: Continuum.

Wilson, V. (2000) *Can Thinking Skills be Taught: A Paper for Discussion*. Scottish Council for Research in Education *http://www.scre.ac.uk/scot-reserach/thinking/* (accessed 4 May 2007).

Wolf, A. (1995) *Competence-based Assessment*. Buckingham: Open University Press.

Wolvin, A. (1984) Meeting the communication needs of the adult learner, *Communication Education*, 33: 267–71.

Woods, R. (2006) The next step in brain evolution, *Sunday Times*, 9 July.
Wragg, E. (1984) *Classroom Teaching Skills*. London: Routledge.
Wright, A-M., Sina, A-J., Colquhoun, S., Speare, J. and Partridge, T. (2006) *FE Lecturer's Guide to Diversity and Inclusion*. London: Continuum.

Index

Locators shown in *italics* refer to figures and tables.

TEACHING AND TRAINING IN POST-COMPULSORY EDUCATION
Third Edition

Andy Armitage, Robin Bryant, Richard Dunnill, Karen Flanagan, Dennis Hayes, Alan Hudson, Janis Kent, Shirley Lawes and Mandy Renwick

Review of the second edition:

> "... clearly written, well organised, easy to use, practical and accessible for both new and continuing teachers."
>
> *The Lecturer*

The third edition of this bestselling text examines the breadth of post-compulsory education (PCE) from Adult and Further Education through to training in private and public industry and commerce. Revised and updated throughout to include recent initiatives and developments in the field, it is the definitive textbook on learning, teaching, resources, course planning and assessment in all areas of PCE.

The authors examine key areas in post-compulsory education through topical discussion, practical exercises, theory, reading, analysis, information, and examples of student work. Popular features of the previous edition such as the chronology of PCE have been retained and fully updated.

New features include:

- The new framework for teacher training, including the new Lifelong Learning UK professional standards, CPD provision, mentoring and subject coaching

- The revised 14–19 agenda and the developments involved, including specialised diplomas, functional skills, personalised learning and thinking skills, changes to GCSE and A Levels, work related learning

- Developments in information and learning technology, particularly electronic teaching and learning resources

Contents: *Acknowledgements – Abbreviations – Introduction – Working in post-compulsory education – The Lifelong Learning teacher: learning and developing – Student learning in post-compulsory education – Teaching and the management of learning – Resources for teaching and learning – Assessment – Exploring the curriculum – Course design, development and evaluation – Developments in post-compulsory education – Bibliography – Index.*

2007 304pp

978-0-335-22267-4 (Paperback) 978-0-335-22268-1 (Hardback)

A LECTURER'S GUIDE TO FURTHER EDUCATION

Dennis Hayes, Toby Marshall and Alec Turner

This book offers a unique and provocative guide for all lecturers committed to providing the best education and training possible in the changing world of Further Education. The authors examine:

- The key issues in FE
- How teaching in FE differs from others sectors
- The motivations of learners
- The use of new technologies in the classroom
- The techniques adopted by college managers
- The changing assessment methods
- The introduction of personalised learning
- The politics behind the training of lecturers
- What the future holds for FE

Written in an accessible style, every chapter presents a different and challenging approach to key issues in Further Education.

A Lecturer's Guide to Further Education is essential reading for all new and experienced Further Education lecturers.

Contents: *Introduction: The perverse consequences of further education policy – A beginner's guide to lecturing – The McDonaldization of FE – What's motivating students? – Educating the digital native – Key skills or key subjects? – The rise and rise of credentialism – The transition to work and adulthood – Teacher training for all? – Symposium: The future of further education*

2007   200pp

978-0335-22018-2 (Paperback)   978-0-335-22019-9 (Hardback)

ADULTS LEARNING
Fifth Edition

Jenny Rogers

- How do adults really learn?
- How do I handle the first class or session?
- How can I get my material across in a way that will interest and excite people?

Completely revised and updated throughout, the new edition of this friendly and practical book is the guide on how to teach adults. Written in an accessible style, it unravels the myths of teaching adults, while explaining why it is both a rewarding and a complex task.

Using case studies and examples from a wide range of sources including higher education, adult education and management development, *Adults Learning* answers questions such as:

- How do I deal with a group of mixed ability?
- How can I can I manage the conflicts that may arise in a group?
- Which teaching methods work best and which are least effective?

The author includes new chapters on problem-based learning and action learning, updated and extensive new material on handling groups, and a revised chapter on coaching, providing plenty of points for further discussion.

Adults Learning is a must-read for anyone involved in teaching adults.

Contents: *Introduction – Adult learners: what you need to know – The first session – Giving feedback – Understanding your group – Facilitating – Action learning – Problem-based learning – Coaching Role-play and simulation – Delivering information: lecturing, demonstrating and blended learning – Design for learning – Evaluating.*

2007   272pp

978-0-335-22535-4 (Paperback)